JUST
TIME

Just Time:
A Journey Through Britain's Fractured Justice System

By Stephen Jackley
© Stephen Jackley

ISBN: 9781912092413

First published in 2023 by Arkbound Foundation (Publishers)

Cover image by Tasmin Briers

This is a true account of the author's journey and the publisher considers it of public interest to ensure a full record is made readily available to readers. However, any opinions expressed herein are those held by the author and the publisher holds no liability for any inaccuracies that may have inadvertently arisen.

* * *

Arkbound is a social enterprise that aims to promote social inclusion, community development and artistic talent. It sponsors publications by disadvantaged authors and covers issues that engage wider social concerns. Arkbound fully embraces sustainability and environmental protection. It endeavours to use material that is renewable, recyclable or sourced from sustainable forest.

Arkbound
Redbrick House
York Court, 6 Wilder St
Bristol BS2 8QH

www.arkbound.com

JUST TIME

A JOURNEY THROUGH BRITAIN'S FRACTURED JUSTICE SYSTEM

STEPHEN JACKLEY

Writing · Publishing · Diversity · Inclusion

Foreword by
Eoin Mclennan-Murray

I joined the prison service in 1978 on their graduate entry scheme, working for 37 years and serving in 10 prisons in a variety of governor grade jobs. I was governing governor of 3 prisons, my last one being HMP Coldingley. It is here that I became aware of Stephen.

When he entered the wing office, I could see he was apprehensive and everything about his mannerisms were defensive. He began to explain the issues he had at Coldingley. As we spoke, he became more relaxed and some of the issues he raised, if true, were not unreasonable. I told him that I would check what he was saying and, if he was right, resolve the issues he had raised. He seemed a bit surprised at my calm and rational approach and I went on to ask him about his custodial history. He reeled off all the prisons he had been in, sometimes pausing to give further details which were not complementary. Despite his pent up anger, it was clear to me that he was an articulate individual, but also awkward in company. Little did I know then that my dealings with Stephen would develop into a very positive relationship which, within the constraints of prison and my role as governor, would lead to a collaboration following his release, where I became patron of a charity he helped create.

This book catalogues Stephen's journey through many of the penal institutions in England. He had only committed the offences to fund and fulfil a project that would begin to correct the imbalance of power and wealth that was so obvious to him, both in the UK and throughout many of the countries he had visited. He had been dubbed by the press as the Robin Hood robber. Although his intentions were pure, his actions were criminal, and it was only the criminality that he thought the judge had taken account of. During the course of his incarceration, he wrestles with the injustice of his sentence length on one hand and, on the other, the need to be punished for the harm he has caused to innocent people who were on the receiving end of his robberies.

He describes how he oscillates between fighting the system and conforming with it. Various interactions with staff and courts either push him more in one direction or the other. He spends a lot of time reflecting on his life, on the wasted years, on the idealism that burns deep within him. As the years roll by, the ambition of escape evaporates and he turns more to fighting the system through litigation. This was the point at which I encountered Stephen and everything told me he was a soul worth saving. However, he now stood in danger of sacrificing the rest of his life because he got entangled in fighting a system that would and could swallow him up. I needed to get him to see that there was the possibility of a life, a good life, after prison - if he would only look to the future and plan for his resettlement.

It would not be easy for Stephen to abandon his modus operandi. It had served him well as a survival mechanism but it would now really hinder his progress. He had been labelled by the prison service as a high risk prisoner who posed as an escape risk. His new probation officer not only endorsed that label but, had he had his way, would have prevented Stephen from progressing to open prison, which offered the best chance of preparing for a successful release.

I wanted to write this foreword because it gave me the opportunity to comment on the changes that Stephen made through his penal journey. He started off as an angry young man, preoccupied by the injustice he felt had been dished out to him. Many of his encounters with the inflexible and uncompromising elements of the prison system fuelled his desire to fight back, even though by doing this he diminished his chances of ever getting an orderly release from an open prison.

My intervention was to try and protect Stephen from himself, to use logic and common sense as the tools for him to navigate his way through the system. Life is a compromise and Stephen had to learn this in order to work with me to achieve what he really wanted - his freedom. This book charts, in entertaining detail, the ebb and flow of Stephen's passage through the turbulent waters of an imperfect criminal justice system. There are lessons in it for all of us.

Eoin McLennan-Murray
Former Chair of Howard League for Penal Reform, President of the Prison Governors' Association and Governing Governor

Contents

Prologue

A year has passed in American custody. It had started on 19th May 2008, when a quiet 21-year-old University student entered a Vermont gun store looking for a Glock. Thereafter, a police search in the UK uncovered enough evidence to issue a warrant for multiple armed robbery offences on banks and bookmakers. Escorted from JFK airport in New York, from one prison system towards another, the journey starts half-way across the ocean...

Part I:

ENTERING THE DARKNESS

*"All we have to decide is what to do
with the time that is given to us."*

Gandalf to Frodo in the Mines of Moria,
'The Lord of the Rings', J.R Tolkien

Chapter 1: Return

The Atlantic's glittering blue expanse passed far below. I sat unchained, yet the two American agents beside me were a constant reminder that I remained in custody. One was a tall, lanky Caucasian man in his mid-thirties; the other was black, with a thin moustache, who clearly spent more time going to the gym than his colleague. This was their job, I guessed. Escorting felons and undesirables they didn't want in their great nation back home. Their kindness at JFK Airport, letting me loiter in one of the shops and buy food I hadn't tasted for a year, now gave way to silence. Not that there was much to talk about. I had given one-word answers and nods to their jovial questions, knowing it was all a façade to put me at ease. Those cosy assurances that I would be free once the plane landed could not hide the ice in their eyes.

I fingered the British Embassy letter in my loose brown Federal Prison trousers.

'You will not be arrested on arrival', it promised.

Next to me, the white agent made small talk with a woman in the row behind. It went on for well over ten minutes as his colleague thumbed through a magazine.

"I need to use the toilet."

The white agent glared at me. "Again?"

"It's okay," his colleague said. "I'll take him."

Their need to escort me on a plane flying at thirty-two thousand feet was irritating. Where exactly did they think I would go...?

Safely locked in the toilet cubicle, the same question taunted me. I bent down to examine the screws connecting the metal toilet to the floor, wondering again how Frank Abegnale had managed it. He had embarked on a criminal career when just a teenager, becoming wanted across many countries and even escaping from a plane's under-carriage after removing the screws of a passenger toilet. Here, they were bolts. There were no removable panels either – only a little swinging bin that led to a plastic bag of used tissue paper.

Someone hammered on the door.

"Come on, Stephen. The plane is landing soon."

I popped it open, glancing briefly at the black agent's waist. The gun was not there, but secured by a vest strap under his jacket. Both had subtly made it known they were carrying firearms when they collected me.

Back in the seat, imagination took over. Maybe the Embassy wasn't lying. Perhaps the agents were only telling me what would happen. There was nothing to worry about, really.

With seatbelts buckled, the plane descended.

From bright sunshine to grey skies, I felt the tyres bounce onto the English tarmac and wished it had not been so smooth. Almost immediately, against a fuzz of wind-lashed rain, the strobing lights of a following police van penetrated the cabin.

They kept me back as other passengers began to exit. I tried, once, to get up and join the flow.

"No," the black agent said, grasping my arm.

Then it was time. With the plane emptied, they led me down the aisle and past two nervously smiling flight attendants.

I clutched the crumpled Embassy letter in my right hand like a passport ready to hand over for inspection. There was barely time to take in the white corridor ahead. A large group of British police suddenly appeared, pouring in from a side door. Handcuffs snapped around my wrists as a long line of words flooded over me.

The useless letter hung loosely. I glanced back at the two agents, their faces solemn.

The police frog-marched me through Heathrow Airport in a long file, flashing ID badges at customs with no questions asked. There were no queues or stops. I thought they would be taking me to a holding area, but the cordon kept marching through Heathrow's brightly lit corridors, past the glitzy displays of duty-free shops, at a pace hard to match. Then again, I was practically being dragged. Occasionally officers in front boomed orders to passengers who were too slow to get out of the way, causing even more stares. It felt as if the entire airport had paused in its usual conveyor-belt frenzy to scrutinise me. A group of elderly women shuffled away in horror whilst kids pointed wide-eyed.

The cordon swept through the last set of double doors, and cold, wet English air greeted me. Just as I remembered, leaden skies hovered overhead, with puddles scattered around the pavement.

I was pushed into the back compartment of a car next to a police officer who resembled a Sumo wrestler.

"If you make any moves, you will be sat on."

Sirens roared to life. The unmarked car was in-between two other police vehicles, and within minutes I heard the blades of an overhead helicopter.

I stared out the window, pressed close to the Sumo police officer, in total silence. As the convoy left London's skyscrapers behind, I pondered. First arrest, then prison. The year in America had been barely bearable. How much longer lay ahead?

They took me to Worcester Police Station. Some initial 'booking in' questions were asked before I was subjected to a strip search and placed in a cell. Typed papers slid under the door, and I slowly read them: twenty-two separate charges, most carrying maximum life sentences.

***

Was it morning, afternoon, or night? I awoke to windowless fluorescent light, an all too familiar sight. The metal door swung open, revealing four policemen.

"What time is it?"

"Time for you to see the magistrates," one said expressionlessly.

I rubbed my eyes and offered my hands, like a sacrifice, for their cuffs. They took me through a long corridor of white bricks, then up some stairs and into a small courtroom. Behind a reinforced glass screen, three elderly figures peered down upon me.

The only thing they asked me to confirm was my name.

Next came the solicitor, Andrew Childs. He was tall, in his fifties, with thin grey hair. We went over what evidence the police possessed. "A great deal," he said.

"Where will I be taken next?"

"Oh, probably to the local prison. They will then transfer you to a higher security one."

Sure enough, within an hour, I was led to a waiting white van. The guard shoved me into an open compartment and removed my handcuffs, locking me in.

Immediately voices leapt to life. I struggled to understand what they were saying, but a persistent remark seemed to be about felines.

"I will be a D Cat in a year," one declared.

"My bro's an A Cat," another replied.

It must be some slang criminal term for people, I thought, *perhaps relating to "status".*

As the van steered away, I caught a glimpse of TV cameras and a large crowd.

"What are they here for?" a voice shouted.

"Hey, who is on this bus!"

I sat there silent for the entire journey.

When the van slowed and made a series of turnings, I knew the prison was close. It passed a sign, 'HMP Hewell', then stopped before a large gate with eighteen-metre walls on each side – a change from the multiple rows of rolled razor wire I had seen in the last American State Jail.

Through the gate, we paused in an enclosed area. A guard

boarded and checked all compartments, then left. The van then crept forward, through another gate, into a large courtyard.

One by one, the guards opened the compartments. I was led up a ramp and into a doorway with a sign above saying 'Reception'. Inside, a guard behind a huge desk asked me to confirm my name, then another escorted me to a holding cell.

"Would you like tea or coffee?" he asked.

I paused, checking he was talking to me rather than to a colleague. Was it a test? A joke?

"Er, tea, please."

He even asked if I wanted milk and sugar, to which I replied yes.

The holding room had a TV in one corner of the ceiling behind a plastic cage and two long benches facing each other. When the guard brought back a cup of tea, he also ushered in someone else.

"You come from court?" the prisoner said, sitting opposite.

"Yes."

"Looking at doing long?"

"I'm not sure."

After slurping away at our drinks and watching the TV, keys jangled in the door again. "Jackley?" a new guard looked at me.

I nodded.

"Guv'nor wants to see you."

He led me into a small office where a woman in her thirties sat. She had long brown hair and a thin smile. The silver label pinned to her suit read 'Managing Governor'.

She pointed to the chair. "You must be tired after your journey."

I did as she asked and glanced at a pile of paperwork with my photo on the top page.

"I have been advised to put you in Segregation until you can be assessed for a higher category. Do you have any questions?"

The uniform behind me coughed. I didn't need to know what 'Segregation' meant: solitary confinement, a prison within a prison.

"How long will I be there?"

"I'm not sure," the Governor said. "Maybe a few days or weeks, but we'll move you as soon as possible."

The guard was joined by two others, who directed me into a small room. They ordered me to remove all my clothing – the tan trousers and brown t-shirt I had been given as a federal prisoner – then threw some other clothes on the floor. They looked like pyjamas, with alternating blue and yellow patches.

After I changed, the guards marched me through another door. Sunlight hit me, the air fresh and warm, as bees zipped between bright flowers lining an outside walkway.

They led me to Segregation, its grey slabs of stone oozing coldness in the shadow. This would be my home for days, for weeks... maybe longer.

It may have been another prison halfway around the world, but the Segregation block smelled the same as those I knew before. A mix between stale air and disinfectant. It reminded me of the secure psychiatric wards I used to visit to see my mother as a child after she had been 'sectioned' for another couple of months due to her schizophrenia, except here the stench of despair was far more prominent. They could paint the walls as colourful as they wanted – here a kind of faded blue – but nothing could hide the purpose of this place. The same rows of metal doors, the same iron staircase leading to another level, the same cameras planted like one-eyed Gargoyles staring at the remnants of broken lives.

The guards led me to a cell on the second tier. Behind came an echoing tombstone *clank*. Stale, stagnant air seeped into my lungs as I pressed my forehead against the grilled-over window, vaguely discerning a concrete yard.

My eyes scanned the white-washed walls. In America, in some cells, there could be found sparkling gems of insight and inspiration – the poetry of loss and hope, pain and redemption – but here, there were just faded initials and the outlines of dick drawings.

A bag containing soap, a toothbrush, toothpaste and toilet roll lay on the bed edge. I only lacked for a pen and writing paper, which a guard brought later.

Questions circled like vultures. *What would happen next? Why did I let this come to pass? When would an Opportunity for escape present itself?*

They knew I was an escape risk. Even if it had not been for Interpol designating me as one, the US Marshals would have made sure to pass it along. Yes, right now, the odds were heavily in their favour. But since when did the odds really matter?

My pen traced words once so strong and confident:-

To bring justice to the beaten and broken,
To bring opportunities to the masses long denied,
To give a voice to those unspoken,
And an end to the inequality of wealth.

Even in the cell, my shattered dream could be remembered, if never again to be enacted.

***

Mind over matter, thoughts over actions, memories over events. If you can sketch a hell like heaven and glimpse light in darkness, seeing rainbows in the darkest storms, hope can be found. *It is your mind that creates this world.* But, while I could be content for many days with only paper and a pen, I could still experience immense frustration that sometimes erupted into fire. Developing a routine of in-cell exercises, yoga and meditation helped, but it didn't always work.

On the third day of Seg, I became accustomed to its little routine: one hour out of the cell, which could be spent pacing an outside concrete yard or showering. Then three meals collected at a hatchway served by an orderly. The food was better than the American State facilities I had been in, but I decided to spice things up that third day.

"Time's up, Jackley," a guard said during exercise.

I did another circuit around the yard. Then another.

The guard marched out with his taller colleague.

"Inside," the tall one ordered sternly.

I strolled past and returned to the cell, ignoring their hostile stares. A few hours later, a senior officer stormed into the cell.

Like in America, prison officers generally split into two backgrounds: former military or failed civilian 'professionals'. With his rigid upright walk, it was obvious which one this guard belonged to.

"Everything all right?" he growled.

"Well," I replied, "is there no way to open this window?"

He marched up to it. "No, there isn't. And even if there were, I wouldn't open it for you. You're an escape risk."

I glanced at the thick iron bars beyond the metal mesh and back at him.

"How long do you think I will be in Segregation?"

"As long as it takes Head Office to assess whether you should be Category A. Once that's done, we'll ship you out to the big boys. In the meantime, keep your head down and don't cause any trouble."

I expected him to leave, but he just hovered there, scrutinising me.

"And stop calling my staff 'COs'. Refer to them as 'Officer'."

COs were 'Correctional Officers' – what I was used to. Apparently, the British officers took exception to the term, which might have explained why my previous callings of "Yo, C O!" did not get any responses.

Sometimes it was possible to glimpse other prisoners by looking through the gaps between the door and metal frame. Their accents were hard to understand: HMP Hewell was close to Birmingham, and I was more accustomed to the flowing twang of New Yorkers than the dense spiel of 'Brummies'. Later, when collecting my evening meal from an orderly, I had to ask him twice to repeat a question.

"I said, man, do you want more custard?"

He meant the thick yellow goo that accompanied a small slice of apple crumble.

It actually smelled quite good, so I nodded.

As he dolloped another scoop, I glanced at a pile of books and newspapers to the right of the servery hatchway.

"Can I take one of those?"

He stared. "Yeah. Why else do you think they are there?"

For the papers, it was a choice of The Sun, The Daily Mail and a heavily stained copy of The Mirror. There wasn't much choice of books, given there were only two.

Back in the cell, I regretted asking for more custard. It had a weird metallic taste, with – no, it wasn't worth thinking about. In prison, you either ate or starved. I scooped away the excess yellow gloop, flushed it down the toilet, and ate the rest of the crumble. Then I turned to The Sun.

Despite being a week old with random pages ripped out, the paper elicited immense interest. I hadn't seen a single bit of UK news for over a year, and it seemed the country was close to another General Election. There was much talk of the failings of Prime Minister Gordon Brown and positive reference to Conservative Opposition Leader David Cameron. Ironically, there was also a small piece about prisons. According to the writer, prisoners were being treated very well indeed – access to a gym, special courses and day releases, with food better than that served in schools.

Chapter 2: Downgraded

After one week, a guard brought over some paperwork and new clothing.

The paperwork stated that I was no longer 'Potential Category A' and downgraded to 'Category B', with references to my 'age' and 'no prior convictions' as the reason.

In the UK, prisoners were put in four categories (the 'Cats' referred to by others before) from 'A' to 'D', with the higher ones considered riskier (regarding their propensity to escape and what would happen if they did). The risk, somewhat aptly, included reference not just to the public but to 'national security'.

I had expected to be made the highest category and transferred to what would, in America, be the equivalent of 'maximum security'. The relief that this was not happening quickly gave way to the trepidation of what would happen next. For all its boredom and deprivation, Seg also represented a mental oasis. You didn't have to worry too much about what was happening around you; you could get through an entire day by barely saying a word. That suited me fine. At the same time, I was pleased to be leaving.

I changed into the new clothes – a blue t-shirt and grey cotton trousers – then followed the guard outside Segregation and along a wide walkway. We passed a few other people, walking a few hundred meters, before approaching another set of doors.

Inside was a large, noisy hallway. On the ground floor were pool tables, a ping-pong table with a missing net, and groups of prisoners talking loudly. Like with the Seg unit, there were two levels of cells. The guard led me down some stairs and pointed to one in a corner.

Eyes scrutinised me as I walked towards it, the usual sizing up. I avoided their gaze and blinked into a dimly lit space no bigger than a small bathroom. What stood out immediately was the television and kettle.

Someone coughed. I turned around, straight into the face of a guy around my age, with closely cropped fair hair.

"Hey, you good?"

"Yes, thanks."

Brushing past me, he flicked a button on the kettle, then looked back. "My name's John."

"I'm Steve."

"Where you from?"

"England," I replied.

"Oh, you sound American."

I explained that I had just spent time in American prisons, and he began quizzing me on the whole experience. This would be repeated for each subsequent prisoner, but at least it provided a talking point when there might have been awkward silence.

The second surprise was the early lock-up. In America, it was usually around 10 pm, sometimes later for different facilities. In England, it was 5 pm. It meant joining a long queue and collecting dinner from a common hatchway, overseen by watching guards, then taking the food back to be eaten locked in a cell.

Fortunately, the TV made the evening more bearable. Before long, I was engrossed in my second film – none other than *The Shawshank Redemption*.

My cellmate sat up and peered up at me. "I guess you've been through all that shit, right?"

***

It turned out HMP Hewell was one of the UK's few 'super cluster' prisons, consisting of three separate establishments. The other two were a Category C Training Prison (formerly HMP Brockhill) and a Category D Open Prison (formerly HMP Hewell Grange).

The part I resided in was the Category B 'Holding Prison', used to keep prisoners awaiting convictions or transfer to other establishments. Its former name – Blakenhurst – was still used by many inmates and guards.

Short of being released, everyone wanted to get to the open prison. It didn't take long to find out why: it was said to have no bars on the windows, not even locks on the doors – prisoners could literally just walk away. The chances of me being moved to such conditions in the near future were, I knew, pretty slim. Nonetheless, the mere existence of these 'prisons' gave hope.

I didn't know it then, but I was now part of a national population seventy-three thousand strong – a number only set to grow in the years ahead. They told me I was in the 'Induction Wing', a place for new arrivals, where prisoners learned about the regime and were assessed for any special interventions. That was the theory, anyway. My induction, meant to last a full two weeks, ended up being three days.

I joined a small group being led to a new wing. They all chatted among themselves contentedly, some hoping to 'pair up' in sharing a cell.

Unlike the Induction Wing's relatively light and airy feeling, this new one had three cramped 'spurs' leading off from a central point where the guards had an office. Every spur had four levels, and with most of the cells holding two prisoners, I reckoned there were at least a hundred people. The design was based on a progressive social reformer, Jeremy Bentham, who devised the concept of a 'panopticon', whereby a single guard could observe all inmates. The prison didn't need to worry about him paying an inspection – he'd been dead for over a hundred and fifty years.

On the ground floor, to my amazement, was a darts board.

Isn't that dangerous? I almost said aloud as a pointed dart flew past the face of a standing prisoner.

"Right, move along; I haven't got all day," the guard behind grumbled.

We ascended the stairs right to the top floor.

"Your cell's over there," he pointed.

I watched him march along the walkway to one of the gateways that led back onto the central area of the wing – the 'opticon'. He had a strange, sideways lurch.

The cell was slightly larger than the last. A bald man who could have been in his thirties lay on the bottom bed watching TV. He sat up to greet me.

"I'm Simon; nice to meet you."

"I'm Steve, you too."

He turned down the TV volume. "How long you been here?"

"About a week," I replied, glancing briefly at the photos he had put on the wall. "Just come from the Induction Wing."

"Which prison were you in before?"

"Varick Street Detention Centre." I smiled inwardly, wondering what his reaction to that would be.

"Where the hell is that?"

After recounting my journey, Simon said he had spent time in an infantry brigade but now served time for possession and dealing of 'Class A' drugs. The photos on his wall, lining the whole length of his bottom bunk, were of family members. Of these, his six-year-old son took precedence, followed by his wife and parents.

Sharing a cell meant talking was practically mandatory, especially with the long lock-up hours between 5 pm and 8 am. When we didn't speak, the TV provided constant chatter, deluging us with programmes that dulled the mind. It had been well over a year since I watched TV, and initially, it was a novelty. As the days passed, however, it became an irritation. Aside from some films and the odd documentary, it had the effect of massaging my thoughts and emotions. Only this was no pleasant massage on a Thai beach after a long day swimming and hiking, but a constant prodding and pulling at the mind.

Even during unlock hours, Simon rarely left the TV. There

were several periods of 'association' whereby prisoners could mingle, play games, and use the phones at the ground level to call approved contacts via their 'phone credit'. On weekdays, these were a few hours in the afternoons and evenings, whereas the weekend was one long period of association, save for the lockup from 4 pm to 9 pm.

Whether locked up or on association, boredom was the main challenge. Some had jobs, which I also applied for, but everyone had to wait. The rest just drifted around, talking to each other or playing games of pool or darts.

In prison, three questions were always raised at some point: where you are from, what you are 'in for', and how much time you were doing. The answers to these questions had a lot riding on them. Being from a particular area often led to the expectation of knowing certain people or, more importantly, being known *by* them. To understand why this is so relevant, you must know that most of the prison population – roughly three-quarters – comprises repeat offenders. There were people on their third, fourth and upwards sentences, which was considered perfectly normal. Indeed, the more times somebody went to prison, the greater their chances of returning. For 'holding prisons' especially, many inmates knew each other on the outside or had some connection they could draw upon to find out who a person's identity and, more importantly, what they were 'in for'.

That second question – the crime you had committed – crossed each person's mind when they first looked upon each other. Certain offences were viewed understandingly, others even admiringly, but a few were met with hatred and disgust. I would discover to what extent these categories could impact the experience of custody, but for the time being, my response of being 'charged with armed robbery' got met with a degree of respect.

And that's where the third question came in: how long were you in for? The fact is, I didn't know, but anyone being tried for multiple counts of armed robbery was not going to breeze out the gates in a few months.

"You've got years ahead of you, mate," one prisoner jovially said, cigarette poking out his mouth. "Might as well get used to it sooner rather than later."

I exercised to release my anxiety, doing push-ups and sit-ups in the cell and running up and down the stairs. The latter drew a fair number of stares from guards and prisoners alike, but I didn't care. In fact, despite the cramped space and air so thick with tobacco smoke that it could have been a carcinogenic petri dish, exercise was about the only thing I did when not reading or writing.

More importantly, I had a goal. They all thought I had 'years ahead' in this system, but they'd be proven wrong. Looking outside the barred cell window on a summer's day, smelling the fresh gusts as they pushed aside the rancid prison air, I could not relinquish the idea of freedom. No matter how small, the next opportunity for escape would be embraced with the blaze of the last fire that burned within me.

***

I guess things would have been fine with Simon if not for his TV obsession, which he also preferred having at a high volume. After a week, I asked why he had to have it on so much.

"Is it bothering you?" he asked.

"No, it's just – well, you could do other things."

"Yeah? Like what?"

I rubbed my eyes. "I don't know. Read a book. Play pool. Something."

He glared at me, then back at the TV.

The next day, he said his nephew was coming onto the wing, which could well have been the case. After all, a few cells down, a son was sharing with his father, both in for accessory to murder. One of the guards asked if I'd be willing to move, and that's how I found myself on the opposite side of the spur, practically in line with Simon's cell.

"Better the devil you know than the devil you don't" is a cliché you often hear in prison. However, in this case, I was relatively lucky. Dwaine, cellmate number three, was around my age and massively into his gym. And this was another thing I discovered: UK prisons really did have gyms, and Hewell's left me amazed. There were all kinds of machines – most of which I had no idea how to use – and dumbbells that went up to 50kg.

To access this array, I had to fill in a 'gym slip' in the morning and hope there would be space on one of the evening sessions. Handing in the slips as fast as possible was essential because the guards decided who went on a 'first come, first serve' basis. I usually managed to get on the list, despite the manic morning rush, with Dwaine and me taking turns to hand in our slips.

Dwaine came from Jamaica, and aside from helping me in the gym, he went to great lengths explaining what items were essential to buy from the prison's canteen – which prisoners could mark on a sheet to order from their 'spends' account each week. The 'Jamaican Spice Bun' came top of Dwaine's recommendations, although when it arrived a week later I was disappointed to get what looked like a squashed fruit loaf the size of a sandwich. Still, the taste was pretty good.

When I told Dwaine what I'd been arrested for after speaking at length about American prisons, he stared. "Seriously? You don't look like an armed robber. I had you down for fraud or drugs."

It wasn't the first time I heard this, and a reason why I chose not to wear glasses – save from when watching TV or writing – even though my eyesight was pretty poor. To survive prison, you didn't only have to be strong; it was also necessary to *look* strong. For many, simply looking the part was enough for them to avoid the worse trouble.

Dwaine became my 'gym buddy', showing me various exercises that left my muscles burning for days. He also ate a lot, which wasn't a plus regarding toiletry requirements. Each cell had a toilet with a curtain that could be drawn around it, and although prisoners tried to do shits during unlock time, it wasn't always possible.

Another thing about Dwaine was his obsession with two prison officers. One he hated – the guard with the lurching walk who had first shown me onto the wing, referred to as 'Crabman'. The other, Miss James, he seemed besotted by. In America, the female guards tended to have close-cropped hair and were overweight. In contrast, Miss James could have been featured in a modelling contest. She had even allowed me to use an office phone to call my mother when I was still waiting for 'phone credit'. Afterwards, she took me aside and asked how I was getting on.

"Okay," I replied shyly. "Just waiting for news on my first court date."

She smiled. "It must be a difficult time. I understand you were in American prisons, too?"

I nodded. Even some guards, it appeared, found my history curious.

"Well, I hope you find it better here than there."

Although I said yes, I really didn't know. So far, the only outside 'exercise' consisted of 30 minutes every day pacing anti-clockwise around a concrete yard. Unlike Orange County Jail, where multiple hours could be spent outside, looking up at the blue sky or doing exercises, Hewell felt more like being squashed into a mackerel tin. The little time spent on exercise was something I nonetheless treasured: breathing fresh air, feeling the wind, seeing the tops of green trees poking above the jail walls.

One evening, shortly before one lock-up, I heard a mixture of angry shouts. It was not the first time I heard a disturbance, sometimes preceded by alarm bells and early lock-up. Dwaine flew into the cell, sweating profusely. Seconds later, the face of 'Crabman' appeared with another guard. "You feeling better now?"

"Fuck – "

The door slammed before Dwaine could complete his sentence. I asked him what had happened.

"He's a racist bastard," Dwaine replied, not providing any detail.

Later that night, a slip of paper got passed under the door, which Dwaine immediately snatched up and ripped into more pieces than I thought possible.

The next day, he was moved early off the wing.

That same afternoon, my solicitor visited. He brought a stack of paperwork that the prosecution would use, consisting of witness statements, forensic reports, photographs, and numerous diary entries. They had everything they needed: I knew that already. *But this?*

Those bittersweet memories from so long ago cast me back in time. From the grey photocopied pages, another figure leapt out – free, young, and with every prospect open to him. Days had been spent wandering through quiet forests listening to birdsong or cycling along river paths with the evening sun ahead.

I blinked. Like a dream, it all disappeared.

Alone in the cell, I sat hunched against a wall. Legal papers spread out around me: every space, even the two bunk beds, were covered.

I longed for a chance that would never come again; even for the cold embrace of the Atlantic Ocean, which had passed beneath me barely a month ago.

A dull pain spread across my forehead as the hours shifted towards morning. It wasn't just the diary entries, but something I had never considered before, which crept like an octopus through the maze of my tangled thoughts.

Knocking reverberated from the door.

"Are you okay, Stephen?"

An angelic face framed the window slit. Miss James.

I paused, not knowing what to say. I hoped she couldn't see the tears running down my face.

"I'm... fine... thanks, just going through some legal paperwork."

She smiled. "Okay, don't stay up too late!"

The window shutter closed gently.

Ultimately, I only had another three days in that cell. They relocated me to the Remand Wing, where I was supposedly meant to be from the beginning as an unconvicted prisoner. Everyone on this wing was technically innocent, given they had not yet been proven guilty – including me. I suppose the prison system tried to reflect that by granting a broader range of freedoms: more access to the gym and time out of the cell, plus broader visiting privileges. However, everything else was the same – save for one guard. For every action, there is an equal but opposite reaction. Having met Miss James, I was now about to encounter her opposite.

Chapter 3: Savouring the Darkness

I can't quite see them
But I know they are there
Shining light years away
Blazing in ancient glory –
The stars.

At first, the new wing seemed better. I was placed with someone who worked as a 'wing cleaner' – a large man in his forties called Mark.

They also gave me a kitchen job. The first few days revolved around washing dirty dishes; then, after being bossed around by the kitchen staff, I graduated to preparing the potatoes. They came in barrels of salty liquid; round pale things that were slimy and cold. I had to feed these through a processor and then hand over the sliced debris to the fry-up man, who encrusted them with a layer of used oil.

One day I returned to the wing after a long day handling potatoes to find all my belongings had vanished. Clothes, books and paperwork were nowhere to be seen.

It took five minutes to locate Mark, playing pool.

"Didn't anyone tell you?" he smirked. "Go speak to a screw."

Confused, I found myself talking to Miss Savoury. She shared the blond hair of Miss James, but her face was wrinkled, with a protruding nose bent slightly on one side. When she spoke, it was harsh and mocking.

"Up in Cell 15, Jackley."

Even before entering, I could hear the TV blaring at full

volume. Inside, my belongings had been dumped onto a bed, with a man opposite.

He ignored me, his eyes glued to the TV.

"Hello!" I shouted.

He turned, then smiled weakly.

With a spread of thin grey hair around his bald head, I guessed his age between fifty to sixty years. He pointed to his ears and said something.

"What?!"

I stepped closer, straining to hear.

"Sorry, I'm deaf," he said.

I felt sorry for him. It could not be easy being deaf in prison, but already his blasting TV made it hard to think.

"Can you turn that down?" I asked twice.

He reached forward and adjusted the set so it was only marginally quieter.

"Do you know why they moved me here?"

He shrugged and gave another weak smile.

Now, for once, the noisy prison wing seemed relatively quiet. All the shouting, smashing of pool balls and slamming of gates could not compete with the deaf man's TV. Down by the pool table, I noticed my old cellmate, Mark, briefly glance up and then say something to two others. They burst out laughing.

I had only shared a cell with Mark for less than a week, and, with my kitchen job, I really just saw him from the evening to morning. That may sound like a long time, but for prison it is about equivalent of two colleagues meeting briefly at work. Like most, he spent a great deal of his time watching TV, while I read and wrote. Perhaps it was this difference that caused the move, or maybe I had inadvertently insulted him. Then again, wasn't it up to prison officers who moved cells rather than inmates?

"Miss Savoury authorised it," an officer later said. "You should ask her for the details, not me."

He pointed over to Miss Savoury.

Even from a distance, she emanated disdain. I imagined if Miss James aged twenty years and had a problem with alcohol, it might approach Miss Savoury's appearance. In her eyes, instead of understanding and fairness, was judgement and vindictiveness. I had seen that look before, many times, but then this was in a different system, thousands of miles away. Here they all seemed nicer, to the point of offering a cup of tea when I arrived. Boosted by this perception, I approached Miss Savoury and waited as she finished a long conversation with another inmate.

"Excuse me, Miss," I said, as the conversation finished.

Her eyes locked on me. "Wait, Jackley. I'm speaking to somebody." Even when the inmate walked away, she acted like I wasn't there.

"Excuse me."

She scowled. "What?"

"I just wondered why I was moved to another cell – the other officer said I should speak to you."

"What does it matter? I have the choice in which cells I allocate to prisoners."

Her lips twisted slightly. "Oh right...," I stammered. "Then can I move into a new cell? It's just the other person is deaf, and the TV is very loud."

"I've made my movements this month, Jackley. Now go away and stop annoying me."

She turned her back and wandered off. The exchange had been carefully watched – by one group in particular, with Mark in the middle. He said something, and those around him sniggered.

My options were limited. Being returned to segregation for some act of disobedience was one, but that would damage the chance of coming across an opportunity for escape and potentially affect my sentence. The solicitor had already noted how the prosecution would use anything they could to argue for the harshest possible sentence, including behaviour in custody.

The second option, to simply endure a month or more in the same cell, lost its appeal rapidly. Not only did the deaf man depend on noise, but he also started to mark the walls. When I returned from work, rows of x's and hearts had materialised above my pillow. The move began to take on new dimensions. I was on the Remand Wing – an unsentenced and unconvicted prisoner. And the same applied, for the most part, to those around me. Just what could the elderly deaf man be charged with?

In America, they called people convicted of sexual offences 'snappers'. In the UK, it was 'nonces'. I was not about to leap to conclusions – and yet.

This cell had two 'flat beds' rather than a bunk bed, so we slept only about three feet apart on the same level. His nightly toilet visits also grew in frequency, with long pauses before he returned to bed. Sometimes I saw him standing in the shadows, turned in my direction. On one occasion, I spoke, asking if 'there was a problem', but he remained silent. The unease grew, and my requests to move cell to different officers were all denied.

In the background of all this was my swiftly approaching 'plea hearing' – the point at which I would either plead guilty or proceed to a full trial. There didn't seem much choice: they had enough evidence to convict me. And yet it was not a straightforward decision. Once that 'guilty' plea was entered, the inevitability of being sentenced to prison would follow, with no going back.

You've got years ahead...

The words kept repeating like taunts, suffocating all other thoughts. And this was not Orange County Jail or a federal prison with plentiful time outside. I was barely twenty-three years old, forced to share a six-by-nine-foot space with someone more than double my age, who acted deaf and was quite possibly a predator.

And what if escape failed? What if an opportunity never even arose?

I sometimes returned to the wing when everyone else was locked up because the kitchen shift went beyond 5 pm. One evening

Miss Savoury escorted me to the cell. She said nothing, as did I.

She paused as she unlocked the door. Maybe she thought I would ask her – again – if I could move cell. The anticipation on her face was evident, as was the cruelty.

I walked in, silent.

"Jackley. Grow up and stop writing on your walls."

Before I could respond, she slammed the door in my face.

The old man watched the TV at its usual volume, but the bang was loud enough to be heard by him. I looked at his smiling face, then at the new line of x's above my pillow.

My fists clenched. I began to say something – then stopped. *You've got years ahead.*

***

There were times in prison when you would awake, forgetting exactly where you were. Times when your mind rebelled at the present circumstances in the free ocean of subconscious and left you longing to return to your dreams. Despite the situation, this often happened to me. I still awoke, clinging to the dissipating dreamscape of something better. Topless on a beach as the tide washed in, hearing the gulls cry in the distance, the warm sun turning the water into a causeway of sparkling gems. Lying on a soft bank of grass beneath the spreading boughs of an oak as birds sang above. Awaking in the safe bed in my room of the childhood home I had once longed to leave, as the smell of breakfast drifted from downstairs.

The darkness gripped me now. The dream was over. I turned, seeing the shadowy figure at the foot of my bed, his features made clear by the first light of dawn. A weak smile played across his lips.

I sat up, staring back at him.

"What do you want?!"

He turned, then drew the toilet curtain.

I imagined grabbing the TV when they opened the doors and throwing it over the balcony, watching as it smashed into silence.

They'd put me in a new cell within an hour, back in Segregation. But, when the doors opened, no TV smashed. Instead, the usual line of prisoners queued up to receive medication and go to work. Like a ghost trapped within its own nightmare, I followed them.

Halfway down the corridor, a voice called.

It didn't seem possible: *didn't she just work last night?*

"Jackley!"

I couldn't ignore it again. Another officer looked in my direction, blocking the way ahead.

I turned.

She stood there, elbows slightly bent, like a wrathful spirit fixed on its target. I wished I had one of those special Greek medallions to ward off the 'evil eye'.

"Come here!" Miss Savoury barked. "What are you wearing?"

I blinked. "Erm, kitchen clothes?"

"No! Your socks need to be over your trousers."

"What?"

"Are *you* deaf now, too?"

I looked at her blazing pale blue eyes and wondered what thoughts ran through her head. Where did this hatred come from?

Pulling my socks over the hem of the white kitchen trousers, I looked back at her and wondered what would come next.

Over in the kitchen, some of my companions were friendly, particularly one called Kev. He was tall, with a fringe of silver hair and an Indian complexion. Of all the jobs, I reckoned his to be the best: preparing vegetarian dishes. It was the only position that didn't seem to involve pouring in tons of oil or used fat. During a quiet period, I approached him as he stirred a big pot of curry, wondering aloud what I could do.

"Savoury's a real bitch," he said.

Initially, I found his thick East London accent hard to understand, but now it flowed more smoothly than the 'Brummies'.

"She killed someone last year," he added.

"How is that possible?"

"Happened whilst restraining him. There was an inquest, and she got let off."

I gawped.

"Don't let her scare you, though. What she did was wrong – they're not meant to move you like that. Put in a complaint. And, whilst you're at it, ask to speak with medical – get a single cell."

"How can I do that?"

"Just say you're a risk to your cellmate. From what you've said, that can't be too difficult!"

I had spent an entire week with the old man, and the thought of solving the situation through paperwork had never occurred to me. Finding the forms and posting them in the dedicated boxes back on the wing didn't take long.

Two days later, the tannoy sounded. Every wing had one – intermittently announcing things throughout the day. "Collect your meds", "kitchen workers to the gate", "X prisoner to the wing office", and so on. For the first time, it called my name.

I walked up to the gate, which a guard opened. He showed me to an office where a woman waited. For a dreaded moment, I thought it was Miss Savoury – she had the same blonde hair and looked in her forties, but I quickly noticed she wore a nurse's uniform.

"Hello, Stephen. I'm from the mental health department," she explained. "I've read your application and understand you are having issues sharing a cell."

I tried to explain. To make out that I felt threatened by a frail old man wouldn't make sense, and describing his 'love messages' would be too awkward. So instead, I told the nurse about the headache-inducing TV and how, with the prospect of a long sentence, I needed time alone. Perhaps it was not my words that made an impact, but rather my face. I had barely slept properly for almost a week.

Getting single cells was not as hard as it would become. Nevertheless, the nurse wanted to know more details. She asked why I was in prison; the reasons behind my offences.

The solicitor's words at our last meeting came rushing back: '*do not give them any reason to justify you as dangerous*'. Therefore, I stuck as close to the truth as possible without going into details.

After an hour of talking, she said a follow-up appointment would be made. "I'm also happy to recommend that you have a single cell," she added.

True to her word, I moved the next day. The first thing I did was crash onto the bed.

***

Guilty.

The hearing was fast. A few minutes standing before a judge, with just that one word spoken. Before, I had spoken to the solicitor, batting options back and forth. The prosecution had already dropped or modified the charges I disputed, save for one general point that made a huge difference. There were nine counts of armed robbery, but not of the banks and bookmakers I had targeted. Instead, individuals were named – tellers and cashiers – as if I had gone out on the streets and mugged them.

I told the solicitor that, under no circumstances, would I be pleading guilty to such misrepresented charges.

On top of that was the greater issue of intent. A crime requires two elements: the *actus reas* (action of doing an offence) and the *mens reas* (the thought or intention to commit an offence). Whilst the *actus reas* could not be denied, I thought the *mens rea* could be argued as lacking. All my diary entries provided substantiated that, as did the money given away.

My solicitor refused to change his viewpoint. He sat there, grim-faced, repeating the same thing he had said weeks ago.

"If you plead not guilty, you will face a long trial, but I do not doubt that you will get convicted with the evidence against you. And then you won't get any time off your sentence that you would have got for pleading guilty."

I thought a conviction could be scuppered if only one person in a jury of twelve could understand my motives and relate to them. If the underlying reasons behind a crime were just, then surely it was not only about whether a crime had been committed? On the other hand, certain things were beyond the faintest doubt. One was that, if I pled guilty at the first opportunity, the time otherwise given would be reduced by one-third. The solicitor never committed to a figure other than saying I was looking at a sentence "possibly in the double figures". Against this likelihood, a one-third discount seemed massive.

I may have made the logical choice in pleading guilty, but even after doing so came lingering doubt. To be charged with robbing individuals was especially difficult to accept. All I saw were the banks and bookmakers – the cornerstones of a globalised capitalised system that was wrecking the planet and enslaving billions to a lie.

But there *were* people. My mind flashed back to the witness statements I had only read once, the night Miss James appeared. They were still in the mountain of legal paperwork, buried amongst diary entries and photocopied bank notes.

My hand reached out – then paused.

"You want a cuppa?"

It was my new cellmate.

Leaving the Remand Wing after entering my plea had one drawback: there were not enough single cells to go around, so I had to share. However, my new cellmate – Number 6 – was from Russia, very clean, and polite. I helped him fill out the many application forms that every prisoner had to navigate: from simple things like getting a medical appointment and using the gym to more complex issues like arranging visits and obtaining a new job. Practically every activity had its own application form, with few provisions available for those who could not speak English well.

Meanwhile, I still worked in the kitchens. It had been Kev

who helped secure my fast move to the new wing, since he spoke to a staff member. I had a lot to thank him for – no longer was I plagued by the presence of Miss Savoury. As usual, he stood over a pot of steaming curry.

"Can you pass me that chilli there?"

I handed him the huge container and watched as he dolloped red powder into the steaming pot.

"Isn't that a bit too much?" I remarked.

"Nah, if they can't take it hot, they shouldn't order it in the first place."

He dipped a spoon into the pot, blew on it, and tentatively sipped.

"Better, but far from perfect."

"Doesn't smell too bad," I replied, holding back a sneeze.

"I could make an award-winning feast from the crap they haul in here," Kev chuffed. "But by the time this lot has had their hands on it, the crap turns out even shittier."

He had a point. Whether because of health and safety standards or simply because they didn't care, kitchen staff consistently ensured that any vegetables were heavily overcooked. They also had an apparent obsession with oil and fat. Almost every menu option apparently required gallons of the stuff, as cheap and nasty as possible. As for the meat – let's not go there! Scrubbing the grease-oozing detritus of the kitchen's leftover meat trays was enough to make you a life-long vegetarian.

The fact that some of Kev's dishes could leave prisoners pouring with sweat wasn't a problem for me: I liked spicy food, having acquired a taste for it in Thailand.

Working in the kitchens also meant I could have a wider choice of food, although some kitchen staff took exception to prisoners eating anything other than what they had selected on their 'menu sheets'. These were handed out every month, with four different types of food listed for each day. An X was placed next to your desired option and then collected at mealtimes.

Back then, there were two hot meals a day – three if it was a weekend. The breakfast consisted of a cereal packet, one small carton of UHT milk, and an assortment of sauces you could spread on sliced bread put out by the servery. The choices of lunch and dinner generally consisted of 'vegetarian', 'healthy', 'meaty' and 'Halal' options. A 'full English breakfast' (with vegetarian option) was provided on Saturdays and Sundays.

My new wing was quieter and more relaxed than the other two, and for the first time I noticed a few chess games being played. Kev also mentioned that somebody was doing an Open University course, but it took me a while before I went up to the second floor and knocked on the door of Cell 47.

"Come," a voice called.

Upon entering, it didn't look like a prison cell. Larger than any other I had seen, it could have been an ordinary room with a carpet and curtains. A full-size desk fit against the window, with a stereo and rows of CDs above a single bed. A man in his mid-thirties sat on the end. He had closely cropped blonde hair with a long tattoo on one arm. His piercing gaze almost made me leave immediately.

"Erm, hi," I said sheepishly. "A kitchen worker told me you are doing an Open University course."

Suddenly the door behind opened.

"Joe, have you got that other Queen CD, mate?" another prisoner asked.

"I'm in a meeting. Return later."

He rapidly disappeared.

"So," Joe said, scrutinising me. "You're that bank robber, aren't you?"

I nodded.

"Spent time in America? Used to be a university student?"

"Yes."

He gestured to a chair. "Take a seat."

I sat down by his desk.

"You see that book there," he pointed to a thick textbook on the desk. "It's what gets me to sleep each night."

The book had some long title about psychology written along the spine.

"Oh, right," I replied. "How did you start doing an Open University course?"

"Whatever you heard is wrong. You can't do an OU course."

I felt offended. *Is he saying I'm stupid?*

"You need to be sentenced and doing over four years to do one," Joe continued, "so you have to wait for that. Plus, you need to be in a training prison."

"What's that?"

He ignored the question and took a sip from a pottery cup with a bulldog picture. All the other cups I had seen were blue plastic.

"You did all those bank jobs alone, I hear."

I wasn't sure how to respond.

"To answer your question, a training prison is where you will be sent after you get sentenced. You'll be sent to a B Cat to start with, like me. I'm waiting for Lowdham Grange."

"Is that better than here?"

Joe laughed. "This is a shithole. Yes, Lowdham is much better. Do everything you can to get there."

Someone knocked on the door, and the head of one of the more muscled prisoners appeared. "Oh, sorry, thought you were by yourself."

"That's alright. Steve was just about to leave."

I later learned that Joe was a 'drug kingpin', a former millionaire with the right contacts in prison to continue his status.

It was already becoming clear that a sentence consisted of more than just time. Conditions could vary drastically from wing to wing and even cell to cell. Meanwhile, I was adapting to the environment. The ways of speaking and mannerisms in British prisons differed from America, together with all kinds of cliques and sub-groups. Some revolved around keeping fit and going to the gym; others to recreational diversions like playing cards, pool, or building match-stick models.

Ever the loner, I unwisely did not belong to any of these groups. Bullies targeted those without associates. Perhaps it was less of a problem to me because of being seen as relatively high on the prison hierarchy: facing counts of multiple bank robberies bestowed a certain level of credos.

Socialisation had always been difficult. From school to university and now prison, it was only a matter of time before my 'credos' evaporated. Indeed, the fact that I had already moved to seven cells in just two months should have told me something. Talking, blending in, finding common ground and avoiding being irritated by 'little things' continued to be major challenges. The noise and constant pressure to interact confidently with others left me stressed and anxious, just as much as the forthcoming sentencing hearing.

One day I went to see the prison psychiatrist, Dr Dinesh Maganty, arranged by the nurse I spoke with on the other wing. The meeting lasted about an hour. At the end of it, he mentioned something called 'Asperger's Syndrome' and went through some symptoms: the tendency to have obsessions, to need a routine, and to be sensitive to noise. Despite seeing the connection, I was uncomfortable with being given a label. I had witnessed the consequences with my mother, who had been diagnosed with schizophrenia and always seen through the lens of being mentally ill, causing prejudice and turning people away. Nonetheless, Dr Maganty said that he thought the condition was important and should be brought to the attention of my solicitor, who could arrange a formal assessment.

This was in July 2009, and many judges felt compelled to apply a form of sentence called the IPP. It stood for 'Imprisonment for Public Protection'; instead of being a set sentence, it was indefinite. Those receiving IPPs were only released when the authorities deemed it safe. When introducing the sentence in 2003, then Justice Secretary

David Blunkett presented it as an improvement to public safety. No longer would dangerous criminals re-enter society only to re-offend. Instead, they would be provided with courses and work to address the factors behind their offences, steering them away from crime and making it safe to release them. That was the theory, anyway.

Despite the full consequences of IPPs not yet being appreciated then, my solicitor prioritised avoiding one.

"We have to be careful," he said. "While it's true that you have no prior convictions, your offences were also serious and quite numerous. Receiving an IPP is something you should be prepared for. Any factors that might make the judge consider you more dangerous, such as a medical condition, will increase your chance of getting it."

So, despite Dr Maganty's opinion that I had Asperger's Syndrome and this needing to be raised with the court, we did not explore it further.

I would never know what difference it could have made until much later.

***

The days passed. And with each passing day, I gradually changed as well. It was a change that came in stages, sometimes faster than others. All those hours locked in a cell, with the company of cold walls and uncaring strangers, brought room for inward contemplation.

As much as I resisted it, the stack of legal papers had one section that required re-reading: the witness statements. As I grudgingly re-turned the pages, it was clear that something critical had been carelessly set aside: people had been harmed because of my actions. People who were simply leading ordinary lives, with jobs to pay their bills and support their families. Then I arrived, masked and armed, bringing only fear and trauma. Yes, these people had *feelings,* a simple understanding I had never appreciated before. Years ago, they were just actors on a stage who would experience no loss. Back then, the only 'victims' I saw were the gigantic gambling corporations and banks, whose money I stole represented practically nothing. The £1 coin I left behind was more than a calling card; it was my debt being repaid, for £10,000 was worth the equivalent of £1 to the banks and betting groups.

But between the maze of my logic were individuals who wanted no part of the plan. And some, as the witness statements detailed, had genuinely suffered. One statement, in particular, left me in tears – showing the actions of an evil man who deserved punishment. And that man was me.

Such a realisation was worse than any prison disciplinary punishment, worse than the sadism of guards or the ever-present stress of the environment. However, unlike these things, the change it brought to character could only be positive. This did not alter how I looked upon the world and my ability to see where it headed; that, essentially, it was dying. Inequality continued unabated, enslaving millions to mindless cycles of production and consumption, with only a tiny minority really benefiting. And all this was driven by a globalised capitalist system that put monetary profits first and life last. To steal from banks and betting shops, hoping that would be the start of fighting back and creating something new... Back then, it seemed the only way.

I deserved to be punished for that mistake and the resulting actions that caused harm to others. The intentions were good, but that alone was insufficient for exoneration.

Standing before the sentencing judge, HHJ Cavell, on 21st August 2009, I wondered what he made of me. A ruthless armed robber bent on destruction for his own personal gain, as the prosecutor portrayed? Or a kid from a fractured family who launched a crime spree with the deluded aim of wanting to change the world?

The United States of America vs Stephen Jackley.

Now it was *The Queen vs Stephen Jackley.*

Above the judge hung not a flag of stars and stripes but a coat of arms, with a Latin slogan underneath: *Dieu et mon droit* – By

God and My Right – the motto of English monarchs going back to the time of William the Conqueror. I wondered how often it had been raised to justify oppression, murder and enslavement. How many times had the Kings and Queens of centuries ago, confident of their divinely appointed positions, lived in luxury whilst huge segments of their people starved and suffered? How could one person hope to change such a system?

I agreed with the prosecutor: I deserved the harshest possible sentence. Not a life in prison, but total exile from the United Kingdom, to be cast loose, without provisions, in some remote wilderness of another land. That, or the death penalty. It was exactly what others had faced for countless generations before me. I had even written a letter to the judge, setting out these options, only to be convinced by the solicitor to completely re-write it. Those options, he pointed out, were not even possible for the judge to give out. The only thing that would be achieved is to risk increasing the time spent locked up. Against all this was my mother – someone who had already suffered enough in her life without her only son locked up and made out to be a dangerous lunatic. So, the letter got re-written, with the only part kept being where I set out my apology and remorse to those impacted by my offences.

Judge Cavell stared down at me from his seat.

"I can't begin to imagine what possessed a man of your obvious abilities to resort to this appalling series of serious crimes," he began. "You set out to terrify such employees and customers who happened to be on the premises. When one man dared to stand up to you, armed as you were, you slashed at him with a vicious bladed knife."

I stood there in silence, phasing away from reality, tracing the outline of the unicorn in the royal emblem above the judge's head. When he pronounced the sentence, I barely heard it.

Only afterwards, in the court's holding cells, did the solicitor confirm what had been handed out.

13 years.

Chapter 4: Bedding In

Whether you are in your early twenties or not, coming to terms with the fact that you will spend the next six and a half years[1] of your life locked behind bars is not easy. Initially, I did my best to minimise the duration, believing that 'open prison' was accessible within four years. But my ability to accept the sentence eroded by the day.

I looked up to the more rebellious prisoners, yet I felt isolated from them – indeed, from anyone – for in my heart remained a belief that I was different. Whether or not I had Asperger's Syndrome was irrelevant; it was about being someone who had sought to resist a system itself rooted in criminality.

Every week, there were departures and arrivals on the wing: people who were taken to court and never returned, others who were transferred to different establishments, and a few who got moved around within the prison. Aside from these, some always remained as prison grandees for months, if not years. The Listener Sam, with whom I now shared a cell, was one of these icons – known and respected by guards and inmates alike.

The Samaritans ran The Listener Scheme and trained prisoners to support their peers when depressed. The objective was to reduce suicide rates in the prison population more than anything else. It worked. Day or night, a prisoner could ask to speak to a Listener. This often meant the guards unlocking a cell in the early hours and taking the occupant to the 'listener's suite' – either a dedicated room or the Listener's cell.

---

1   At that time, a determinate sentence was split in half – 50% to be spent in prison, and the remainder 'on license' in the community.

Now I was in such a cell full time. Apparently, it was normal for those newly sentenced to over ten years to either be kept on suicide watch for a few days or paired up with a Listener. At first, Sam (cellmate #7) didn't seem too bad: a man in his fifties doing a life sentence for murder, with long grey-black hair tied into a ponytail and a London accent. Intricate match-stick models were spread around the cell: a gypsy caravan, a Harley Davidson motorbike, and little houses with windows and doors. This was what Sam did in his spare time. Unfortunately, he also did something else to make the hours pass more easily: smoke. One cigarette after the other. They were not even meant to pair non-smokers with smokers, but that wasn't the worse part. I didn't notice it the first night – I wouldn't have been able to sleep even if I wanted to – but his loud snoring became an issue on the second. Earplugs, given to me by a nurse, did little to dampen it.

Efforts to move cells were fruitless.

"You've just been given a sentence of thirteen years," one guard stated. "If there is one place you need to be, it is in a Listener's cell."

I was sick of it. Of everything. On the night of 27th August, I thought, again, of Fate. Was *this* always bound to happen? The cold mechanisms of chemistry; our every move shaped by actions and reactions set in motion before we were even born? Like the Constants of Physics, which dictated how particles and forces behaved, or the grand mathematical numbers that defined how shapes curved. The Golden Ratio, The Mandelbrot Set, Pi.

I fought back the tears. *No!* There *were* choices, and I threw them away, taking the path that led to prison. But no, again, I'd rather have...

"Pi!" The word exploded from my lips.

I didn't care that it awoke Sam.

So why not wake everyone else up, then? I thought, mind careering into madness.

I shouted Pi repeatedly, even as others mutter clear their annoyance until misty sunlight filtered into the cell.

Sam just lay back smoking for all those hours. He didn't look at me or speak a word.

On unlock, like some robot that unthinkingly repeats its programme, I got up and joined the queue for work. Hostile glances bored into me, but I was in a kind of fugue state – mind blank, yet body moving. At the gate, an officer stepped in front. "You need to remain on the wing."

I wandered back to the Listener's cell. He still lay there, cigarettes trailing smoke in his overflowing ashtray.

A year ago, I was in The Hole of an American State prison. Despite the constant strip searches and harsher conditions, I had my own cell – a place to write and read and dream. Now, even that small glimmer of endurance had been removed.

I went to the barred window and looked to the blue sky.

Behind, the shadows enveloped me.

What was there to lose?

I stood on a knife edge, tilting in the direction of darkness. The anguish was overwhelming.

Segregation would have been next, and after that...

But someone intervened. She came into the cell and asked me to sit down. Then she sat next to me on the bed. It was not her words but her tone: understanding, rational, sympathetic. She pulled me back from the precipice, getting me an appointment to see Dr Maganty that afternoon, who authorised a single cell straightaway. The officer was called Miss Colman, and what she did represented not only an act of humanity but also of courage. Not all officers on the wing agreed with it. Her rank as Senior Officer (SO) gave her superiority, yet it would have been for nothing without the desire to make a positive difference.

***

Thirteen years. The barrister had argued the closest case to mine was for a man sentenced to eight.

Even being in a single cell, the days and nights dragged.

Around me, other prisoners utilised ways to get through their sentences: games, talking to each other, and going to the gym. I had to do similar, if only to blend in, but the pi-shouting episode did nothing to boost the opinion of others. Friends of the Listener looked at me resentfully, while others were envious that I was allotted a single cell. Still, hiding away wasn't an option.

One weekend I summoned the confidence to play chess with another prisoner called Martin. He did not talk about 'Pi night', nor even my crimes. Indeed, I was more interested in directing the conversation towards *his* crimes, for Martin had been sentenced for money counterfeiting.

If I ever aspired to any crime, it was his, for there were no indirect or direct victims. The only loser was the state, and with it, some would argue, the economy, which impacted everyone. However, I disagreed with that perspective, especially if the money went to good purposes. The monetary notes we use daily are nothing more than a lie, declaring to be of value when, in reality, there was none – save to the extent of a collective acceptance that they can be exchanged for real goods and services. I saw no harm whatsoever in counterfeiting such lies, only admiration for the intelligence and foresight of those with the audacity to, quite literally, make money.

"How did you do it?" I asked.

He moved a knight across the board. "It's pretty easy. All you need is the right equipment."

I tentatively nudged a rook forward. "What kind of equipment? Would it not be really expensive?"

Such are the conversations whereby amateur lawbreakers become professional criminals. Yet Martin was not forthcoming with information. Perhaps he did not trust me, or needed to get a better feel for my sanity.

"I *spy*, with my little *eye*, something beginning with P!" a voice boomed.

I looked around into the eyes of Martin's cellmate - a short, muscular guy in his mid-twenties.

The chess game was almost complete, and at that point, there was no advantage to either player, but the distraction caused me to make a critical mistake.

"Pie!" the prisoner shouted behind me just as Martin took my Queen.

I turned around and stared. "Are you all right?"

"Me? Yeah, fine. Are *you?*"

A gate clanged shut as an officer strolled onto the wing. Martin's cellmate slinked away.

"Thanks for the game," Martin said, collecting the pieces and putting them into one of the prison's plastic cereal bags. A few metres away, his cellmate smirked at me.

Word spreads fast when you are shown disrespect in front of other inmates and do nothing. Some conclude they can also be disrespectful, escalating into bullying and building momentum into a daily nightmare.

For now, things were not quite ready to head in that direction. The resulting media coverage after my sentencing hearing – from newspapers to BBC news – 'topped up' the former credos I experienced for being a bank robber.

As for the officers, some of them seemed to be in their jobs to actually help people. Miss Coleman, for example, made a point of trying to speak with me whenever she was on duty. Others could be seen routinely talking to inmates informally, even joining in the occasional game of pool. Aside from those with no other career prospects, what led to someone wanting to work in prison? It baffled me. Was this their way of making a difference, of turning broken lives around? Or was it more about relishing the power of locking up other human beings and inflicting punishments that even the highest-ranking police officer wouldn't be capable of?

One thing had not changed since my imprisonment, and that was curiosity. I constantly needed to find reason within irrationality, to bring understanding to what previously appeared incomprehensible. I mixed with other prisoners with brevity and forbearance, yet in those interactions I sought to understand their individual journeys. Some resembled flotsam on a current, going where fate had deemed to deposit them. Others had a burning will to forge their own paths, even if that led to crime. What defined all their journeys was the illusion that society had indoctrinated them into believing: money.

Their choices were built on acquiring it. When they were prevented from doing so through the rules or were not content with the little they could gain lawfully, they strayed into burglary, robbery or dealing. They also had morals. One burglar spoke proudly of how he only targeted 'commercial properties'. Another prisoner, a twenty-two-year-old former university student spending his first sentence for an assault, reminisced on the respectable life he once led – destroyed by one impulsive act.

Meanwhile, while some judges were content to sentence single parents for victimless crimes, it was not so much the parent that suffered but those who were completely innocent. The lives of some who might have made a positive difference to the world were instead drawn into a quagmire of loss and alienation, with many simply following in their parent's footsteps.

As important as these things were, they also occurred within a microcosm. Beyond that was a small society, itself part of a little nation and, looking to the wider world itself – as beautiful and incredible as it is – that too is minuscule compared to the rest of the universe.

Occasionally, I saw past the glare of floodlights and glimpsed the faint impression of Venus or the silver smile of the moon. Behind bars, these celestial objects were a reminder, painful in its comprehension yet reassuring in its constancy: they would remain, undimmed – even as humanity surrendered its grip on the Earth. Ultimately, my entire life was insignificant and transient – a single drop in the ocean, a sand grain in the Sahara, as the planet continues to circle the nearest star. Within this strange existence, we all drift to currents never entirely of our own making. Like embers caught in a fire, we float, upwards or downwards, until we vanish unseen into the darkness or come too close to the flame, blinking into the same depthless unknown.

A day will come – sooner than we think – when even those who roam in good conscience within the borders of man's laws will be prisoners of their society's choices. They are choices that prize greed and acquisition above sharing and compassion, which wantonly destroy the natural environment and exploit the vulnerable in order to keep a minority in control.

**

This was a time before the prison budget had been cut to the bones and when there remained some legacy of treating prisoners like human beings. Labour were still in power, or rather New Labour. A prisoner could easily access work, gym, exercise, training and even classes like art – which I enrolled upon. Held in the evenings, the tutor was in her mid-thirties, with long braids of auburn hair and a soft voice that always praised the artwork.

After asking me what I would like to paint, she said I should try some watercolour pieces of natural landscapes. The others were all stuck into doing various portraits, some using crayons and others oil-based paints. Only in October did the art tutor's focus suddenly shift, encouraging us to do pieces around Black History Month. Not much encouragement was needed: the grand prize of £10 phone credit equalled a week's wages.

The classroom had an old computer with a version of Encarta 1998, and I began doing a special poster from Encarta's images, as well as helping another with his. Nicknamed 'Dred', of African-Caribbean descent, he praised my drawings when they were derided by everyone else.

"You must be descended from Van Gogh," he chuckled with his

big belly laugh, looking over my shoulder at another botched attempt at a lavender field. Another prisoner across the desk scowled, filling in the lines of a piece resembling a rendition of *The Scream*.

Dred experienced great difficulties with written English, so most of my time was spent helping him write sentences for the poster. Overall, we were both proud of the piece he subsequently produced.

A few weeks later, I received a slip under my door. Lo and behold, the competition's winner was not Dred, but me. I had hardly put any time into my poster, and Dred's was much better. So, as a fair shared prize, I brought over a few chocolate bars I purchased from the canteen for us to munch on in the art class.

Not long after, I had to visit the dentist. Two of them practised at Hewell – one allegedly being a beautiful woman, the other being a bald old man. As if to balance out my luck with the art class, I got the man.

"You got some good gnashers there," he said, peering into my mouth with a mirror.

I found it ironic and a little worrying that his own teeth were in major disarray.

"But – but – but!" he exclaimed frenetically, "it looks like we've got one that may need digging up."

I sat up slightly, eyes widening. That could mean going to an outside hospital...

"No, no," the dentist said, mistaking my reaction. "It is nothing serious, just a little removal. As long as you don't let it get compacted by sugary food, it shouldn't get any worse."

The first thing I did when back on the wing was to search out a doughnut.

"Hey, Pie-Guy."

The irritating nickname had been given by some of the inmates – including Joe.

"You put in a transfer request yet?" He was in one of his active moods, pacing the bottom landing and watching the pool games. Most days, he was just an invisible presence, reading in his cell or going to his job as a Segregation orderly.

I nodded.

"You'll be moved soon enough," he advised. "Have they told you where you are going yet?"

"No."

"Hmm. You should ask for Lowdham Grange."

"Yes, you already said that. They won't respond to my applications about it."

He laughed – a booming roar that ricocheted around the wing. "You just put in an app? You need to *talk* to them, make them your friends. That's the only way to get things done."

"It's not a pleasant prospect," I said, "being in any prison for another six years."

"What if you had a cell with a stereo and a PlayStation? If you were doing an OU course and in a decent job? Plus, tons of gym? You'd feel better about it then, I bet."

He strode away.

Joe may have been right, but I made no attempts to 'befriend' the guards. It was hard enough with other inmates. I had to constantly remind myself of 'Rule Number Two': Don't Let the Bastards Bring You Down – and occasionally resorted to calling the Samaritans on one of the wing phones. This was one of the few free numbers; standard calls were paid via a canteen credit system.

Occasionally I also went to Chapel after being persuaded by Dred. They held regular meetings for people of different faiths, but I only attended Sunday service. It was a relatively small space, so only a few wings could come at a time. A stained-glass panel, about the size of a car windshield, hovered above the altar. Blue, red and green lines merged with the figure of a white dove, as if flying in through the glass – or out of it. I often sat next to Dred, although this meant being in the front row rather than my favoured position at the back. I didn't like the awkward proximity of the preacher. At least the smell was better up front, though, with small incense sticks brought out for each service.

On most Sundays, a guest speaker conveyed their 'journeys to Christ' – some were former prisoners and gang members; others were leaders of community groups. Not that it made much difference to most attendees. The Chapel was renowned as a place for exchange, more of gossip and illicit items than anything else. Prisoners from multiple wings could mingle relatively unobserved, so it was often busy. Some, like Dred, sang loudly to the hymns or happily volunteered to read from the Bible. And there were others, like me, who just looked at the dove.

Chapter 5: The World, Behind Glass

"Jackley, pack your shit!"

In October, the long-awaited transfer finally came. But where?

I got the answer from a pleasant and plump 'OSG' lady. Operational Support Grade was the tier below regular prison guard: the lowest rung on the ladder.

"You are going to Garth," she said.

"Jackley! Your shit still not packed? You need to get down to Reception in five minutes!" It was the same guard whose ugly face had greeted me first thing.

It took only a few minutes to pack everything, mostly paperwork.

Kev came beetling over. "So, you're leaving?"

"Yes, going to Garth. Do you know anything about it?"

He frowned. "Can't say I've ever heard of the place." Turning around, he called to another prisoner. "Hey, Tom, you heard of Garth?"

"Some Northern prison."

On one level, I felt pleased to be moving after so long. But on another, I was deeply anxious. Going to Garth had never been indicated before. I thought they would send me to a Southern prison or Lowdham Grange; instead, none of the three options I listed had been selected.

I was placed into a holding cell with two others from different wings. They hardly said anything, and neither did I. One looked like a blonde-haired scarecrow, and the other was well into his thirties with short black hair.

Despite the previous haste, it took well over an hour before we were loaded onto the white G4S transport van. It had two staff: a driver and someone in the prisoner compartment. Within minutes of leaving, the driver cranked up the radio, and his colleague started handing round packets of crisps. My eyes were glued to the small plexiglass window, heavily reinforced and scratched.

I could see *the world*. There were birds, trees, fields, people, and cars.

Above, ever-changing cloud formations skimmed the sky. Sunrays cascaded across every floating pinnacle, breaking up contours into striations of colour. Countless shapes, faces, mythical beasts and ocean-washed coasts materialised in that vaporous aerial world. But sadness swept over me when I glanced outside on city streets, seeing university students – young, free, happy – a life that had been mine.

A knife plunged into my stomach, twisting its dull blade around and around, dragging in its wake the entrails of a past that could never be repeated. I looked up at the small hatch. It was some kind of escape panel, perhaps in case the van overturned or caught fire. Standing up, I pushed.

It wouldn't budge.

I peered into the van, trying to see the G4S guard, but could only glimpse the blonde-haired guy in the compartment next to me.

He glanced over, met my gaze, then looked away.

The risk was clear, but I tried, nonetheless. Standing on the plastic seat, I braced my whole body – pushing from my feet upwards until my head pounded.

No use. I doubted if even the strongest American prisoners, perhaps not even Schwarzenegger in his Terminator 1 days, could have forced open that teasing rectangle to freedom.

Whether the other prisoner saw my efforts or not, he didn't react. Instead, he gazed out into the world, behind glass.

Looking, but also maybe dreaming of the past and despairing at the present. The small compartments were barely the size of small phone booths, and mine had tiny indentations. I imagined all the previous occupants banging their heads and fists against the plastic in anger and loss.

By now, the van had travelled for well over two hours, and I was desperate to pee. Nor was I alone.

"Alright, alright," the G4S guard huffed, stumbling down the aisle between the compartments. "Here are some piss bags," he said, sliding something under every door.

I tore open a small plastic bag to find another bag inside.

Had other drivers been looking, I doubted they could picture us three taking a pee, somewhere in the middle of England.

The guard casually collected each bag, snapping off his gloves as he dumped them into a bin.

"How long we got left, 'guv?" the blonde-haired guy asked.

"Hmmm, I'd say about another hour."

I sighed. That could mean anything from between two hours to half a day. But to my surprise, the van soon pulled off the motorway, taking a series of country roads before finally coming to a halt outside a giant prison complex.

'HMP GARTH', a sign declared.

The sketchy blue sky with white clouds had changed to uniform grey. There were no trees, shrubs or any other sign of life. Just one long wall, slightly curved at the top, with a crow perched above a tall camera post.

We crept into the prison gatehouse. Officers prowled around the vehicle, and one boarded to check our names. Instead of the jolly Brummie accent at Hewell, his was a dry northern one.

"Welcome to Garth."

The van passed another rolling gate and then waited outside the reception building. Like at Hewell, an officer stood behind a desk and asked me to confirm my full name. He added a new question that would be repeated many times hereafter: what crime I had committed and how long I was serving. Yet all the paperwork lay right there before him.

Was it really necessary to repeat something he knew and recite the length of my sentence like I needed to be reminded of it? Briefly, I considered telling him I was serving one week for smoking a joint, but then thought better of it. The guards were different than Hewell, speaking in clipped, terse tones and not bothering to ask if I wanted tea or coffee. However, they brought trays of food about an hour later. It must have been around 4:30 pm – the usual serving time for dinner in British prisons.

"Better food here, at least," the blonde-haired guy said, wiping his hand across his mouth.

The other said nothing. He looked outraged and deeply lost in disturbed thoughts.

"You know what this prison is like?" I ventured to the blonde-haired guy.

"Nah, you?"

I shook my head.

"Doing long?"

"Thirteen years," I replied. "You?"

"Ten."

I had not met many prisoners doing double-figure sentences before, but Garth was a Cat 'B' training prison for long-termers. If our sentences had been shorter, we might have gone to a Cat 'C' establishment.

About an hour later, we were escorted along a series of corridors, through multiple barred gates, until arriving at the Induction Wing. It was quiet, for lock-up had already happened. My cell was comparatively large, with lots of shelving, a table, and a single bed – with a pile of neatly folded bedding at the end. A plexiglass and barred window looked out onto an exercise yard surrounded by a high fence. Further away, I saw another prison wing and, beyond that, a high wall through a razor-wire fence. Multiple rows of intensely bright floodlights overlooked it all, with crows perched on many of them.From within my plastic bag, I withdrew some paper and a pen. *Mind over matter, thoughts over bars, hope over despair, light overcoming darkness...*

I stopped, listening. No shouting between cells or clanging of gates.

I flicked the TV on and the screen fizzed into life. Another world, behind glass.

***

There were more lock-ins than Hewell. Occasionally I caught a glimpse of the blonde-haired guy who came with me, playing pool and talking, whilst I remained alone and aloof. It was only a matter of time before this raised suspicion. A quiet prisoner who did not communicate could belong to that most hated of tribes – 'nonces'.

At that time, there was extensive media coverage of a paedophile and baby killer – the case of 'Baby Pete', whose murderer had just been announced to receive five years in prison. Meanwhile, a university student with no prior offences and a non-violent character who never intended to cause harm and pled guilty at the first opportunity was given thirteen.

After being sentenced at Worcester Crown Court in August, I queried my barrister about the prospect of an appeal. "Is there not anything you can do?" I had asked in anguish. "You told me it would be eight years."

"No. That is the case which I compared yours to – the case of *Naidoo* – but this judge chose to give you a higher sentence."

"What about the mitigation that was never mentioned? The issue Dr Maganty raised? The important diary entries – the ones *not* mentioned by that prosecutor? All the other stuff, the fact I never sought to cause harm... doesn't any of that matter?"

He explained that he would look at an appeal, and within a few weeks I received his formal written advice. Now, in the cell at Garth, I took that six-page document out again and stared. Not only was it pointless to appeal the sentence, he wrote, but also risky. An appeal found to be without merit could result in time spent in custody as an 'appellant' not counting towards a sentence.

I felt like ripping it up.

Chapter 6: Garth

God, give me the strength to go through
These troubled times with an uplifted heart,
The will to go on despite my surroundings,
And the peace and knowledge which comes
with understanding.

As a 'B' Category inmate, the cost of my incarceration was around £32,000 at that time, more than the cost of going to Eton. How much would be saved if a small percentage of this was spent on preventing people from committing crimes? So many had ended up in prison through fragmented family circumstances, poverty, drugs, poor education, childhood abuse, unemployment and poor mental health – a host of factors that could have been mitigated through thoughtful investment into public services.

I was different from other prisoners, notwithstanding that a majority were assessed to be suffering from mental health issues, according to the Prison Reform Trust. I differed in how I interacted or, indeed, my lack of interaction. Nonetheless, I sought to give meaning to being cast into the dungeon, trying to fashion it as a challenge and test; an opportunity for self-betterment.

There were others, I thought, who would be in similar situations: working on an experimental submarine with no shore leave; being a prisoner of war; going into a coma after a bad accident; living underground after a nuclear war; residing at an Antarctic outpost; being an animal in a zoo... and thus the hypothetical scenarios piled up, giving me false comparisons that quickly faded.

After a week on the Induction Wing, a guard came to escort me to a completely different part of the prison. With each metre, my trepidation grew. We came to some wing doors, and behind was a layout I had never seen before. Instead of an open hall with rows of cells on each side, a maze of cramped corridors lay ahead, all with cells facing each other under fluorescent strips. Other prisoners glared at me in silence. Jobless, they locked me up all day whilst others roamed around in the corridor chatting to each other. One started sweeping bits of detritus under my door, kicking it randomly and then striding away. He looked around thirty, ripped with muscle, and boasted loudly in conversations with his mates about people he had 'carved up'.

When I went to collect dinner later that evening, I was pushed and shoved until consigned to the very end of the queue, only to discover almost no food remaining at the servery. I left the tray by a bin, my plastic plate fringed by some green and white stuff that might have been kale with mashed potatoes.

Within the closed estate at that time, approximately seventy per cent had previous offences. 'First timers' were consistently more likely to face bullying, manipulation and 'criminal indoctrination'. On the other hand, repeat offenders could better navigate the system, drawing upon support from others and forming sub-groups. These could often be predatory by nature, reaffirming deviant behaviour yet escaping the attention of prison officers.

Even at night, taunts were thrown from behind closed doors. One prisoner, in a mock growling voice, kept repeating variations of the same phrase: "new kid should suck."

It was only a matter of time before I'd have to fight – yet, against such opponents, how could I win? They were all older, bigger and seasoned by prison. With Garth's poor conditions on top, and with so far ahead in hell, there didn't even seem any point in surviving. The fire that had seen me through the worst of America had somehow faded. I began not even bothering to collect meals, which continued for three days before a screw appeared at my door.

"Not eating, Jackley?" he quipped.

I shook my head sadly.

"Well, up to you," he grinned, slamming the door.

Within minutes the lead bully launched a few kicks, returning later to sweep some old cigarette butts, still trailing smoke, into the cell.

Outside, through dense bars, I could barely see the grey-black sky.

Thirteen years.

I longed to be standing at the crest of Huka Falls in New Zealand or atop the red Devonian cliffs of my home. To die young and free rather than lay defeated in a prison cell. Death, either way, began to seem like the greatest escape. To merge with the flow and force of nature, like a raindrop returning to the sky; one form dissipating and transmuting into others. No longer to struggle and feel such aching loss and pain. Only two threads suspended me above the path of suicide: my mother and the prospect of freedom.

You have to hang on. You have to keep going.

How many have spoken the same words in the depths of their despair? After the torturer has had their way, as the victim lies helpless on the cold, blood-stained concrete floor, how often have these words floated soundlessly into the air above? And who has listened? As the wounded soldier lies dying on the battlefield, calling upon God to return him home to his family and loved ones – how often have these words drifted unheeded into the uncaring night?

I had plunged head-first into a kind of zombie state: not eating, not even writing, just waiting. But the pressure built. I would erupt in a blaze of glory, fighting my tormentors to the death, or seek a quieter exit. There were many ways of committing suicide for the solitary prisoner, and I began to run through these: making a rope from the prison bedding or slitting my wrists with a snapped prison-issue razor blade.

My mother... but what of her? I was her only son, her only close relative. After the death of my father, she was effectively alone. But instead of supporting her, as a good son would, I travelled around the world, went to university and committed a crime spree that bought the whole family into disrepute.

Who was I, to make the easy choice of death?

And who was I to carry on living?

It must have been about a week on that wing before a Senior Officer called me up. Frowning from her desk, she asked why I wasn't eating.

My answer, to be transferred to another prison – closer to my mother – drew a long sigh.

"I can't sort that out for you. Have you made an application to OMU?[2]"

"Yes," I replied weakly. "On the Induction Wing, but I never got a response."

"I'll look into it. In the meantime, are you going to eat?"

I just looked down.

"If you don't," she paused, "we'll have to take certain steps you wouldn't like."

She took me back to the cell, with the usual bunch hanging around.

"What are you lot doing here? Shouldn't you be at work?"

"We are, Miss. I'm the wing barber, and he's a landing cleaner."

"What about you?" she turned to the lead bully.

"I'm a cleaner too, Miss," he said politely.

She nodded curtly. "Then you should be wearing more than just a vest and shorts. What do you think this is, a beach bar?"

Their conversation continued after the Senior Officer locked me in the cell. Fortunately, I did not have to endure their presence

---

2   The Offender Manager Unit handled prisoner allocations.

much longer. Within a few hours of the SO's meeting, a guard came and told me to follow him with my belongings. I walked back along the corridors towards the newer part and the Induction Wing. At a juncture, he directed me left, along a strange, windowed walkway, until coming to another set of doors. I heard a faint noise beyond – shouting and the noise of balls clinking against each other.

Another wing.

Except this truly was a wing, rather than a series of cramped corridors. Two landings of cells overlooked an open area of tables with groups playing cards. It resembled the Induction Wing, with a cardio room and an officer's station overlooking it all.

The guard pointed to a cell – big, clean and bright. At dinner time, I broke my fast, expecting a battle to reach the serving hatch, but I found the queue orderly, as had always been the case at Hewell.

The veggie burger and chips tasted delicious.

***

After a week on E Wing, I was given a job in the 'Braille Workshop'. It involved translating books into braille for blind people, which the prison then printed and sent out. Despite its social objectives, the job was tedious, making the long hot afternoons of pruning fruit in Australia seem comparatively interesting. Occasionally I received letters, but they did not always bring positive news. Out of curiosity, I had asked a friend to send in any press cuttings about me. However, when she returned a batch from various sources, including one from the *Daily Mail*, none attempted to understand my crimes, solely portraying them as destructive and selfish.

Cast out from society, demonised by the media, consigned to waste my remaining youth in jail – why not just be given the noose or firing squad? An enemy not of the people but of the state. If my past plans had been realised, people forced into a life of poverty and waste would have been rescued. The global economic system, nothing more than a corrupt corporate oligarchy, would have answered for its wrongs. They deemed the

Organisation I had sought to build a fantasy – yet all things, *all things*, begin with ideas. First, we imagine; then, we plan; then, we build. The step between making ideas a reality was simply about having the *will* to act and then *doing it*. I had crossed the divide that millions of others dared not transgress, even when their hearts protested at the injustice.

But, while taking action, I'd stumbled. Some of it was down to mistakes and poor planning, but in other respects, it would have arisen no matter what. Was I really the freedom fighter I'd hoped to be, or instead, just a deluded criminal?

I wavered back and forth but still clung desperately to the former – if only for survival.

Part of me wanted to defy the system yet again by escaping its clutches, knowing it had committed crimes far worse. It was the same system that had ushered me down a path of crime for the injustices it disposed; that had rejected me as a citizen and then ruthlessly hunted and punished me as a lawbreaker.

Later, at Braille, I sullenly completed the tasks allotted by the instructor.

"You're not liking this, are you?" he asked.

"I don't like any of this," I shot back. "Not the prison, the sentence, nothing."

A few of the others turned round and stared.

The prison's procedures only intensified my frustration. Sometimes there were sudden unannounced lockdowns, with all inmates confined to their cells and strip-searched. It happened four times in one week. Whatever Garth's regime, it varied according to who was on duty. Even the uniform requirements shifted, such that when I left the wing one day, I got barked at to go no further without wearing the tight-fitting green trousers instead of the loose tracksuit bottoms. On other days, random workplaces and areas were closed off. Then there were the radiators, which they chose to crank up at maximum in the day but left stone cold at night. It was impossible to change the heat – each cell had a radiator pipe running across an entire wing. I could only try and cool it down by draping wet towels over the pipe.

Despite the irregularity of some procedures, others remained unchanging across the prison estate. One was how prisoners could not receive any items sent from the outside, save from a minimal list, such as books and paper. As for the rest, they had to be purchased through one of the Prison Service's 'Approved Suppliers', supposedly for security considerations. However, I thought their financial arrangements with these companies (and their grossly inflated prices) also had something to do with it.

I discovered this first-hand that December when called to Reception about a 'package'. My friend had sent in various food items: chocolate, packaged biscuits, nuts and cakes. I watched as three officers sifted through it, my mouth watering as each item was lined up.

"You can't have any of this. We don't allow prisoners to receive food from outside the prison, or any other items, unless ordered on the catalogue."

"But I am on Enhanced IEP level," I responded. Only those prisoners on the highest level of 'incentive and earned privileges' could have an expanded list of permitted items – duvets, curtains, health supplements and the like.

"Doesn't matter what IEP you're on, we have to dispose of these items. I'm sorry."

The apology came unexpectedly, and I suddenly became aware that the officers were just ordinary people in a shitty job having to follow procedures they had no say over, probably on low wages with little time off over Christmas. The anger I had felt previously at 'the system' crumbled in their presence. I would never see this food, but why should it be binned?

"You know, I'm happy for any of you to have it if you want."

A look of surprise came over their faces. "No, we can't do that. Don't worry; it won't be touched."

"No really, I don't mind."

They were silent for a while as they bagged up the items. Then one spoke up. "Surely it won't matter if we let him have some of this packaged stuff? It's already factory sealed – we can put it through the X-ray to double check."

"You know that isn't possible, Tim," his colleague responded, handing the bag to the third officer.

Tim wandered off, muttering something about "DHL[3] making a fortune".

Back on E Wing, an envelope waited in my cell. As I tore it open, my heart leapt. It was from Worcester Crown Court, announcing that my sentence was being reviewed as excessive... that important factors had come to light and needed to be considered... that the prosecutor was arrested for lying to the court and perverting the course of justice...

No, it was just a confiscation hearing – some procedure about taking money from offenders that was alleged to have been acquired from criminal activities. If someone gained X amount from an offence and happened to have X in their bank or assets, the law's position was that money belonged to 'the Crown'.

At least it would mean leaving Garth.

Outside, the usual sentinel crows perched atop the elevated floodlights, like silhouettes against a backdrop of clouds. I hadn't seen a ray of sunlight since arriving at this prison, but around the edge of one cloud shone a golden crest of light.

They say birds have incredible binocular eyesight and perhaps one of Garth's crows would have looked into the many cell windows and seen a single prisoner, his pain somehow pushed aside by a smile.

---

3   The Prison Service's main chosen supplier for catalogue orders at that time.

Chapter 7: Gloucester

I awoke feeling groggy and weak. Eight days had passed, and in those eight turnings of the globe, I had moved south again, back to HMP Hewell. At Reception, a guard singled me out.

"Hey, Jackley. Good luck!"

What the hell did he mean?

For the whole journey to the court, I pondered that question. Back in America, I clung to a mad hope. I had thought someone, likewise committed to changing the system and seeing my plight, would storm in and rescue me. A crazy, childish fantasy, but its embers remained. No, it would never happen. The only way to achieve freedom would be through my own actions. Court was the opportunity I had been waiting for. If it went wrong, it might mean longer time, placement in worse conditions and exclusion from open conditions. But against that was the prospect of *Freedom*!

In the holding cells, I paced back and forth, heart rushing. The hours passed, a plastic-bag lunch got served; I coughed and sneezed into thin toilet paper. Acquiring a cold a few days before had been the last thing I needed.

Then the cell door opened, and two G4S guards beckoned me out.

It's coming...

Up the stairs they marched before reaching a plain wooden door.

Almost nineteen months in hell had passed, confined to a slow decay. Now that hellscape was about to end.

Surely they must be able to hear my heartbeat? I thought.

Then they removed my handcuffs and led me through.

It is impossible to convey, save to those who have seen it, a courtroom from the position of a prisoner or accused. It is not just the layout – the rows and rows of benches, all overseen by the high bench of the judge, above which is the seal of the United Kingdom. There is a sense of an immense force bearing down, centuries of tradition and law confronting you with disapproval. But now there was something else.

Unlike before, glass completely enclosed me from the courtroom.

The two guards pushed me down; I had only barely been aware of the judge entering and ordering everyone to "be seated".

Meaningless words were exchanged between my barrister and the prosecution, followed by the judge making some indecisive remarks. Then the guards returned me to the holding cell.

Once the door closed, I slumped to the ground. It was like being sentenced for a second time, as the brutal knockback of being denied freedom overcame me. I stayed hunched on the floor until I heard footsteps, then leapt up.

It was just another prisoner returning from his hearing, bellowing absurdities about wanting more crisps.

I turned to the wall and punched it, sending a searing wave of pain up from my fist.

By the time the guards came, I had regained some composure, but my solicitor immediately saw through it when we spoke alone in the lawyer's room.

"Are you all right? You know this hearing wasn't about your sentence, I presume?"

I couldn't speak for a few seconds, then looked up. "Yes. I've just got a cold. So, what's happening with this confiscation thing? What did the judge say?"

"Well, I think it's pretty hopeless that you will be able to hold onto this money. The hearing was just to determine if you would consent to it being taken, which you told me you wouldn't, and I conveyed the arguments you raised with me."

I sniffed. "But he didn't order it to be taken."

"No, it just means there will be another hearing for him to do so."

"What… another hearing?"

"Yes."

"When?"

"Probably not very long. You don't need to come if you –"

"No, no, I want to come. Will it be here?"

"Erm, it should be, yes."

"Can't it be held in another court, like where I'm not encased in glass?"

He paused.

"I mean, it doesn't look very good, does it? It makes me look guilty and untrustworthy."

"Hmm… but you're already convicted. It's normal."

"There must be a way. Please. It means a lot to me to appear in a court of law and not look like a criminal. It's probably hard for you to understand, but…"

I trailed off, unsure what to say.

"I'll see what is possible. The court sometimes transfers cases to nearby venues when overloaded, which is very much the case this time of year. I'll see what the clerk says."

"Thank you," I smiled.

We then discussed my thoughts on an appeal and prison life in general. "I'm not finding it easy," I told him, "especially with the prospect of another six years ahead."

"I understand. But I have to agree with the barrister's advice, and would strongly recommend against appealing your sentence."

I bit his words down and rubbed my fist.

"Have you hurt your hand?"

"Oh, just a little," I mumbled.

"Okay, well, keep in touch."

He got up, shook my other hand, and left.

Back on another van within an hour, I vaguely heard them mention going to a different prison. Shivering and coughing, barely able to move the fingers in my right hand, I felt like shit - more mentally than physically.

Had I looked carefully through the curtains of rain, I might have glimpsed an old sign that said 'HMP Gloucester'. Unlike the other establishments, it was based in the heart of a city, within about two hundred metres of Gloucester Cathedral. Originally built as a County Gaol in 1792, it now acted as a 'Category B' Local Holding Prison, similar to HMP Hewell's (Blakenhurst).

In Reception, one of the officers asked the standard question of whether I needed to see a nurse. It would have been stupid to refuse, and besides, I always liked seeing nurses.

This one did not disappoint. In her mid-twenties, with long blonde hair and blue eyes, she spoke with kindness and concern.

"You have a bit of a cold by the sound of it."

I nodded, then mentioned my hand.

She examined it, letting me relish the touch of her warm skin.

"How did you do this?"

"Punched a wall," I blurted.

She laughed, a sound like a clear waterfall over rocks. "Why ever did you do that?"

I just shrugged.

She put some cream on the hand and bandaged it. "I don't think you've broken anything, luckily. But if you have any more problems, put in an application. And don't go punching walls again!"

It quickly became apparent that HMP Gloucester was a crumbling Victorian-era hell pit. In just three years' time, it would be permanently closed after a series of negative Inspectorate reports, only to be used as a site for ghost tours. There were said to be around a hundred and twenty unmarked graves of former prisoners dotted around the site – men who had been sentenced to hanging or who had died in custody.

The wings were dark, rimmed by rusting iron fences, and the cells resembled medieval dungeons with high vaulted ceilings and cellar-like windows.

Mine had no light, neither artificial nor natural. I could only write by the fuzzy blue illumination of the television, which my cellmate spent his days glued to. Some of the screws – for screws they were – had already shown a worrying degree of animosity. Between each other, they laughed and joked in their brightly decorated office. A solitary Christmas tree stood outside as an unwanted reminder of the season, decorated with red and blue baubles.

The poor conditions and lack of proper medicine all prolonged the illness. My cellmate (number 8) – a thin man in his fifties doing a short sentence for burglary – wasn't very happy with it, and he soon got the same. Not that I was alone in bringing in some kind of lurgy; half the prison was coughing and sneezing.

If prisoners didn't spread illness amongst each other, then the vermin did. They were everywhere: various bugs, cockroaches and even the occasional rat. Indeed, I once woke up hearing the pitter-patter of little rat feet on the cold cell floor. These animals were highly flexible, able to squeeze through gaps into a cell. One prisoner even boasted of keeping one as a pet, only for the screws to release it from his 'custody' during a cell search.

Gloucester had plenty of lock-up and very few work or educational spaces. The other prisoners were subdued, and a few were on suicide watch. Someone had killed themselves the previous week.

After a precursory 'induction' consisting of completing four forms with tick-boxes and speaking to an orderly, I got moved to another wing. It was meant to be more modern, with warm single cells, but mine was surprisingly dark. A thick metal mesh obscured the barred window, allowing only pin-pricks of natural light to filter through. The wing itself was laid out in corridors – like the 'Bullies' Den' at Garth. None of the cells had sanitation, so using the toilet (located at the end of each corridor) meant pressing a button and waiting to be unlocked.

The thirty minutes of daily exercise was regularly cancelled, often for no good reason. When less than 1mm of snow drifted down, 'health and safety reasons' prevented it. When incidents occurred on other wings, it caused total lockdowns.

Walking around a small concrete yard may not sound much until realising it is the only time spent outside in the course of 24 hours. Everyone walked in an anti-clockwise direction, like at all the other jails. No prison regulation required this – prisoners just did it. Woe betide anyone who went the opposite way, for you would get nothing but row upon row of scowling faces.

Sometimes I did exercises in the middle of the yard or in a corner as the other prisoners sauntered around. None cared how close they came; some just brushed past, despite the space on their other side. But I did not get any stick, as such. With a bandaged hand, they probably concluded I had been in a fight.

Without work, books consumed the hours – first, *The Word and the Void* series, then *Papillon.*

A legal letter arrived in the second week, which some prison officer had scrawled 'Opened in Error' on the envelope. My eyes jumped to a date: the 4th of January 2010, the next hearing. Just three weeks to go!

To hell with thirteen years. Papillon might have done the same after escaping a life sentence, but even his time seemed easier. In a French penal establishment over seventy years ago, he got out into the sun, worked, and could even swim! I would have rather toiled ten hours in the burning sun and eaten a fried rat for dinner than sit in a cell all day wasting.

***

Cathedral bells rang every Sunday, and they did so even more for Christmas Day. Did anyone going to the service look up at the towering prison walls? Did anyone out there care? Even as their merry bells echoed off the prison, I doubted it.

Christmas inside is pretty dismal. It can help to have friends or at least acquaintances, but at Gloucester, I had neither. A fair degree of outdoor exercise and gym also helps, but these were cancelled. So, most of my time was spent in the cell.

Through the heavy metal window mesh, I could glimpse the sun-drenched sides of the Cathedral, reminding me that it was a pleasant day for some. Whereas outside people may feel some buzz of goodwill to all, in prison, it was reversed, with inmates transferring their frustration and depression onto others. The servery workers wore grim faces, doling out meagre portions of some oily, half-cold breakfast. If you didn't eat meat, you had the delight of two cold thumb-sized 'vegetarian sausages', a waffle shaped like the bars in the windows, and a slice of white bread.

The only thing that never got cancelled was chapel. I had no intention to celebrate Christmas, but at least it offered a chance to get off the wing, and maybe there would be some special treat thrown in as well.

On arrival, it was crammed. Instead of incense, a lingering smell of tobacco and body odour dominated. People pushed and shoved to get in; each man pressed against another. I ended up being squashed between an obese prisoner and another with food stains spread across his blue prison-issue clothing, but the one behind made me regret coming the most. Throughout the whole service, all he did was spew Satanist words against the priest and other speakers - just outside their hearing, but well within mine. Tiny mince pies about the size of an Alcoholics Anonymous medallion were given out at the end, but the resulting scramble caused me to avoid getting one.

I thought of my mother and what she might be doing. She had some good friends living nearby, a Christian couple with an autistic son, and I knew they had invited her round for Christmas lunch. The thought cheered me up. Since lockup came earlier than expected – 4 pm instead of 5 – I didn't get a chance to call her. All day long, the three phones downstairs were stacked with inmates trying to use them, and instead of hemming myself into a tight queue, I had planned to call when dinner was being served. None of the screws cared, of course – they didn't even explain why lock-up was earlier than usual. I guessed they just wanted to get home.

The day ended with the same question I'd asked since handcuffs gripped my wrists at Heathrow Airport: *how much longer?* Without escape, a nightmare ninety months lay ahead. I was still only twenty-three years old, meant to be the prime of life. And what was prison but something that should be reserved for those who are indeed a danger to society? I did not think I was one of them.

In the sparse exercise periods and library visits, it became clear that HMP Gloucester's perimeter lacked the tight security of previous prisons. There were gaps. The top of one building came within jumpable distance of the wall, notwithstanding the presence of barbed wire. By scrambling up a drainpipe and padding the wire with extra clothes, I might have got out. However, the best route was via the next court hearing. As for what happened after – the need for documents, money and transport – I pushed it aside. There was a way for all of it.

There had to be.

Until then, it was twenty-two hours lock up per day: half an hour of exercise (if not cancelled), a brief period of unlock to collect the two meals eaten in one's cell and an hour of 'association' that I usually eschewed. Still, it became hard to forego a whole precious hour unlocked, and soon I began playing chess with another prisoner. He must have been in his early forties, with cropped black hair that receded at the sides, and an occasional twitch in his left eyebrow. I did not ask how long he was doing or what for. My interest was in Hereford, where he came from – the same place where my solicitor said the next court hearing had been moved to.

"You want to know more about Hereford?" he asked after the second chess game. "I live nearby, up the river."

Desperation can quickly eat away at caution. Before long, I

asked probing questions about the courthouse.

"You thinking of doing a runner?" he asked.

I laughed as if he was joking.

"That court's pretty easy to escape from," he smiled. "One of my mates did it a year ago, although he was caught straight after."

"It's got no glass then? For when you come before a judge?"

"Nah, none of that."

The tannoy announced end of association."Thanks for the chess games," I said.

"No problem. Let's talk another time?"

"Sure."

Now I had a contact, not only someone who knew the court but local to the area. The question was: could he be trusted?

Despite my experience in America, where I was betrayed after making enquiries connected to escape, I still thought that inmates did not typically inform on each other. Indeed, this was one of the top unspoken rules of prison life. If an informant – or 'grass' – was found, the consequences would be severe.

The chess-playing prisoner had no job, just like me. He was locked up most of the day and acted nice enough. So, the next day, I played chess with him again, and the day after. He kept losing, so I let him win a few times. And he gave more answers.

I'd only been to Hereford once, scoping it out for a potential heist. It had many banks, with old avenues that could facilitate an easy escape, and was surrounded by countryside. And now the opportunity I had been waiting for so long lay on the horizon – freedom would be mine!

***

December came and went, but just before the New Year a slip got shoved under the door. I read it and frowned.

Another prisoner had committed suicide.

Whoever he was, whatever he had done, his life was now

over. Like the one the month before, another man had chosen death rather than life behind the walls of HMP Gloucester. He was the sixtieth prisoner to do so – a figure that, five years later, would more than double[4].

As the year shifted to 2010, the bells were replaced with bangs. We all heard the fireworks in Gloucester at midnight, and many hammered on their doors, just like at the Metropolitan Detention Centre in New York. Around the world, a million or more iron doors of men and women thrummed with the hopes of something better, just as my own heart rushed to the thought of escape being four days away.

Only, when the 4th of January finally came, nothing happened. My solicitor wasn't sure of the reasons, nor could he specify when we would get another date.

With the prospect of more time at Gloucester, I lodged more job applications and queried the officers, but they simply said there were only enough spaces for one-third of the population. Every day I expected to read a slip declaring another suicide. It made me appreciate the precarious nature of my own situation: I had come close to suicide barely a month ago at Garth. So, I applied to enrol on the NHS Organ Transplant register. At least if I died in custody, or during the process of escape, it could help someone else.

The prison, however, thought otherwise.

Just before lock-up that evening, a group of guards encircled the cell, demanding I accompany them.

"What's it about?" I asked, heart pounding.

"Just follow us."

Two grasped my elbows on each side, then marched me off the wing and back to the prison's older part. Here prisoners were already locked up, with a few shouting through their cell doors.

The guards unlocked a door in the corner of the wing. It

---

4   https://www.statista.com/statistics/314689/prison-deaths-rate-in-england-and-wales/

looked like a single cell: the standard flatbed with a metal toilet, a little table (minus any TV) and a small, barred window. It smelt of fresh paint and, in one corner of the brilliant white ceiling, protected by thick plexiglass, was a camera.

"What's going on?" I gasped.

"You're a suicide risk," he said. "You'll be here for at least forty-eight hours."

"What are you talking about! This makes no sense at all."

After doing a meticulous strip search, they left me alone.

I crashed onto the brick-like plastic mattress, yawned, and then gestured towards the camera. Whoever saw the two stuck-up fingers didn't bother coming to reprimand me.

In the morning, an officer entered to explain I had been placed on an 'ACCT' ('Assessment, Care in Custody, and Teamwork') – their word for suicide watch. He said it would last for two days, 'subject to behavioural review', and came about due to my enquiry about being put on the NHS Organ Donation Register. Perhaps they were being extra cautious because of the two suicides, or maybe they just wanted to make my time even more difficult than it already was. All attempts to reason with him and convey that I was not suicidal failed. But then he started asking a long list of questions I didn't expect, writing my answers down on a document with an orange cover. Before leaving, he announced I would be attending a cookery class. I didn't even realise UK prisons had such courses, let alone one like Gloucester.

Another officer collected me later that morning, and we walked over to an old building linked to the prison library. Once inside, he ushered me into a large room with extended shelves and several cookers. Despite its size, only four other prisoners were there, overseen by a middle–aged, plump lady with short brown hair. The officer told me to wait at the door, then handed the lady my 'orange file' and said some words I couldn't hear. Then he left.

"Hello, Stephen," the lady said. "Have you ever cooked before?"

I blinked. Had some kind of dimensional folding occurred, transferring me to another country or time?

"Erm. Yes, a little."

"Fantastic! Today we have already started making some caramel shortbread," she beamed.

Even the other prisoners – a mix of ages, shapes and ethnicities – were smiling. Not only could we bake actual food, but we were allowed to eat it. Before long, the room began smelling delicious. I watched as, tray by tray, long wedges of chocolate-covered caramel shortbread were taken out. It had proven easy to make: eggs, flour, plenty of sugar and cooking chocolate mixed just the right way. The lady, who said her name was Diana, had spent the entire time ceaselessly buzzing between one person to another, giving out instructions like "oh, a little more sugar, sugar!" and "one more egg and you'll be fed!"

It was like a younger version of Miss Doubtfire: she even wore glasses, which kept misting over.

By the end, I had eaten so much caramel shortbread that collecting lunch on the wing was not an option. Diana even allowed each of us to bring back a plastic container of shortbread slices, most of which I gave away to prisoners and guards alike.

"Mmmm, delicious!" one of the larger officers said.

I would never have imagined it. Not only had I just baked something in prison, but the guards were actually eating it.

Chapter 8: Alcatraz

'A man is never lost. Whatever he may have done, there's always some moment in his life when he has a chance of retrieving himself and becoming a good and useful member of the community.'

Papillon, 'Banco'

It was February 2010, and I was no longer in mainland England. The Isle of Wight lay off the southern coast, with regular ferries running from Southampton and Portsmouth. It was a popular holiday destination, speckled with sandy beaches and sleepy villages. Lesser known were its three prisons. In 2010, they were separated out as HMP Albany, Parkhurst and Camphill. Parkhurst had started life in 1778 as a military hospital and asylum before changing to a prison for children, many of whom were later transported to Australia for trivial offences. After that, it housed the Kray twins and the 'Yorkshire Ripper'.

It was a prison unlike any I had been to before. '*Abandon Hope, All Ye Who Enter Here*' could have been carved above its stone portal. It was, in many ways, the Alcatraz of England. High walls hid the rows of razor wire fences behind, with the tops of foreboding buildings peeking above. At one point, it had been an 'A' Category prison, only to be downgraded to 'B' Category when three inmates escaped in 1995. The trio had managed to copy a master key and, after hiding in the prison's gymnasium, used a ladder to scale the perimeter wall.

I had been to the Isle of Wight once before on a school trip, visiting a ruined Roman villa. Ironically, this coincided with the escape of the three prisoners, and the aftermath of that trip was marked by fears that they would lurk in every shadow, ready to grab any innocent pupil as a hostage. But now *I* was the prisoner, and the one marked out from the rest. For on the long transit they made me wear handcuffs, even within the locked cubicle, which had never happened before and none of the others had to endure. On arrival, I was quizzed by a group of hostile guards about my time in America, the robberies and custodial behaviour. One was from the 'security team' and fingered a large file with my name on it.

What else was written in that file? Why had I been handcuffed the entire journey?

I could not know the answers, but they filled me with anxiety.

Like all UK prisons, Parkhurst required new arrivals to go to a special induction wing. This was the time to apply for a job and to work out the regime. Induction offered a small degree of respite and readiness before movement to the main prison wings.

"Whatever you do," one of the orderlies advised, "try not to go to B Wing."

The orderlies' job was to induct new arrivals whilst performing other duties like cleaning and being on the servery. They were older, all with London accents. They were also pretty generous: the servery helpings were enormous, sometimes even offering seconds.

A large hall adjoined the Induction Wing filled with natural light, and one day I attempted to best my Metropolitan Detention Centre 'burpee' record using a mat in one of the corners. In America, it reached a total of 1500 press-ups across 500 burpees, but at Parkhurst I struggled to get past the 400th set. Perhaps I was just getting older, or maybe it was the interruption of a nun who came across me half-naked and sweat-drenched in the hall, wanting to know if I would be attending chapel.

After the first few days of induction, where prisoners were

unlocked to have their appointments, twenty-two-hour lock-ins followed. Through the door gaps, I glimpsed a new batch of arrivals – all over 30 years' old. One constantly sang off-tune on the landings, gazing upwards at nothing, whilst another hovered ominously over the wing toaster – inserting slice after slice of bread, which he then cut into little triangles.

The official unlock time of 14:00 could be 14:30 or 15:00 or not at all. Despite this, the screws had no issues with unlocking the doors of a minority of prisoners, who wandered around chatting or playing pool. It was especially annoying as I'd planned to call my solicitor, who wrote in a letter to call him at 14:30.

I pressed the cell bell – an electronic button that a prisoner could use to summon an officer when locked up. They made very clear on induction that it should only be used for emergencies. "I need to make a legal phone call," I told the screw whose face framed through the door hatch.

"Unlock is not until three."

"Why? There's others who are unlocked."

"They're on induction," he hissed. When the door finally got unlocked, closer to 16:00 than to 15:00, I was immediately bellowed at. "The prison doesn't revolve around you!"

"Unlock is written down as two o'clock," I responded.

"Two o'clock, three o'clock – we decide!"

In all these delays, only I showed any degree of annoyance. No other cell bells went off or doors hammered with fists, as would have happened in America. Yet such passivity had a good reason, for the screws frowned upon any kind of 'misbehaviour', none more so than when it arose from their own breaching of procedures. Being moved to a bad wing was one way they dished out punishment, as I discovered the next day.

It could have been an entirely different prison. The shouting was cacophonous as I passed through the two heavy barred doors. So this was the notorious B Wing, with five levels of cells reached by two iron staircases on either side. Mine was on the third floor – about the same size as a single cell at HMP Hewell, but it already had someone inside. Ventilation consisted of a five-inch grill on the window, which he chose to keep shut. We exchanged a few words after lockup; then he started to use his PlayStation.

BANG... EXPLOSION... "RELOAD."

Apparently, the game was impossible to play on anything but the highest volume. I lay down on the top bunk and sighed.

Between gaps in the game's audio, I could hear prisoners shouting between the locked cells. Clanging gates opened and shut amidst it all, marking the presence of guards who circled the wing to do their regular checks. Even without those gates, it was often possible to tell when they were nearby due to their footsteps and radios. That was how I heard a group of them approach before the cell door was unlocked.

"I hate to be the bearer of bad news," one said. "But you're going back to the Induction Wing."

Why I almost blurted. But, in prison, you soon learn that asking such questions is pointless: you are often ignored, and when answered, there's a high chance it's a lie. Moreover, I was happy to be moving – regardless of the reason. The game-playing inmate barely glanced away from his TV screen as I grabbed my bag of belongings and followed the guards back to induction.

Days followed of lock-up. Despite the relative peace compared to 'B' Wing, anger began to boil. One long afternoon, I gazed out the small glass-pained window, revealing a bright blue sky of another Spring day and a privileged party of orderlies undertaking gardening work. All the pain at losing freedom surged to meet my rage at the system, where unlock times were just ignored, court dates were inexplicably cancelled and movements to different cells were done without explanation. My fist hit the glass, splitting it into fragments and leaving a jagged shard impaled between my knuckles. Unlike other cells with unbreakable plexiglass, those on Parkhurst's Induction Wing – which dated back to when the prison was first built – were made of real glass. Thick blood began to run down my arm.

I tore out the wedge of glass, then wrapped a prison-issue t-shirt around my hand. Realising they would see the blood anyway on unlock, I hit the cell button. The guard who appeared looked like he was ready to add to my injuries; only on showing him the blood-stained t-shirt did his expression change and the door got unlocked. After being marched over to see a nurse in the medical center, who casually sewed up the wound, I came back to Induction. All inmates were still in their cells. I was beckoned into an office filled with screws, all talking and laughing, then shown into another room where a single officer sat behind a desk.

"Take a seat," he said.

The man was muscular, in his forties, with closely cropped hair and a military bearing.

"I've been reading through your file. First America, then here. What is it you're playing at?"

I just stared.

"You think I don't know," his voice rumbled. "I was here at Parkhurst when it was an A Cat, and before that worked in the Maze Prison, then the Special Housing Units. I've seen plenty of hard cases, and I'd say you're on a mission to join them."

The Special Housing Units, or 'SHUs', were notorious: prisons within prisons, which were reserved only for the most dangerous and unruly of prisoners. As for 'The Maze', it was where IRA members had been subject to one of the most brutal prison regimes documented in Western Europe.

"All I did was punch a window," I said meekly.

He looked at me piercingly, then his desk phone rang.

"Yes? Oh. I'm just talking to him now, actually. No, I wouldn't go that far. Yes..."

The conversation went on for a few minutes before he hung up.

"Who was that?" I ventured.

"You're pretty young," he responded, "but old enough to know better. *Don't* cause any more problems. Talk to some prisoners who have been here longer than you, and you'll get out once you serve your sentence. But if you continue down this line, you might not get out at all."

"But..."

He cut across me. "That was from the Governor of Security. You just need to know you were moved from B Wing because you are deemed unsafe to share a cell with anyone, as you have extremist views."

Extremist views? What was he talking about?

"You will be moved to C Wing, where you will have a single cell. Behave yourself. If I have to see you again... well, we won't go there."

That same evening they moved me to 'C', to a cell located on the top floor near one of the wing's corners. This made noise levels much lower than they would have otherwise been, even though the wing as a whole was quieter than 'B'.

The walls were painted sea blue – my favourite colour – and it had the largest desk I'd ever seen in a cell, perfect for writing. Outside the window, beyond the iron bars, rolling countryside with scattered houses and sunny fields receded distantly. In contrast, the prison's concrete exercise yards and buildings were layered in darkness.

When I came out of the cell after giving it a clean, a flash of colour greeted me. On the landing rail, barely a metre away, sat a green budgie.

Its eyes blinked a few times, as did mine.

Then there was a whistling noise, and the bird flew down to the landing below to perch on a prisoner's shoulder.

I watched, dumbfounded, as he vanished into a cell.

This was my first encounter with a prison budgie. Only some establishments allowed them, and they were restricted to longer-term prisoners, primarily lifers.

Like the bird, I didn't stay long. Barely a week passed when a slip arrived telling me I would be transferred for a 'court appearance': the long-awaited confiscation hearing had finally come! The next day, after many hours in holding cells and the usual G4S journey of discomfort, I entered HMP Winchester.

It was a local remand jail, similar to Gloucester, with a crumbling, Victorian-era veneer that had overseen the incarceration of thousands. I got assigned a cell with someone looking at five years for drug offences. His table was lined with rows of intricate origami birds, which he made to pass the time and occasionally managed to exchange with other prisoners for chocolate bars. He explained how the careful folding of paper was done to create a 3-D shape, and after many failed attempts, I managed to make a little green bird. It reminded me of the Parkhurst budgie. The next day I went to Reception with it, drawing a few bemused stares from staff when I asked to take it on the van with me, for fear it would otherwise get damaged. They refused, throwing it in with the rest of my paperwork.

The bird was crumpled and squashed by the time it was given back at HMP Hewell. I tried unfolding it and remaking the curves but could only arrive at something lop-sided that resembled a frog.

Was it a sign of what the future held in store? Was I to be crumpled by seven and a half years in prison, unable to re-enter the world intact? The worn faces of other long-termers already whispered the answer. They had been through the system, entering as men and fading as shades. Their hopes, their dreams, their lives... were gone. Husks of men, powerless and beaten. It would suck up my life, just as it had theirs.

Only one thing would change that fate.

***

Worcester Crown Court: Round 4. Part of me deflated when they announced it, but hope remained. Of the three times I had been there before, only once had there been a glass screen.

"I'm sure you know what to expect by now," my solicitor said.

"Yes. Did you give the judge the letter I wrote?"

He shook his head. "I don't think it would have helped. The money doesn't have to be proved as coming from your offences – it is enough that it matches what you stole. As I wrote to you, the law is quite clear on this."

I shrugged. "What's the situation with this glass enclosure?"

He pulled on his ear.

"The screen," I clarified. "We talked about it last time."

"Oh, yes. I honestly can't remember if this courtroom we are booked in has screens for prisoners."

At that remark, he excused himself.

Minutes later, they marched me up the familiar flights of stairs and along a corridor. It was a different door from last time. Row upon row of benches faced the highest one, seat of the judge.

No glass! Only a wooden barrier that could be vaulted over with ease. I looked quickly for the exit – then my heart dropped. Two guards stood by it, both staring at me. I looked at the tall windows – all far too high to reach.

Judge Cavell swept into the courtroom. I knew him upon sight. Sure enough, he pronounced his judgment, yet again: that all my assets be taken and paid to 'the Crown'.

When he rose from the bench, with every other person in the courtroom doing likewise, my muscles twitched to leap and run. Perhaps I could get past the two guards – and then there was the judge's door. Could I go through there... and get out?

The chance passed too quickly. Within seconds the guards marched me back out, re-handcuffed, and back down the stone stairs.

They slammed and locked the holding cell door, where another prisoner already sat on the bench. I turned to the wall – the same cold concrete I had punched in blind despair two months previously. Was there a mark on that cold stone or just the faintest streak blood? No, it was flawless in its solid death – unmarked, uncaring; a symbol of the system. Nothing I did would have an impression upon it, nor would it regard me with mercy or understanding.

I sat on the wooden bench beside the other prisoner. Eyes closed.

***

Back at HMP Hewell again, they moved me from the Induction Wing to the 'Enhanced' one I knew from before. Kev, Joe and a few others I recognised were still there. This time, I was paired up with a man from Bangladesh, Ali, serving twelve months for 'passport fraud'. I guessed it was his first time in prison, and we sometimes spoke about his home. He told me he simply intended to live and work in the UK, yet could never do so without the right passport. Remaining in Bangladesh, he would have been condemned to poverty. Now, he would be condemned to that anyway.

Ali was my first cellmate (of nine) who used the desk more for writing than watching TV. He used to sit there, hunched over another letter, with cheap blue glasses slipping down his nose.

Once again, I saw Dr Maganty, who bore a striking resemblance to Ali. When I told him about my sentence length, a frown creased his forehead.

"I'm very sorry to hear that. It is unfortunate that your solicitor did not decide to arrange a full psychiatric evaluation."

"It was something about not risking an IPP sentence," I replied.

Someone knocked on the door. "Just a few more minutes, please."

I watched the doctor thumb through some papers.

"You can still get a report done," he observed.

I nodded, uncertain.

"In the meantime, to help this be done, I will put you on a medical hold for six months. Is that enough time for you?"

Remembering Parkhurst, I said it was. "You can put in a medical slip if you need to see me again."

I thanked him and got up.

"One other thing," he said as my hand touched the door. "You may wish to consider applying for a therapeutic community. It might help deal with some of the issues you told me about."

I'd never heard of such a place, but when I asked Kev about it later, he said there were only a few dotted around the UK and that it was hard for prisoners to be accepted for them. Joe, in contrast, dismissed them as 'places for nonces and grasses'. "You'll be better off going to a decent prison, like Lowdham, as I told you."

"I tried that, but they said I'd be returning to Parkhurst – at least I would be, if not for the medical hold."

"Well," Joe said, "I'm hoping to be transferred to Lowdham next month. Can't bloody wait."

I was still down for evening art classes, so I went back and dug out a painting half-finished months ago of bluebells in a wood. It was based on a place I used to visit with my mother as a child, and I planned to send it to her once completed as a special surprise. Other paintings were stuffed below it, and I immediately recognised one by Dred. It showed three men hanging on crucifixes, with a ray of light cascading from red clouds onto the central figure. He wasn't in the class now and the female tutor had been replaced by a thin, elderly man who kept coughing slightly every minute as if clearing his throat to say something.

I wondered if Dred was still in the prison and if I should take his painting to the chapel. It was too good to be lying on a shelf, forgotten. I decided to speak to the chaplain that Sunday before doing anything.

***

The next morning, three days before my birthday, the cell door crashed open.

"Jackley, pack up! You're being transferred."

I looked up at the guard, barely awake.

"But there's a medical hold," I started to say, only for him to walk out. "Medical will confirm that I have a hold on the transfer!" I shouted after him desperately.

A uniform materialised from an office door. He was a 'Principal Officer' grade – the tier above Senior Officer – peering out like a troll seeking its next meal.

"Ya don't have no hold." He glared at both the other officer and me. "Get him down Reception."

"Right," the screw said, swaying slightly from side to side. "Pack your shit and get here in five minutes."

I went back to find my cellmate still in bed.

"What's going on?" he queried.

"They are trying to transfer me, despite having a medical hold."

"Ah, not good, that isn't," he frowned. "You should tell them this; maybe you don't go."

I felt like replying that it didn't matter what I said or did, yet it was something different for this to happen barely days after being told by a doctor that no transfer would occur. Then I remembered Parkhurst, whose paranoid security department already saw me as an escape risk and 'extremist'.

"You ready then?" the same screw appeared.

"No, you have made a mistake. I won't go. You might as well take me to segregation."

He paused, peered into my eyes, then turned around and returned to the wing office.

"Oh," my cellmate said, getting out of bed and slipping on his glasses. "What will happen now?"

I began reassuring him that everything would be fine; he wouldn't get into trouble because it was only to do with me, and when I heard other prisoners being unlocked it seemed the officers had finally listened and contacted medical.

The illusion quickly faded. Three guards suddenly appeared, yelling the same order. I just said nothing.

"Right then," the tallest one said. "We'll take you to segregation."

They marched me out and along the walkways as other prisoners stared.

Back to the same Seg I had started my UK sentence, I caught a glimpse of Joe before being thrust into a bare cell.

"Pie-Guy. What are *you* doing here?" he asked through the door gap.

"They want to transfer me, but there is a medical hold. The doctor told me only a few days ago."

"Hmm," he paused, looking around. "I don't think you'll accomplish much by coming here..."

He trailed off when a screw reappeared – or rather, four of them.

"You are going to Parkhurst," the lead one said. "The bus is waiting."

These weren't wing screws but part of the dedicated security team – former military personnel. But I just looked at them and shook my head.

"There is a medical hold. I am not meant to be transferred. Medical will confirm this."

The screws moved into the cell, towering over me. "I've already checked with medical. There is no hold. And even if there were, you are still going to move."

I backed up.

"You either come with us now, or you'll be twisted up and put on a special van."

One stepped forwards menacingly, bumping a huge fist into his palm.

Part of me wanted to resist, even if the outcome was inevitable. I'd felt it all before in America - blows, restraining belts, bare concrete cells and nightly relocations. I'd seen what happened when power confronted powerlessness. There I barely survived a year of it – here, six more loomed ahead.

"All right," I told the lead screw, "I'll go in the van."

"Good choice," he said.

As I walked past the fist-bumping screw, he swung a savage underhand blow into my side, sending me crumpling to the ground.

"Oops," he blurted.

The other screws laughed and grabbed my arms, dragging me

to the van and practically throwing me on board.

"What's going on?" a prisoner cried.

"Shuddup!" the lead screw responded, passing me to one of the G4S guards and handing over a thick document.

Probing questions were soon fired at me by the other prisoners as the van rolled forward, but I could hardly speak. I just sat shivering, feeling like a wad of gum blocked my throat.

After ten minutes of croaky breathing, I called to one of the guards.

"*Asthma?*" He made it sound like he'd never heard the word before.

"Yes. I need my inhaler."

It was amongst my belongings, somewhere, and I could only hope they had been collected from my cell.

"There's no inhaler here," the G4S guard said. He shouted to the driver. "Hey, Maggie, someone says they have asthma."

The driver called back something about not taking risks, then announced they were returning to Hewell.

"What the fuck," one of the prisoners shouted, "we've already been waiting for ages!"

And they waited longer as the van was kept stationary outside the prison gate. I recalled what a nurse had told me as a child: *"Breathe calmly, slowly, don't hold it."* In this way, the tightness in my throat eased.

Amidst a cacophony of angry shouting and after another hour, HMP Hewell told the G4S guards that I "did not have asthma" and had no reason to open the gates. The van duly turned around and headed back out on the road to the further moans of its prisoners.

Then came another shock: the destination was not Parkhurst but Wandsworth, in London! The journey took around five hours, by which time piss-bags had been handed out twice. Eventually everyone was offloaded within the confines of HMP Wandsworth late into the evening, with the reception screws not even bothering to confirm our names. They acted tired and impatient, barking orders out threateningly.

I was put in a large holding cell with the others. The loudest again complained about how long he had waited at Hewell. He was not that big, but it soon became apparent he had two 'friends', whom he laughed and joked with. A fourth prisoner just sat there in silence.

"It's your fault it took so long," the loudmouth confronted me, with his two cronies behind.

"Yeah?" I replied. "Well, I didn't ask to be here, did I?"

He shoved me.

I pushed him back.

"Fucking cunt!" he cried, launching a fist that struck sideways against my jaw.

I staggered, then the adrenalin kicked in, and with it came the anger – not just at him, but at the prison guards who violently dragged me onto the van, the breaking of a medical holding order, and the justice system itself. Just as his mates were on the verge of joining, I threw a whirlwind of blows, sending him backwards.

He glanced at his two friends. If they joined, I might be lucky to escape with minor injuries, but I could not know how far it would go.

"Come on then! What are you waiting for?!" he yelled, striding forwards.

Suddenly the hatch in the door cracked open.

"What's going on in here?" a woman officer said.

I stood back, as did the loudmouth. "Nothing, Miss," he replied. "We're just having a chat."

"Yeah," one of his friends added, "just a bit of energy, you know."

The officer looked at me. "Is that so?"

"Yes," I confirmed.

"If I come back and you boys have caused trouble, you will all go to Segregation."

With that, she left, and within seconds the loudmouth came forward – only to be held back by one of the others. "Come on, Mav; he's not worth it. I don't want to end up in Seg."

I kept my eye on him as he paced the cell, mumbling a few

insults and then increasingly louder 'jokes' to his friends that were clearly about me. The officer's return could not have come sooner.

"Good boys," she said, looking around.

We filtered out and followed her through a series of gates.

"What the fuck is this!" the loudmouth exclaimed.

"Mind your language!" the officer said. "We haven't got any room on the other wings, so you'll have to spend a night on the VP Wing."

The wing was immediately recognisable as different from the others due to a cardboard 'wall' that lay against the bars, intended to hide those behind from view of the general prison population.

The loudmouth managed to get a cell with one of his friends, but the rest of us had to be paired up with existing inmates. Needless to say, I didn't sleep that night – conscious that the person lying on the bunk below could be a serial rapist. He was a large man in his 40s and tried to make conversation when I first entered, but my mono-syllabic answers quickly put it to an end.

The next day we were brought down to Reception. My jaw felt sore and I didn't relish the prospect of another altercation, but loudmouth hung back with his two friends on the opposite side of a holding cell, barely looking at me. He was quickly loaded onto a van bound for HMP Swaleside. His two friends were going to the 'C' Category HMP Camphill on the Isle of Wight. The fourth prisoner remained as quiet as me.

Part II: SURVIVAL

"A man's life can pivot on the smallest hinge of time. No minute is without potential for momentous change, and each tick of the clock might be the voice of Fate whispering a promise or a warning."

'The Good Guy', Dean Koontz

Chapter 9: Working it Out

Was it some kind of joke? First dragged to the top of England, then right to the bottom again, before yo-yo-ing back and forth to the middle. Now it was Parkhurst: Episode II – Attack of the... Screws?

I was put in a holding cell with the other quiet prisoner who came with me on the journey from Hewell, who introduced himself as Chris.

"Those were some real idiots," he sighed.

I looked at him, surprised. The trio had ignored him, and his shape probably had something to do with it. Bigger and taller than me, he was nonetheless around the same age. His closely cut brown hair met with a small scar on his left temple.

"How long have you been in prison?" I asked.

"Two years. Got another seven to do. What about you?"

I told him.

Chris said he was 'doing time for attempted murder' but wouldn't give details. He was more interested in Parkhurst's conditions. "It's okay," I replied non-committedly. He went to the Induction Wing and me to C Wing – back to the same blue cell they had placed me in just a few weeks previously. Then it was lock-up.... nights and days of lock-up.

My twenty-fourth birthday came and went. It was possibly the quietest, most non-eventful birthday of my life: a lie-in until late morning, followed by writing letters, finished off by an aptly named film – *'In Hell'*. Here the protagonist (played by Jean Claude van Damme) contended with a hostile prison environment, pushing his limits to survive. One line jumped out:-

'You need to find that dark place deep inside,
Forget the world you come from,
Embrace the world you're in.'

If the time ahead was to be truly endured, I had to rediscover the strength of heart and body I first embraced in America. Just a few days previously, I barely avoided losing a fight – but how many more might lie ahead?

Accordingly, I began an intensive workout regime. When exercise got called, I used every minute to sprint up and down the sloped concrete yard, as well as do frog leaps. C Wing also had a small gym, usually open for 'Association' times in the evenings and on weekends. I used this whenever I could, notwithstanding the antics of some inmates. One group used to bring in a stereo, blasting out racist rap music, with one bare-chested man making exaggerated dance moves. At first, I thought the 28kg dumbbells were a decent weight to be bench pressing, but then I noticed another prisoner happily pushing 35kg beside me. Several used a variety of things they could order from the canteen, like milk powder and cans of tuna, but this depended on having money, which – jobless – I lacked.

Of course, the gym was generally a noisy, crowded, and intimidating place - the opposite of writing and reading alone in my cell. But, once I overcame the initial reluctance, it became a vital outlet for stress, anxiety, and anger. It provided something to aim for, with direct results you could see when everything else in prison was intangible. Gym also represented the only arena where inmates could better themselves in a way almost equivalent to those outside of prison. Indeed, this could be where we had an advantage due to the stringent diet, ample time, and compelling need to be strong. There wasn't any option of partying on weekends, with no access to alcohol or decadent foods.

For the tabloids who decried even the concept of prison gyms, they forgot the consequences of imprisoning young men against their will. Such facilities were not only beneficial to mental and physical health, when so many other vital avenues were denied, but also to the prison authorities themselves. A closed or non-existent gym equated to much higher tension levels, with inevitable violent outbursts on other prisoners and staff alike. This was also why gyms often organised competitions between different wings, together with team sports like football and volleyball.

Every day, I plunged into military-style exercises. When the gym was unavailable, I used the net brackets above the stairs to do pull-ups. Burpees, sit-ups, and push-ups could all be done in the cell. When the gym was open, I trained solo – flying through sets and working multiple muscle groups until my entire body burned by the day's end.

One afternoon, halfway through some exercises, the door burst open, and two guards entered the cell. They started moaning about 'untidiness' and some graffiti I had scrawled on the walls. They also asked about my applications to the IMB[5]. I confirmed it was not about them or the prison but my transfer from Hewell. "Although," I added, "it would help to have a job by now." They proceeded to do a careful strip search, then made me stand outside as they went through the cell inch by inch.

Another prisoner came up to me later. "So, you've been burgled," he remarked.

'Being burgled' meant having a cell search, for it usually resulted in the confiscation of items. In my case, a few cardboard boxes and plastic 'pop bubble' lining had been taken, which I had used as an impromptu exercise mat. The other prisoner said his stereo was removed for some reason.

"Haven't they given you a job yet?" he asked.

"No. I put in for gardens but heard nothing."

"Just gardens?" He chuffed. "Not many people get that job.

---

5   Independent Monitoring Board – a quasi-inspectorate body consisting of members of the public who visited a prison, that prisoners could apply to speak with.

You have to be here for years."

Gardens was my first choice in every prison I had entered. Of course, no ordinary prisoner could benefit from using the gardens, a fact seemingly lost on the prison administration. I could only walk through them on escorted movement to the chapel every Sunday. There was even a fishpond, overlooked by trees and beds of multi-coloured flowers. On one occasion, when there was a long queue outside the chapel entrance, I casually walked over to the pond and sat by it. For a few minutes I was at peace with nature, watching the golden-hued fish swim in circles as birds sang aloud, before a guard ordered me back.

"Not just gardens," I told the other prisoner. "Something else too – craft shop."

"Oh," he grinned. "Pottery. That's where I work. There's loads of spaces! I'll talk to the instructor for you."

"Thanks."

"No problem. My name's Geoff, by the way – yours?"

"Steve."

"Nice to meet you. Now, I've got to speak with the old quack."

I watched him disappear into the cell next door. It was occupied by Brian, a tall man in his sixties who was a former professor. We had spoken briefly on two occasions, and his educated voice and cultivated demeanour immediately struck me. With a goatee beard, glasses, and a full head of grey hair, my first concern was that I had some kind of paedophile in the cell next to me. However, he was actually serving a life sentence for murder – something he later referred to as "*the* miscarriage of justice". Whilst he rarely left his cell, someone always sat in there chatting with him. Apparently, he advised on legal issues or sometimes just with writing ordinary applications. I often used to hear him hammering away in his cell at night, using an old typewriter that might have come straight out of a sixties era movie.

When I spoke to 'the professor' about my own writing

endeavours, noting that I was in the process of writing a book, his face lit up.

"I'm the editor of the prison newsletter," he said. "Would you like to contribute an article?"

I nodded enthusiastically.

Parkhurst wasn't just filled with murderers and armed robbers. In fact, the majority were doing time for a range of non-violent offences: Geoff, for example, was serving double digits for dealing drugs when he had never been convicted before.

Consideration of mitigating factors varied from judge to judge, resulting in mismatched sentences for similar offences. When Naidoo had embarked on a string of armed robberies, he was given eight years. That was the closest case to me, yet I had been given thirteen years. As for looking beyond to happened to offenders after they are condemned – to the places of incarceration that were meant to be part of the justice system – judges didn't care.

I tried to convey this in the articles I gave to Brian. He told me they were good but were not something he could publish. "For one thing, they wouldn't let me," he said. "For another, they are both immensely long!"

I thought of sending both to *Inside Time*, a national prisoner magazine.[6]

Behind me, someone coughed. It was an overweight, bald man with a Cockney accent: Geoff.

"I have spoken to Ron, the pottery instructor," he said, "and you are due to start next week."

"Really? That's great! Thanks for your help."

***

Despite settling in at C Wing, I still hated Parkhurst. The average lock-in was twenty-two hours a day, and work was postponed due to

---

6   The present day chief director, John Roberts, later instructed his staff to exclude the Arkbound Foundation, despite over 20 pieces written by the author being featured in their magazine.

the instructor's absence. Getting transferred therefore remained a high priority, which required speaking to my 'Offender Supervisor'. He needed to draw up an OASys (Offender Assessment System) report linked to the 'sentence plan', an important document that could impact what a prisoner would do in custody and where they would go. For those serving 'life' and indeterminate sentences, this document was also critical to their release.

When facing sentencing, I was warned about indeterminate sentences – particularly IPPs. At Parkhurst, many prisoners were serving over their 'tariff' periods, often for absurd reasons. One man was being denied release because of not completing an 'offending behaviour programme' on his OASys. Yet that programme was only available in another prison halfway across the country, which he couldn't go to because it was a lower security category, and they kept him 'B' Category. There were many other examples of perverse irregularities, although most didn't get as far as being criticised in the House of Lords (which the IPP sentence did on multiple occasions).

Some of the prisoners who went to consult the professor were looking at appealing their sentences and convictions.

"You don't seem like the typical armed robber," he told me one day.

It wasn't the first time I heard this.

"Are you not appealing your conviction or sentence?" he added.

"Well, no, although it annoys me that the judge disregarded important mitigation and put me on a culpability level the same as a serial rapist or murderer…" I trailed off, remembering he was in for murder.

"But that's the way it is," I finished.

"Indeed," he smiled.

"How have you got through your time in prison?" I asked him. "Don't you ever get… down?"

"I don't let it get to me. I keep myself busy – writing and helping other prisoners to write. And I read. In fact, I've just finished a book, which you might like."

He entered his cell and came out with some kind of textbook. On the jacket was written 'Chaos', by James Gleick.

"Chaos surrounds us," he observed, "so we might as well try to understand it."

Not long after, I requested an even thicker book from the chaplain, Father John. Most chaplains were dour and detached, but on hearing his first sermon, he projected an honest belief in the power of redemption – seeing his congregation not as prisoners but as men. He gladly gave me a Bible on request, noting my name and location. I had read the book before, all of it, when in America. But I felt like rereading it, or at least parts.

Father John was the first prison priest I encountered who spent more time on the wings than in the chapel. He often used to stop by and chat with Brian, and one weekend he gently knocked on my door.

I welcomed him in somewhat awkwardly.

"You didn't come to chapel this morning," he said.

I paused, trying to think of an excuse that didn't involve going to the gym. Then I realised that lying to him would be no better, so I just came out with it.

"Well, you wouldn't be alone. I dare say you didn't miss much."

He glanced over at the Bible I had on the desk. "How's your reading going?"

Part of me wanted to convey that it was a struggle to reconcile my knowledge of science with religion and how so many parts of his book didn't make sense or even contradicted each bother, but instead I just said "it's proving to be interesting."

The priest smiled. "Well, I hope to see you at the next service. I'm throwing in a little extra, so don't miss out!"

***

On the 12th of April, after over a month of waiting for work, I began my first day in the 'craft shop'. Geoff walked with me and I met the instructor, a tall dour man in his forties called Ron, with a pock-marked face. He went over some common-sense rules, then said I could "have a go at making some coils". This consisted of rolling pieces of clay and then coiling them around on top of each other. Using a wooden knife, the coils were then pushed down to create a smooth surface.

There were around ten others, but the majority just sat and talked. The usual annoying questions were asked about my sentence length, crime, then what American prisons were like, and so forth. As usual, being previously in American custody generates a certain level of kudos, which translated into them giving me some peace.

Geoff was an orderly who spent his time banging together large wads of clay "to get rid of air pockets". He had a friend, Neil, who spoke with a high-pitched Scottish accent and buzzed around the workshop doing various things. With fine white hair and a chubby, smiling face, I would guess his age to be between fifty and sixty.

A lot of talk in the workshop was about the forthcoming 'integration' scheme. The prison was handing out forms to all prisoners, with three options: a) they agreed to stay and 'get on' with VP prisoners; b) they would stay, but they did not want to associate with VP prisoners; and c) they did not want to stay and did not want to interact with VP prisoners in any way. At first, this seemed an easy 'get out' ticket from Parkhurst, but then I learned one of the main destinations was HMP Garth. Needless to say, Lowdham Grange and Dovegate were not on the options. Both establishments were privately run and meant to be significantly better, confirming what Joe had told me at HMP Hewell. Dovegate also had a 'Therapeutic Community', mentioned so favourably by Dr Maganty. I had already applied to go there, but they required my OASys to be completed.

With a job and a stereo purchased from the prison's 'catalogue' for £19.99, the hell-scale of Parkhurst got adjusted to '2B'. Music alone could make a tremendous difference. I already had a few CDs that had been sent in by family and friends, so I could fill numerous hours without resorting to the radio. One of the first songs I played was *Vive La Viva*, first heard in a cell on the seventh floor of New York's Metropolitan Detention Centre. Bitter were the tears that came with that song, the aching pang of loss, of knowing things would never be the same again, no matter how hard I tried. All my youth – wasted. All my dreams – destroyed. It was an origami model, a little bird, and no amount of re-folding would restore its wings.

The work helped. On one giant vessel, I inscribed the following lines from Longfellow's *A Psalm of Life:* -

Lives of great men all remind us
We can make our lives sublime,
And, departing, leave behind us
Footprints on the Sands of Time.

Footprints, that perhaps another,
Sailing o'er life's solemn main,
A forlorn and shipwrecked brother,
Seeing, shall take heart again.

Others had suffered for their dreams – dying in bloody battles, tortured in dark dungeons, or being executed to the braying of mobs. People like Papillion had seen through the hell of prison, coming out able to start again. Could I leave something behind, if only a story for others to learn from? Few, if any, would be able to understand why I had chosen the path of crime – but at least the insights I gained afterwards might be related.

No matter how bitter the memories or how taunting the 'what ifs', perhaps a meaning lay in the nightmare. Mistakes were there to be learnt from, not cursed; trials and tribulations to be fought through, rather than blamed.

Chapter 10: Shepherding

The prison started to transfer those who said they would not be mixing with VPs. On the form that had been put under my door, I had marked 'Option B' – to tolerate but not interact with them. I had no time for rapists or child molesters. Yet if they kept out my way, there would be no problems.

Father John addressed his shrunken congregation about this very issue. "Should we judge others so easily," he remarked, "when we ourselves have transgressed?"

He then launched into a series of parallels that I listened to with increasing annoyance. Did he not realise that there was a crime... and a crime? Under his logic, someone who broke the speed limit when driving was the same as an armed robber – the same as me! These 'nonces' he alluded to went out of their way to prey upon the most vulnerable in society. Their perversity scarred lives forever. And they generally received lesser sentences than those convicted of 'commercial crimes', who simply sought to obtain money.

It was pointless arguing with him, though. He just referred to a few verses in the Bible, then looked me in the eye more keenly.

"Has it occurred to you that some people, reading the newspapers about what *you* did, might think of you as a savage man, unable of reform or repentance?"

"Yes, but –"

"Similarly, you are quick to sweepingly categorise the VP population."

"Well," I replied, thinking of something else, "I think this connects to the way that first-timers should be separated from serial offenders, as well as the more serious criminals having differing conditions."

It was true that someone who committed a string of vicious assaults could be in the cell next to a person who had dealt drugs. More insidiously, a serial murderer and rapist could end up next to a young man who had committed burglary and never been to prison.

The priest just listened and nodded. "I see all men as children of God, through eyes of love, no matter what they have done. Everyone is capable of forgiveness."

He glanced at the stack of books in one corner of the cell, with the Bible he had given me perilously near the bottom of the pile.

"Erm, I forgot to give you back that Bible," I said, withdrawing it from the other books and hoping he did not see the position it had been consigned to. Only, in my haste, most of the books toppled over.

He helped reorganise them. "That's all right. You can keep it. You might want to reread it."

He made some small talk about the weather and forthcoming General Election, then returned to the matter of integration.

"From what I understand, all those prisoners who did not choose the third option will be moved," he said. "You would probably go to B Wing temporarily, then transferred to another prison some months later."

"How can they do that?"

"Oh, quite easily, Stephen. You should know by now the Prison Service essentially has total control over prisoners."

"So, the only ones left here will be non – I mean VPs – and those who like VPs?"

"There're more people willing to integrate here than you might think. And you don't have to like people to live with them."

We talked more about it, but eventually, I fell back on the fact I had already submitted my form. To this, he said I could put in an application saying I had changed my mind. He even wrote down what to put on it.

I did not want the total shithole of B Wing and then potentially returning to Garth. So, I put in an application using the priest's exact words.

In the background of all this was a forthcoming General Election. David Cameron, leading the Conservatives, excelled in the polls. To my surprise, several prisoners also said they would vote for him. Not that anybody could: there was a blanket ban on all prisoners being able to vote, which had been declared unlawful by the European Court of Human Rights ('ECHR'). Some of those on C Wing were part of that lawsuit, but none stood in line to get any compensation, nor could they expect any changes. What the ECHR objected to was the nature of the blanket ban, meaning no prisoner could vote irrespective of their circumstances, crime, or length of sentence. They would have been satisfied if the British government had just given the vote to people serving a few days. Yet, the tabloids simplified and twisted the issue to fit with whatever broader political aims they were aligned to.

"Brussels is trying to force us to allow prisoners to vote", one right-wing newspaper declared. "They would have us handing over our precious democracy to rapists, murderers and thugs." Like so many others, this piece pivoted on the issue of prisoners being able to vote as an attack on the European Union, conveniently leaving out that the ECHR was completely separate from the EU.

The term 'fake news' had not yet been widely applied, but it was very much in action and had been for many years. By over-simplifying complex issues, it was not about making them easier to understand but more about manipulating readers. When had a newspaper ever depicted a crime or sentencing hearing with even the slightest sympathy for the offender? It didn't matter what they did or who they were. It never happened! The reason, I suspected, was political. Having a group who could be demonised and used to stir up hatred and fear in the masses had been helpful for countless regimes across history, and many of those who held power in the UK – to say nothing of those who *sought* power – were the same.

The professor, to my annoyance, hoped Cameron would win. I had a few arguments with him about this, usually after a chess game. Out of six games, I still kept losing.

A few days later, I was surprised to see Chris on the wing, whom I had first met when returning to Parkhurst. We caught up in the dinner queue.

"This Wing seems pretty decent," he said.

"Yes," I agreed. "You can even get a gym session practically every day."

"What? We only had one or two sessions a week on B Wing."

"No," I smiled, "on here, you get around four sessions, and the on-wing gym is usually open for association."

"An on-wing gym?" his eyes flashed. "Where is that?"

I showed him, and before long, he became a regular attendee, whom I trained with occasionally when feeling sociable.

***

At the end of every month, the professor prowled around for some contributions to his 'newsletter' - a twelve-page pamphlet filled with 'updates' from the prison's senior ranks and bulletins from Education trying to fill up placements on an unpopular course. However, that still left around four pages for 'prisoner contributions'.

I proposed two ideas: an imaginative comparison of the 18th century and an evaluation of communism. He didn't seem impressed by either, but I outlined them anyway.

"Just think," I said, looking out across the wing, "three hundred years ago, all this was healthy earth with trees and plants. There were uncharted lands across the ocean, where a man could carve a life where he wished."

"But they were cruder times of whips and nails," he groaned.

"Maybe... yet to me, they seem far more civilised, in the sense that the sciences and nobler arts were put on a pedestal – to be pursued and admired. The baser aspects of free enterprise, globalisation and commercialism were in their infancy. The world population had not encroached upon every coast, turning towns and cities into centres of crime –"

He raised his eyebrow.

"– and inequality... which today have spread like a plague worldwide."

On the landing below, I caught a flash of movement. Someone was running, or more accurately *loping*, up the stairs. We both watched the figure with caution. He veered in our direction, said something inaudible, then turned around and descended the stairs again.

It wasn't the first time something like this had happened.

"An entertaining distraction," the professor said. "You were talking about... inequality, I believe?"

"Yes, and the way the world is uniform. I mean, you can travel a hundred or a thousand miles and further, yet still be in the same place – the same culture, social structure, and rules. The vast differences that distinguished nations in the 18th century have dwindled, with one capitalist economy gripping civilisation in its claws."

"Are you a communist then?" he said. "Some would say the unity you speak of is a good thing – it has brought peace and prosperity unlike ever before."

"I would argue it is the antithesis of unification, for it has separated people from their dreams, placing money as the foremost accomplishment, whilst sundering the role of discovery and curiosity."

"You didn't answer my first question. Are you a communist?"

That is how I had been portrayed in some of the tabloids, who have mutated the word over many years, and even the term 'socialism', as a monster.

"At heart, yes," I replied, which drew a wince from him. "People look at Soviet Russia and think *that* is communism, or

China, or similar states. They are not real communist states, only in name, like Britain is not really a monarchy. True communism is about equality, of sharing. *To each according to his needs, from each according to his abilities* – that is communism."

His response was just a look of doubt.

"If you think capitalism is so great," I continued, "you must agree with the exploitation of the working class – and yes, that class still exists; it's just been relocated to other countries, mostly East Asia and Africa. Along with that exploitation comes environmental destruction, which one day will catch up with all of us."

"So, you would have communism as the one and only solution?"

"Hmm, not as such. The only way for a communist society to work is for everyone to be educated and informed on an objective level so that all can make decisions independently and rationally. To me, communism is the same as a socialist democracy."

"I see. But I really don't think I could put such subjects in the newsletter. First of all, they would be vetoed by the prison censor. And they are way above what most people here care about. Can't you write about, I don't know, your time in America and how that changed you positively?"

It wasn't something I wanted to do, but I gave him an article anyway, and he ended up putting it in the Parkhurst newsletter – some dry story about my flight over the Atlantic and how our choices are important. The sort of thing a school kid could write. Nevertheless, I was pleased it solved his problem of excess space.

**

The wing started to fill up as VPs arrived. One moved into a cell only two doors down – an old man in his sixties.

Other animals also arrived: ducks.

Yes, two ducks and their ducklings had appeared in the exercise yard, using small gaps in the fences to move from one area to the next. Some nights I lay awake, listening to them quack from below. Geoff, who had been here for over a year, told me they had come last spring and were protected by some 'environmental regulation order'.

None of the prisoners on C Wing bothered these harmless animals. Why they chose to come so regularly to our concrete exercise yard when there was grass and ponds available might have been due to the breadcrumbs that some threw out their windows.

During my time at Parkhurst, I watched those fluffy ducklings grow, week by week, until they became ducks – and disappeared.

Behind the bars, I dreamt of everything that made up the free and beautiful world. I remembered those days, the time I cycled the French countryside, and the time I had with Sarah.

Everyone around me were deprived of the touch of a woman, some for much longer than others. A few, of course, directed their desire towards men, if that had not already been there to start with. The most brazen was Gary, who had a cell on the first floor near the screws' office. He used to saunter around semi-femininely, a few times eyeing me, Chris, and other young inmates when we did exercises in the yard. For some reason, this was tolerated, perhaps because he was meant to be extremely rich and serving a long sentence for an international drug conspiracy.

Chris, for his part, didn't seem to care whom he interacted with. Sometimes I saw him in Gary's cell, in the middle of some Play Station game. On one occasion, I queried him on this, but he just shrugged. "Who can blame a guy for adapting to his environment?"

However, one day I was in the showers, which consisted of six separate jets of water hidden from the rest of the wing by a thin plastic curtain. I always tried to pick times when nobody else was there, but on this occasion, Chris came in, quickly proceeding to use the shower opposite.

"Your chest is coming along," he remarked.

"Thanks," I said, "I still struggle above a hundred, though. How do you manage it so easily?"

"Dunno," he said. "Just push harder, I guess."

"No, you just gain weight easier. If I do cardio, it falls off me quickly."

"Ah," he smiled. "You've got a great physique."

"Thanks," I replied uncomfortably.

He stepped forward, still naked and body dripping with soapy lather. We almost touched.

I stepped back.

"Don't you –" he started to say, then looked at my face. "Okay."

I hopped out and got dried as quickly as possible, feeling his eyes on me.

In later days, I only spoke with Geoff and the professor. He noticed I was down and lent me some of his classical music CDs. Even Geoff came up once to ask how I was, bringing his version of a present: a seedling.

"I've been growing it from the ginger we get from the canteen. It started sprouting a few days ago. Thought you might want something to brighten up your cell."

"Where did you get the pot and soil from? Won't the screws confiscate this?"

"Got it from someone who works in the gardens. Nah, I keep plants in my cell, and so do a few other prisoners. If you don't annoy the screws, they'll let you keep it."

I put the seedling on my windowsill.

***

As Spring moved to Summer, I remembered the beaches on the Isle of Wight – some of which I'd visited as a child. Moreover, throughout all this time, I had been getting regular letters from my mother, but now they were shorter and less frequent. Knowing what to write to her and the few others who sent me letters was always tricky. What could one say, still being in the same place? So instead I sent the most upbeat poetry I could write, along with sketches. She had wanted to visit for a while, and I had been putting it off. It was essentially an affirmation of being in prison, whereas contact by letter and the occasional phone call made the situation less real.

Still, going through my entire sentence without seeing her would be worse. Now that I was relatively stable, in a prison not hundreds of miles from where she lived, I completed a 'visiting order'. Prisoners were allowed between two to four monthly visits, depending on their 'IEP' status. This stood for 'Incentives and Earned Privileges Scheme' and had three levels: Basic, Standard and Enhanced. All prisoners were by default Standard but could be demoted to Basic for bad behaviour.

Irrespective of whatever 'incentives and privileges' were offered – no matter the conditions – the mind mattered most. There were no greater boundaries, obstacles, or borders than one's own thoughts and emotions. Everything is part of the world – even the steel bars of the jail cell windows or a wasteland of concrete and metal. And yet it was not the same as being by a waterfall, watching the sunrise, gazing upon a starlit night sky. At best, I was in stasis; at worse, in hell.

I knew it even as I sat in the exercise yard, bathed in sunshine. Alone, and wishing...

"What a beautiful day!"

It was Father John walking through the yard and carrying a few books.

"Too right, Father," another prisoner called back. "Can you ask them to give us a bit longer out here?"

"Alas," he said, "that is not within my power. But you are welcome at the Chapel next week, and you could catch a bit more sun on the walk over."

The other prisoner laughed.

The priest spotted me in the corner and strolled over.

"I thought of you when I finished this," he said, handing over a relatively small book.

'The Philosopher and the Wolf' flowed across its cover.

"Thanks. It looks interesting."

"I hope you like it. Now, I must go... there are a few more *deliveries* I've got to make."

I watched him walk onto the wing.

"Hey, Steve!" the prisoner who asked about exercise shouted at me. "You found religion?"

"Not yet."

He burst into laughter, along with his mate. At least some people were happy.

I got up from the hot concrete and slipped my blue prison-issue t-shirt on. Over by the wing door, a screw stood watch. He was old Swinburne, my 'personal officer', and pretty decent – not all of them let us go topless. C Wing had two groups of screws, with one lot being absolute bastards and the other being relatively nice. Sometimes I saw one screw for weeks on end, only for them to disappear for an equal length of time.

I just hoped the ginger plant seedling would not end up being the casualty of a sadist.

It was doing well, sprouting up about six inches within the space of a few weeks, lovely green spreading leaves with tinges of red in the centre.

***

Sometimes prisoners were transferred to other prisons, whilst others were taken to court, and a lucky few were released. In Parkhurst, movements only really happened for those moving towards the end of their sentences or subject to disciplinary punishment. So, after returning one day from the craft shop, I was surprised to find the professor's cell door had been locked and barred.

"He planned to escape," Geoff explained later.

I gawped.

"Yeah," Geoff continued, "got caught writing coded letters."

The BBC later reported:-

"Brian Lawrence, 67, from Berkshire, planned to escape from Parkhurst last week using helicopter flights at the Isle of Wight Festival as cover. He communicated with his accomplices using lemon juice as invisible ink and codes hidden in sudoku puzzles."

Parkhurst's security department, for all their paranoia, had managed to intercept his letters by unpicking an unusual phrase he used - 'more heat, less light' – which revealed hidden messages by heating the paper underneath. Now he was in some Cat A establishment – perhaps for the rest of his life. One of the last things Brian did as editor of the newsletter of Parkhurst was to include a poem I gave him, called 'Lamentation of a Wolf', inspired by Father John's book:-

> *If you could imagine a wolf in the wilderness*
> *Standing tall and proud*
> *Against all perils, withstanding all pain*
> *With amber eyes gazing*
> *Into an ever-changing distance*
> *To a world where he is not hunted,*
> *Where he can run free,*
> *Boundless as the winds which stir the waters,*
> *Living as one with life.*
> *Alone but for the shadow that walks beside him,*
> *Seeking that soulmate who alone can save,*
> *Who alone can defeat the solitude –*
> *Together, as one, breathing unconquered,*
> *A Will and Independence to defy the very Earth*
> *And yet, connected,*
> *To every root and branch,*
> *From smallest to greatest.*
> *The stars, the insects, the fallen leaves,*

The mountains, rivers, and trees.
On a cold starlit night
With an eerie howl which touches the heavens,
Face uplifted into the black unknown –
Calling, crying, searching...
A floating question mark amidst a mystery.

I hoped he would remember this poem and that it would give him strength as he faced turmoil.

I hoped, one day, against all odds, he too would be free.

***

Summer Solstice came and went. With Father John's help, I enrolled upon my first Open University module: 'Crime and Society'. It meant applying for funding, but the priest said this was almost always given.

On my windowsill, the ginger plant had sprouted to over a foot in height and started to show signs of flowering. It had emerged from a plastic bag, bruised and bashed, a blob of sinewy yellow meant to be chopped up and consumed. From that formlessness, it became something else – a living organism, or rather, a burst of life from an existing organism. But if it had been deprived of light and water or bruised too badly, what would it become? A mere clumsy mass, to be used once and then thrown away.

How much different were people? They were living organisms, yet some had not been given the things they needed to develop, like love, responsibility, trust, security, work, and a purpose. How many here had received those things?

And what of the long-termers, like Brian, who could spend decades inside? What went on in their minds? Some eschewed basic things like exercise and gym – retreating into themselves. Had they given up all hope of ever leaving prison? Indeed, did they even want to? There was a word for this – institutionalisation – and even I feared it.

They all said the beginning of a sentence was the hardest – the first days, weeks, and months. As time passed, as months shifted to years, the fire inside – like youth itself – faded. That was why the highest security prisons, which generally housed those doing the lengthiest time, were often more tranquil than the lowest security ones and local remand jails, where the inmates may only be spending a few months. Factor in how those doing longer sentences had to fight harder to progress through the system, with custodial behaviour making all the difference in a re-categorisation or IEP-level review.

Nonetheless, rebellion occasionally erupted at Parkhurst. It didn't take long for a horde of screws to materialise from nowhere when something happened, even when there were meant to be 'staff shortages'. The last disturbance started after an inmate simply wanted to call his family after being told of a death, but there was an issue with his phone credit. He chose the wrong screw to speak with, who rudely told the prisoner to 'put in an ap' [application form]. It didn't take long for a shouting match to ensue, culminating in the bereaved prisoner being taken to segregation. A decent officer might have offered him a wing phone call or spoken sympathetically, which would have resolved the issue.

Therefore, I only interacted with those who had proven decent. Otherwise, I had to lump it if I needed something – like extra kit or some new prison-issue toothpaste.

Once, I saw an elderly inmate hanging around the wing door as prisoners moved to get their medication from healthcare. I had seen him when first arriving at Parkhurst. He must have been edging into his seventies, with a long white beard. He was bent over, pale, resembling a skeletal version of Santa Claus. He hovered around the door near one of the more sadistic screws, occasionally bending down to pick things up.

They were cigarette butts.

A handful lowered themselves to this habit, desperate for tobacco, but seeing this old man do it made me pause.

The screw near him laughed and joked with a gym orderly. They were openly mocking the old man.

JUST TIME

I stepped closer, not caring that I blocked the flow of others.

"I don't know how you people can sleep at night... treating prisoners like animals, locking human beings in cells."

With that, I stormed away.

Chapter 11: Escape from Alcatraz

What immortal Hand wove this thread –
If Good, and full of Light,
Why this pain and pointless fight?
When all things come crashing down
When Earth, Sky and Ocean join
Will there be peace
Or judgment?

The prison machine churned on, devouring goodness and regurgitating waste. I respected those who rebelled openly against it, even when doing so only extended their pain. People like Charles Bronson, who had spent endless years in Segregation. Was the pain levied by the system such a high price for such a lofty principle? Fighting against the judges, the courts, the prison system, the politicians, the lords, Whitehall, corporations with their hands in exploitation and destruction, banks with their feet deep in inequality... yes, many would fight against them if given the means. And, like the cruellest totalitarian regime, they would squash any meaningful resistance into the dust. They would torment, torture, and diminish those who Stood Up.

I'd seen it. I was looking at it every day.

As June became July, the notes of Bob Marley floated down – words of wisdom and righteousness, reflecting on the injustice of an empire that still goes on. They were hot weeks, those two months in Parkhurst, weeks that I wished would pass sooner as I reflected upon what might have been. Some people found Christmas hard, but for me the worse time was summer. A season where I naturally sought out the sparkling sea, meadows of birdsong and the peace of gently stirring trees. Prison, instead, was grey, hostile, suppressing everything that might grow. My only companion was the ginger plant, and how I loved that little bit of green. I tended it as one might care for a child, taking pride in each new leaf it grew.

Everyone was different: some took pleasure in living things, in helping life, in creating; others hid in darkness, eyes pinned to televisions.

The Philosopher and the Wolf, given to me by Father John, contained some interesting observations; how scheming and deception were at the core of social intelligence possessed by simians (apes, including humans) and how many of the traits we valued – like love and empathy – were seen in all social mammals. The author also wrote of a 'disperser' in a wolf pack: that lone creature who set out to find another pack, often dying in the process.

I wanted to be part of something else if it was not possible to change the pack I was born into, with all its injustices and inequalities. Sometimes I looked up to the stars with a deep, unfathomable sense of longing. Was this what the snow wolf felt when he howled at the moon?

That mysterious longing I still knew deep in my heart. Where did it come from?

No stars were visible in Parkhurst, only the occasional glimpse of Venus through the cell window, its light fighting through the amber glare of the prison's many floodlights: a dead and violent world, an example of global warming at its most extreme. Would, one day, Earth become similar?

I sometimes touched upon such things with Father John, and he spoke simply of his faith.

"God has a plan for all of us," he remarked, "but we cannot always work out the details. Even less so for the entire world and universe."

Nodding, I looked briefly past the bars in the window to the blue beyond. I believed in God, but differently from the priest. I saw God in nature, in the beauty and splendour of the world, even as mankind relentlessly destroyed it.

***

On the 25th of July, I was called to collect some items from Reception. Parkhurst, like most prisons, allowed prisoners to purchase supplements from an approved supplier catalogue, subject to IEP status.

My order was a container of whey protein and creatine, placed almost two months ago when deciding to up my training regime. The total cost of £27.50 represented a fortune in prison, but at least it gave the means to push beyond the limits I had reached in the gym.

On return to C Wing, I got a haircut, which I paid for with a packet of eggs (£1). I also started to get a few orders for pottery products, like plates and mugs. In exchange, they gave me canteen products – principally, tins of tuna or the standard prison currency then, 'burn' (tobacco).

Apart from that, my weekly canteen order usually resembled something like the following: -

Chocolate bar... 99p
Jamaican Ginger Beer can... 49p
Noodles... £2
Fish... £2
Marvel (tinned milk)... £1.80
Oats... 70p

Ron ran the craft shop with a loose hand. We could make what we wanted, provided we produced a few things for the prison shop that sold items to the general public and visitors. There were three pottery wheels he kept glancing at pointedly, but none of us had mastered them. I tried, but the result was a lop-sided jug. Using the wheel could also be time-consuming and tedious; each usage required careful cleaning afterwards. As well as the clay, there were plaster moulds, and I made two complete chess sets from these – plus a few unique pieces that I carefully painted. Ron even let me bring back some pieces to the wing so I could finish them off with little tubs of paint during lockup.

Inside Time decided to award one of the poems I sent to them – about the wolf – a £25 'Star Poem of the Month' prize. Suddenly, I was rich again!

Other inmates noted my contributions to 'their' newspaper, usually positively. A few thought otherwise, however.

"Hey, Steve," a voice called in the dinner queue.

It was Chris.

"Love the poem, but can't you write about something more... interesting?"

A few others sniggered.

I wasn't sure if he harboured animosity towards me for spurning him in the showers. Little things like that could bug me, and I still regarded him as comparatively decent. So later, I knocked on his cell, finding him in the middle of writing something.

"What's up?"

"Nothing, just checking you knew about this whey powder I recently got. It's pretty good and cheap."

"Oh? What's it called?"

I told him, and after a few minutes, he thawed.

"We need to train sometime," he remarked.

"Yeah," I said blankly.

"Hey, about what happened, you know..."

"It's okay," I hastily replied.

"Outside, I had a girlfriend and everything..."

"Look, Chris, it's really okay."

"Good. I'm glad we've sorted that out. Let me know if you need spotting again or anything."

"Sure."

In later days I did ask for his help a few times. One of the best techniques was 'negatives', which focused on the stage where you lower a weight, adding a bit more than you would otherwise lift. Another technique was drop sets, where you did a set, took some weight off, did another set immediately, and so forth. This was especially good when combined with split sets (doing alternating muscle groups like biceps and triceps in the same session). At one point, I wrote an article about such things and gave it to one of the new gym orderlies, a large Jamaican prisoner, and he enrolled me on a special weightlifting course that I could do in addition to pottery.

This news might have cheered me up had he not told me he was likewise doing time for a string of armed robberies.

"Ten years," he added. "You?"

"Thirteen."

"Sheet. You been sentenced for it before?"

"No, first..."

"Sheet!"

***

Changes in the daily routine could happen at any time, and they seemed to cause me more stress than anyone else. One day, I went to the wing office when exercise was cancelled for no apparent reason.

"All the other wings have exercise," I remarked to a group of screws.

"Well, this one doesn't."

"Fine. Hope that makes you feel good."

The screws waved me away.

Subsequently, in my cell, I went through multiple sit-up sets. Halfway through, a knock came from the door, and old Swinburne entered.

"You're still 'Enhanced'," he remarked.

I already know that, I thought, but instead just said, "Oh."

Swinburne glanced casually around the cell, rubbed his red nose, and left.

The remark about being on the 'Enhanced' IEP level was his way of saying, "keep your head down".

Swinburne was an old hand. In a way, they did sentences of their own. He was tall, with slightly fading red hair, and had been given the nickname of 'Rudolph'. I liked him: he just left me alone and helped when needed. In those days, officers and prisoners alike could smoke, although officers were meant to use a special shelter. Swinburne, however, just smoked on the yard. Occasionally I used to glimpse his face when standing there – the look of weariness, of being pissed off. Some were like that: they saw the system's madness and inefficiency.

All these months, I must have made close to forty pottery pieces, not counting the plaster chess sets. Pots and jugs, vases two feet high, pen holders, models of horses and even a miniature prison cell with a solitary figure sitting in it. I had been trying to set aside the best pieces to give to my mother, which Ron had finally authorised and agreed to take to the Visits Hall in advance. I wanted to present all the pieces in person to avoid a long conversation about how I was finding things. If needed, I could spend thirty minutes explaining how each piece was made: preparing the clay, shaping it, firing it in the kiln and painting it to a set design.

Unfortunately, undertaking a visit required a dress code: a striped blue and white shirt and uncomfortable jeans. About sixteen others waited with me in the room adjoining the visits hall – some silent, others talking endlessly about inanities. It helped that Chris was there, too; he told me his sister was visiting, whom he hadn't seen since being arrested.

When we were finally let into the hall, a screw gave us the

number of a table to sit at. Some were slightly larger than others; mine was among the smallest.

Then visitors started to trickle through a door. At first elderly people, but then children, as well as a woman holding a baby. Behind her came my mother and godparents.

We exchanged hugs – that was the only physical contact allowed.

"You look well!" Ken, my godfather, exclaimed.

We spoke about the garden – they said my mother had won another local council biodiversity competition – and just as the conversation started to veer towards 'prison life,' I raised my hand.

A screw sidled other. I looked up and held back a wince. It was the same one whom I'd so strongly condemned weeks ago as 'treating prisoners like animals'.

"Yes?"

As nicely as possible, half hoping he had forgotten about our previous interaction, I told him about the box of pottery brought over by Ron.

"I'll check for you," he replied.

When he reappeared minutes later carrying a big cardboard box, I relaxed.

"Here you are," he smiled, placing the box beside Ken.

I began to explain how fantastic the pottery job was as Ken removed a pot – or rather, half a pot.

The next item had not fared much better, with a heavy chip on one side.

"Oh, I'm not sure how that happened," the screw said. "You'll need to talk to Ron."

With that, he left.

I later found out by letter that more than half of the items were damaged in some way. One, in the words of Ken, "was nothing but smithereens."

Seeing my mother had been both painful and heartening, but the broken pottery almost felt like a violation. I had spent so long making those pieces – sometimes, entire weeks – painting elaborate designs and motifs.

When I told Chris and Geoff about this, they didn't think it was a big deal.

"So, you wound up a screw, and he got back at you," Geoff said. "You're lucky you didn't have the visit cancelled altogether on some made-up excuse, as happened to me once, and at least some of the pieces you made were intact."

***

One evening I heard a knock on my cell door just as I finished a letter.

Chris stood there in prison-issue vest and shorts, a reminder that I missed my usual evening gym session.

"Just thought I'd stop by," he said. "Can I come in?"

"Sure."

"I've got this application," he told me, passing over a sheet of paper. It was about enrolling on Enhanced Thinking Skills ('ETS'), an offender behaviour programme I had applied for myself at Hewell.

"I know you're pretty good with writing, so I wondered if you could check it for spelling errors and stuff. I need to get on this for my sentence plan."

I didn't find any, apart from a few missing commas. "Nothing wrong with it."

"Great, thanks!"

"No problem."

He smiled at me brightly, seeming about to say something else, but then left.

I barely had five minutes until lockup, so I ran down to post my letter, swiftly getting reprimanded by the same screw who'd played football with my pottery. "Walk," he cried, "don't run!"

Seeing him was the last thing I needed after his game in visits, but I bit my lip and took another staircase to my cell – having to walk right around the wing and pass the 'gamblers den'. Here prisoners bet on things like tuna tins, packets of crisps, burn, etc. They hardly glanced as I passed.

I felt alone... in a way far more profound than when free. For inside, there was *nobody* and, worse than that, even the company of nature was deprived, save for the ginger plant.

There was Geoff, but he was nothing like the intelligent presence that Brian had been, and then there was Chris, whom I had known longest at Parkhurst but who I still viewed cautiously.

He returned to my cell a few days later after the exercise yard closed.

I was in the middle of sorting through some laundry, but greeted him pleasantly.

"Just heard I'm on that ETS course," he said, sitting on the bed.

"That's great," I said.

"I got to tell you something else," he said uncertainly. "Can you sit down?" he added.

I thought it a strange request, but sat down anyway.

He glanced down, pausing. "Take it how you want... but I find you hot. I don't feel this way towards most guys – hardly any, actually. Outside, it was only girls, but in here... it's not like we can choose. You're doing a long sentence, too; you must know what I mean?"

It took me aback, but I didn't do anything. He remained seated beside me but had turned towards my desk with all its papers. He looked sad. Whether it was sympathy or something else, I put my hand on his arm.

He looked at me, leaned forward, and we kissed.

I became aware of the noise on the wing. "Erm, Chris," I said, withdrawing. We sat there for a few seconds, silent. Then I spoke. "I'm worried prison messes a guy's head up. I need to find my feet with this."

His eyes were a shade of dark green; the same colour as Sarah's.

"I understand," he said. "If you want to chat or anything, you know where I am."

I wasn't sure what to make of what happened. A part of me wanted to see where it would lead; the other part resisted. Each time I saw him, it didn't help resolve the uncertainty, for he acted just as nervous. I didn't go to his cell, and we both trained at opposite sides of the gym.

***

The 19th of September passed, marking twenty-eight months in prison. I did the usual fast and seclusion, broken by a visit from Father John. He confirmed that I had gotten a placement with the Open University, supported by Prisoners Education Trust funding.

I smiled and thanked him. Whereas regular education offered basic-level courses, the Open University offered a pathway to complete the studies I had started as a student before arrest. It was about picking up the pieces of a life and gluing them back together, minus the same mistakes.

Different prisoners were on similar journeys, all in their own ways. Some, like me, were doing OU courses. Others designed and built immense structures from matchsticks. A few days ago, I watched someone wheel away a huge house that stood over one metre tall and two in length, matching the size of the trolley itself. There were patterns in the match-stick walls, around the windows, trailing along the roof. There were even intricate rooms with furniture and terraces. Grit was glued down in pathways around the outside. He was going somewhere – either to another prison or perhaps even being released – and I wondered how long it had taken him to make such an edifice. For what and for whom?

I would never know the answer, but I knew one thing: if given the tools to build a real house or an entire community, what might he achieve?

And now I was standing on the threshold of yet another change; like the man with the giant match-stick model, I would be wheeling away a trolley and leaving C Wing. In place of a match-stick mansion, I would have a stack of paperwork; in place of matches, I would have pens.

After months of waiting, Dovegate Therapeutic Community had finally accepted me.

When applying to this place, I was so eager to put Parkhurst behind me. But now I wasn't so sure. There were even times when taking the long walk to work across a field, with nothing but blue sky above and grass beneath my feet, that I felt close to freedom. Only the walls ahead, and the tall metal post rising high into the sky with its great vulture eye at the top, shattered that illusion.

The Wing SO confirmed that my transfer to Dovegate would take place on the 12th of October, "like it or not." Perhaps he saw the uncertainty in my eyes. Either way, he would never know that on the same date, I arrived in Bangkok five years ago on a round-the-world student ticket. That past, that journey, could have been another person's life.

What followed was a mad scramble to sort things out. I cancelled a visit I had scheduled with my aunt and uncle. Then, with great sadness, I returned my beautiful ginger plant to Geoff. It had left his cell as a tiny seedling; now it came back as a huge plant showing signs of a bright red flower.

"You take care of it," I told him.

"Of course I will." He put it on his window shelf next to another smaller plant.

We swapped prison numbers and promised to keep in touch. At the last minute, we hugged briefly.

On my last gym session, I told Chris I was going.

"You serious?" he said.

"Yes."

"That's shit, man... I mean, I'm pleased for you, though."

He didn't say anything else but later came to my cell.

"So, you're leaving."

"Yeah."

I wrote down my prison number so we could keep in touch.

Then we hugged.

"Yeah," he said, looking long at me. "Write to me when you can."

On the day of my departure, old Swinburne approached. Our last conversation had been about chess, in which he expressed an interest, referencing its long history. "You have improved from when you first arrived," he said. "I wish you the best."

Then we shook hands.

I could not remember another occasion of such forthright decency – to be treated as a person, a man, even an equal, by someone part of 'the system'.

Chapter 12: "Therapy"

"Show me a sane man and I will cure him for you."

Carl Gustav Jung

The Therapeutic Community concept initially started at HMP Grendon in 1962 and boasted of having a lower conviction rate for those who completed it than regular prisons. The model was based on addressing the thoughts behind offences, seeking to understand and change these through group sessions. From Grendon, it expanded to units in HMPs Channings Wood and Dovegate. The company Serco now operated Dovegate, having won a contract from the government.

Before being accepted into a Therapeutic Community, prisoners went through two stages. First, they must apply from another prison and be accepted for entry. Next, they had to pass two months on the 'Assessment Unit', and if deemed suitable, they would then be moved to a Therapeutic Community Unit; if not, they returned to their sending prison. When I arrived, the Assessment Unit had no spaces, so I was put on what the prison officers surreptitiously described as the '*Pre*-Assessment Unit'. In reality, this was for those who were ejected from the Therapeutic Communities or failed in the Assessment Unit.

The accommodation itself was an upgrade to Parkhurst: each cell had its own small shower, and every morning, when unlocking the doors, a guard placed a carton of milk in the sink. They all walked less tensely and called prisoners by their first names. Most of the time, cells were kept unlocked, apart from evening to morning. Even the meals were more substantial and of better quality.

A week passed with the same boring routine before I got moved over to the *real* assessment unit.

Every day, they held a big meeting involving the whole wing (twenty-two people, plus two or three guards) – which involved votes on jobs (from wing painter to being on the servery) and general 'concerns'. At any point, an inmate could put their hand up and raise an issue, usually revolved around what another had done. In the mainstream prison, such conduct would be perilously close to 'grassing', but it was regarded as usual and necessary here. They connected it to the therapy model of 'addressing negative behaviour', although sometimes I struggled to see how beneficial it was with the divisions and tension it often stirred up.

There were also three smaller groups of seven people each. In these, a single prisoner discussed their offences or issues around their offending, which were then questioned and 'constructively critiqued' by other participants, overseen by a prison officer.

My small group had two prisoners who stood out: Ady, a man of average build in his mid-thirties with black hair and glasses, serving a five-year IPP for robbery and kidnapping with violence. He professed to be a 'sociopath' and a 'Satanist' but, with his twisted wit, I couldn't quite tell if these statements were actually true. Then there was Simon, a boyish twenty-three-year-old who spoke with a feminine voice. His crime was among the most unusual and tragic: setting fire to his own house 'to get the attention of police after a friend sexually assaulted him', only for it to go horribly wrong and the fire killing his own mother.

In fact, quite a few were serving sentences for manslaughter and murder. It might seem daunting to speak with a convicted murderer, but they acted the same as everyone else in most cases. I would even go so far as to say that they came across as more intelligent and polite. Such crimes of passion could be sudden and unplanned.

Brian was an example. He had killed a convicted paedophile in 'cold blood' after the man molested his son. Another inmate, Des, had gotten into a fight and threw a wild punch. Specific punches can cause permanent damage, and his had killed the other man outright. He kept the newspaper articles proving it, one of the things he was criticised about in the small group.

But just as anyone was able to kill, and some of the circumstances of a murder could be related to with understanding, others emanated a different kind of aura. Until then, for the most part, I always saw all humans as innately good, that no person could be 'born bad'. But that perspective was challenged after years in prison because of what I saw inside and because of people like David.

Edging towards his sixties, he was tall – measuring a head over my six foot – and looked like he could care of himself. Listening to him speak without knowing his crimes, you might conclude he was rational, intelligent, and even sympathetic. Then you looked at his eyes. It is often said that a person's eyes are the window to their soul. For what eyes glowed more purely and innocently than those of a child? What sparkle could be mistaken for the deep watery well of sadness compared to a genuine laugh and happiness? People could hide their emotions, but none could hide what was in their eyes.

For David, there was a kind of emptiness. In the morning or the evening, day after day, they remained like black pits into a receding nothingness. I saw that strange void even before discovering why he was incarcerated for multiple counts of murder and rape.

Most across the wing detested David, using the nickname 'Dracula'. However, David was protected because physical or even verbal hostility towards him would result in removal from the unit and disqualification from a Therapeutic Community.

***

Interacting with others, in general, was difficult, as well as dull. What they talked about held no interest: the meaningless drawl of football teams and celebrities over a slow game of cards; the stupid posturing over a game of pool.

At one point, two officers took me aside and said they thought I had 'Asperger's Syndrome'. Of course, I already knew that from Dr Maganty, but they didn't. I nodded slowly at their opinion, realising that a formal diagnosis was probably needed. But if this happened, what would be the consequences? Ever since being sentenced, I objected to being placed on the highest level of culpability – where a person *deliberately* sets out to cause harm. As things stood, I was on the same level as people like David. I was the Dracula who entered banks intent on inflicting pain and suffering, not the kid who embarked on a mission to *help* people, as mistaken and deluded as it may have been. An appeal against the sentence might correct this error, especially if a formal diagnosis was given. However, I still remembered the warning from my solicitors about the sentence being potentially *increased*.

One day I received letters from Geoff and Chris. Geoff's was hard to read – a long scrawl covering two sheets of the prison issue paper. Chris's letter invoked mixed emotions. "I am missing you," he wrote. The rest was about his new training regime and getting a job as an education orderly.

I replied, trying to find witty things to say, but I could imagine a prison officer reading each sentence.

Meanwhile, Christmas edged closer, drawing the usual depression from inmates. The Therapeutic Communities adopted a series of annual games meant to be overseen by a prisoner to liven the atmosphere. Nobody on the wing was interested in the role, so I put my name forward and ended up organising a series of games: pool, snooker, chess, backgammon, and darts. I added a few exercises: the fastest rower (there was a single rowing machine on the wing), the highest number of push-ups and sit-ups, etc. Admittedly, I chose some of these because I knew I would win, but it was not like I got paid for all the organisational effort. A small prize fund of £50 got set aside, and it was up to me to designate how this was handed out.

A week before Christmas, they installed in-cell phones – something that Dovegate was already meant to be famous for. But, because there were 1200 people in the prison and only enough lines for four hundred, they did not work. The result? Endless moaning across the wing.

When the 25th of December finally arrived, Dovegate Therapeutic Community Assessment Wing resembled a television comedy, with elements of Greek tragedy thrown in. I had to act as an 'arbiter' for some games, each with their own antics.

Backgammon saw one inmate throw a cup of tea at the wall when he lost.

The exercise games resulted in two people arguing about the rules to the point where a prison officer had to step in.

Darts almost caused someone to be darted in the back – thereafter barring the game from being played on the wing.

The strangest was when Dracula took it upon himself to play snooker. Fair enough, it was the only game he signed up for, but people were so spooked by him – or blinded by their hatred – that he ended up winning, despite his poor playing. His tactic of slowly drifting towards his opponents or hovering behind them as they lined up their shots sealed his victory even before the end of the first match.

There was also a prison-wide competition at the main gym, with some twenty-eight competing from each wing. It had three elements: a one-kilometre up-hill run (I came first at 5:43 minutes), a two-kilometre row (I came second at 7:04), and a dips/thrusts time-set (second again). Considering I was up against supposedly the fittest prisoners across Dovegate, I was quite pleased, notwithstanding the lack of prizes for second places.

JUST TIME

The New Year's celebrations of 2011 were subdued. Faintly, the noise from other wings – and even more distantly, fireworks – could be heard. Another year behind bars, another wasted year of my youth.

2008, 2009, 2010. There were five more to go: the halfway point had not even been reached!

Had it always been fated to fall into darkness by chasing the light? Was there some cruel hand that penned the lines we are all bound to follow? I looked at my own mortal hand, tracing the scars it held. So faint were the lines from the Khao Yai jungle on my fingers, as the great thorns had pulled down. On the other side, the welt of scar tissue caused by the smashed glass at Parkhurst stood out more strongly. On my knuckles, the slight impression of the court cell wall.

Two sets of scars: one treasured, the other mocking reminders of imprisonment. Yet how deep were the scars within my mind, and could they ever fade in five years? Was that long enough to be... changed... by the system? To sever any possibilities of employment and forever be shunned?

Those who came back spoke of it: the prejudice, the stigma, the challenges – driving them back behind the prison walls, even as their hearts called out to resist.

There were no lands to start afresh. No new countries of virgin soil to build from scratch. The world was already full, and there was no room for criminals. Those who ruled would keep destroying it to maintain their power and privileged lifestyles.

I wondered if anyone would look back and remember. Not just recall the forests and fields before the factories, housing and roads had taken their place, but saw the people who stood up and faced such destruction. Where they failed, their actions would be forgotten. Where they succeeded, they would be forgotten too. Would any look back on my failure, seeing the intentions and dream behind it? Or would it be forgotten, just as the songs of conquered peoples are forgotten; just as their struggles for preservation were crushed beneath spite and greed?

I looked upon the night sky, sundered as it was through the bars. I closed my eyes, still remembering the smell and feel of Earth; the touch of wild winds as they swept across the forests; the crash of ocean waves as they pounded the shore.

They would hold witness if nobody else would, as they had always done silently across the millennia.

And, if any greater Eyes looked down upon them, I willed Their memory to last.

**

Some of the officers were quite friendly, including one called Jane. We played Scrabble on weekends, competing for elusive seven-letter words. In our last game, she achieved the word 'Jailors'.

Irony must have been watching, for I got 'Fugitive' soon after.

She smiled knowingly. Did the same thought cross her mind – of how significant the odds of this happening were; that, perhaps, both of us were pieces in a much bigger game?

I got selected for Therapeutic Community... only just. It was fifty-fifty, with the psychiatrist, Natalie, deciding in my favour. Of the four therapeutic community wings, they allocated me to 'Genesis' (the other names being Avalon, Endeavour, and Camelot).

The premise of therapeutic communities was that behaviour could be changed by challenging 'negative' qualities and encouraging 'positive' ones – eventually reshaping someone's character so that they are less apt to repeat criminal behaviour. Yet this notion – 'criminality' – is itself subject to challenge. A crime essentially breaks the established rules of conduct, but such rules are rarely universal across all human societies and times. Indeed, even within the same community, they are open to different interpretations.

As my new OU module explored, all theories in criminology agreed that criminals are part of society rather than outside of it. The main difference is that they achieve socially accepted goals (i.e., wealth and power) through unaccepted means (i.e., robbery and assault). Alongside this can often be found a process of legitimisation, whereby acts that would generally be regarded as crimes become justified because of authority and power.

The oldest, most universally accepted crimes are those that have their roots in damage and loss: murder (the loss of life), stealing (the loss of property) and assault (damage to a person). Yet, if we accept this definition as an objective classification of crime, we must consider actions that cause harm or loss to communities and the environment. It is possible to do such things and yet never be prosecuted as a criminal. The perpetrators and victims often have an exceptional power imbalance, so the loss or damage can never be challenged. History is littered with examples: native people being forcibly relocated or finding their livelihoods devastated; communities being impoverished through the exploitation of natural resources; pollution from industry causing untimely deaths, and so forth. Such things cause tremendous harm, often on a far broader and lasting scale than recognised crimes committed between individuals, yet instead of punishment they were often instead rewarded. Indeed, the most powerful nations and corporations in the world were built on such crimes.

Evidence of it existed everywhere. Nothing sustainable or ethical keeps such a system running. By its very existence, it is fuelled by extraction, exploitation and greed. It draws with insatiable hunger on the Earth's resources and saps the lives both of other humans and the countless species around them, many going extinct by the day. What we're looking at is no longer a social system but a globalised crime – birthed from taking, refined by colonialism, and finally schooled by capitalism. It's a crime perfected to exploit and destroy, now reaching the heady heights of planet-wide extinction.

Yet the ones responsible for creating and sustaining this state of affairs resided not in jail cells but in mansions, jets and yachts.

Like in all other prisons, the stories of Dovegate's inmates only confirmed how most recognised offences were 'commercial', with around eighty per cent being within this class. And yet the drive for material acquisition, 'to get rich or die trying', created the very pressure that drove someone into crime. People acted according to the greed and self-interest that wider society promotes and rewards.

Of course, the therapeutic communities would never acknowledge these issues. Nobody dared raise the possibility that it might have been 'the system' that at least played a part in their offending. All that mattered was that a person had been convicted of a crime, fitting the mainstream definition of a criminal, and therefore their behaviour needed changing to try and prevent them from committing another offence.

The only way I could frame my offences within the bounds of their comprehension was to relate how drugs impacted behaviour, and the drive to get money.

On my group was Ady; a feisty Liverpudlian called Steve; Simon, whom I had met on the Assessment Unit; a man in his forties called Mark who was built like a brick shithouse; a scrawny budgie-keeping Mancunian called Shane, and lastly a young sandy-haired kid called Craig. It seemed Craig delighted to annoy: he interrupted when people spoke or just hummed to himself and fidgeted. He often blatantly insulted other inmates, yet he would be wrecked if he got into a fight.

Craig's antics already resulted in lengthy arguments within the larger community group, yet for some reason, he was kept on the unit. When he took a small group himself, I was startled to learn his time in prison (six years) had come about when he crashed his sports car into a group of pedestrians, killing one and permanently maiming another. He wore the most expensive clothing I had ever seen on any prisoner, and when the canteen was delivered, you could always tell his bag by the considerable size. In fact, he usually had several bags.

The only thing of real significance throughout this time was undertaking my OU studies. The heavy batch of textbooks formed a pile on my cell desk, and I was well into completing my second assignment – posted each time to a tutor for assessment.

Ady also undertook a course in sociology and we often used to speak, despite his professed 'sociopath' and 'Satanist' alignment. He had committed violent robberies and kidnappings – targeting individuals, often in their homes, rather than businesses. When he participated in a small group, he didn't speak about feeling remorse but rather how he detested vulnerability in others. I pointed out that we are all vulnerable to varying degrees and that his apparent lack of compassion may be a mask that obscures a core of goodness. Ady made a subtle smile when I made these observations. There was goodness in him, somehow. I saw it when he spoke out at a community meeting on behalf of an inmate the others had turned against. I heard it in his speech, even as he struggled to suppress it. He had empathy, and I knew intuitively that he felt remorse.

What had been done to him to make such thoughts and feelings be suppressed and disguised? How did ruthlessness take priority over kindness? We played chess occasionally, and he never touched upon it – not even in his small groups.

***

When you think of prison and music, an instrument that might appear is the harmonica. One had been sent in by my mother within the first weeks of arrival, yet all previous establishments had refused to let me have it (citing the rule that no items from outside could be provided, save from a restricted list purchased at inflated prices from their approved supplier). I thought Dovegate may be different, as it was privately run, so I submitted an application. Weeks later, a Deputy Governor wrote back saying that 'the community need to agree', requiring a general vote. All but Craig and a few of his friends agreed so I returned the application to the governor and he replied saying he consented with the purchase. But then he added at the very bottom that it needed to be 'bought via a supplier'. The price in their catalogue was over £40 – much more than I could afford.

Fuming, I began to rip up the application form – but then noticed a half-drunken cup of tea on top of my OU textbook. It just required a small splash; then, I tore off the wet bit so that the governor's supplier mentioned at the bottom was no longer present.

A week later, after showing the application form to Reception staff, I was handed the harmonica sent by my mother.

Such 'little victories' made a big difference to time in custody: *Porridge* was accurate in that respect. But there were also bigger things to think about. Since I was forced to socialise more than ever, the problems linked to Asperger's were visible to everyone. I was constantly asked why the judge had not considered such a 'mitigating circumstance', even by two of the staff. So, I contacted a solicitor, who reaffirmed the need for a full psychiatric report. The prison medical department said they would not provide a report, so it needed to be done privately. My new solicitor could apply for Legal Aid at that time, but they had to justify there was a 'reasonable prospect of success'. The process was long and complicated.

I might have continued enduring Dovegate Therapeutic Community, perhaps even with a chance of 'completing therapy', but two events heralded a premature exit. First, somebody discovered that my harmonica was not from an 'approved supplier' – promptly informing staff. Two screws stormed into my cell, demanding that I hand it over. The way they acted, it could have been a package of drugs. What followed was an entire community meeting in which inmates constantly attacked me about 'breaking the rules', i.e., having the audacity to keep a harmonica that my mother had sent in.

The next event, merely days later, they orchestrated a vote to 'penalise the rule breakers'. It culminated in fourteen prisoners voting to put me on the equivalent of the 'Basic' IEP regime: more lock-up, less money to spend on the canteen, and so on. Only the staff had the power to do this, which they refused, but now I was a prime target for the entire 'community'. I'd alienated enough on the unit to shift the numbers, and on the lead-up to the vote, there were some discreet exchanges of small canteen items for those who couldn't have cared less – with Craig paying for their chocolate bars and packets of crisps.

It was the last straw, despite all the previous backstabbing and fake small-group discussions. I handed over my notice to withdraw from therapy (the so-called '48'). A prisoner could lodge this at any time, which became irreversible after forty-eight hours. When this notice got read out in a session, Craig took delight in encouraging others to repeat 'Ass-paragus Syndrome'.

Simon, the feminine-sounding arsonist from my small group, called me to his cell afterwards. Inside, he had pinned magazine cut-outs of muscular men to the walls. It felt a bit awkward sitting there at the end of his bed.

"They lie, they cheat, they never bother to understand," he said. "Anyone genuine wants to get out of their stupid game."

"But aren't you doing an IPP? Isn't completing therapy on your sentence plan?" I reminded him.

"I don't care anymore," he sighed.

Ady, who was in the cell three doors down, watched me leave Simon's cell and made an obscene gesture – something he delighted in repeating for days afterwards.

"You sure know how to annoy someone, don't you?" I remarked to him on the weekend.

"Me? I'm a pure angel," he grinned.

The harsh notes of a Metallica song bled from his cell, and I asked if he listened to any other music.

He stared across the wing, then muttered something about the mock 'IEP vote'.

"Fuck them," I replied. "Thanks for voting against it, though."

"Oh, I didn't do it as a favour to you," he said. "I just like the idea of winding-up some idiots and nabbing a free bar of chocolate in the process."

Ady looked at me somewhat differently. "You need to start learning to see people as inanimate objects. Use them to get where you want to be."

"Is that your sociopath side talking?"

"No, that is just me."

I still didn't believe it.

Nevertheless, Ady had a point. In prison, that is what everyone did. It was a game of manipulation arising from the nature of enforced confinement. If you didn't play it well, you would be a pawn used by others – or just an easy target.

***

Does twenty-five mark the age when we see each year as another accumulation of regret and loss? It did for me, but perhaps twenty-one was the more accurate number. For then I had been captured and thrown into jail; my life, as it was, ended. I should have died on that day, the 19th of May 2008, for the loss that resulted. Indeed, in the eyes of most of my relatives, that would have been a preferred option. All but one – my mum – had stood by without accusation or condemnation. She was the only one. I called her on my twenty-fifth birthday, taking more delight in hearing her cheerful voice than any other small perk.

I still wondered how it had happened. Was it somewhere in Cambodia, where I saw the faces of children crippled by landmines, scrambling through the rubbish cast aside by Westerners' hotels? Was it in Exeter, when I watched the betting shops take the last of the old man's pension? Or was it always there in my heart – a need to rebel, to be an outcast, to declare war on a system that would never truly accept me?

I thought of the stars. Did any of it matter? The world had

wonder and mystery, and humans were like ants in the cosmos. Billions and billions of stars… and Earth, itself full of marvels, yet a mere rock orbiting a single sun.

Thinking of such things did not leave me feeling small and helpless but instead gave me hope, for there was perfection in this greater existence, a deeper meaning, which defied the shallow sorrow of my surroundings.

One weekend, after chapel, I spent time in the sunshine while inmates waited to return to their blocks. Yet when I initially asked a guard to go outside, he refused. Only when a few others asked – older, bigger, more assertive – was the request accepted. The experience highlighted the power of groups over individuals and the importance of assertiveness and projected strength. I could see how, in the past, my chosen route was blocked by the lack of companions and the assertiveness necessary to change minds. In fact, I could see how the absence of these things paved the way to prison.

Would I have chosen the path of crime had society accepted and embraced me? If I had multiple friends, a steady girlfriend, and a decent job?

In the background, the British political situation continued as predicted. Brian, 'the professor' at Parkhurst, had been right: the Conservatives were now in power, albeit propped up by the Liberal Democrats, and a year had passed of them holding the reigns. George Osborne, Chancellor of the Exchequer, cut corporation tax and simultaneously slashed public services, whilst outsourcing as much as possible to unaccountable private companies. It was the standard template of a neoliberal economy, even when nearly all expert economists said it was a time of investment rather than cuts. Predictably, this would later pave the way for years of consistently low growth as other countries which had adopted a different path shot ahead. For now, the impacts on prison were starting to be seen in the public sector, going by the letters I received from Parkhurst – with both Geoff and Chris writing of more lockdowns. But for Dovegate, a private prison, these would take longer.

I wrote back, highlighting the peculiarities of life in a 'therapeutic community'. Chris wrote about trying to move to another prison – I suggested Lowdham Grange – but he wanted to stay in the South as that was near his family.

Time's creep was not altogether painful, just as a tattoo needle shifts to a dull soreness after the first few minutes. Ady occasionally emerged from his darkened cell, glaring down from the balcony like a gargoyle. He believed it was all a conveyor belt for prisoners – changing them and destroying their prospects of release so they would return. Like most of his arguments, it was framed by his cynical view of the world. Nonetheless, from my experiences thus far, I saw little evidence of the prison system trying to rehabilitate.

"*Everything* is self-preservation," Ady remarked, noting how the jobs of prison officers depended largely on repeat offenders.

Unsurprisingly, he saw the whole 'therapy' construct as nothing more than a grand comedy, something he only indulged in because it was on his 'sentence plan'. With an IPP sentence, it was his only way of getting out.

Falling into silence, he tracked the path of a screw below. Malice poured from his eyes.

"Some of them are decent, you know," I remarked.

He looked at me, the burning gaze dimming slightly. "The only good screw is a dead one. And *her*..."

His meant Eve below, an overweight white-haired officer who could have been a grandmother. She *looked* nice, but had a nasty streak. A row of hate-filled words streamed out of his mouth, making me wince.

"Erm, I wouldn't go that far. They are just people doing their job."

"Oh, they are just doing their job; they are lovely people; oh, let's kiss their asses," he made a squeaky voice, holding up his hands like paws.

Typical Ady behaviour.

"Fancy a game of chess?"

"Yes, yes," he kept squeaking, "let's go play chess and have a jolly good time as the wonderful people frolic around us!"

After I beat him at the first game, he retreated into his usual sullen stare.

"Want another one?"

"I'll say no to that for now, but I'll thrash you next time."

***

> *Don't let them fool ya*
> *Or even try to school ya, Oh, no*
> *We've got a mind of our own*
> *So go to hell if what you're thinking is not right*
> *The road of life is rocky, and you may stumble too*
> *So, while you point your fingers, someone else is judging you*

Bob Marley drifted through the wing as I completed my last set of push-ups. I was out of therapy, but they kept me on Genesis Wing like a hanging albatross. Now they were extending my lock-up time because of a vote about 'those no longer in therapy still being amongst the community'. No matter how many applications I lodged about leaving, the same answer always came back: "It will happen when there's space in the main prison."

I even enquired if it would be possible to serve my sentence in the military as part of a dangerous mission. The idea was nothing more than a floating castle, but I asked nonetheless, putting in application forms to be met with condescending answers. I would have served the country that imprisoned me, given my life even, if it had only wiped away the waste, shame, and slow decay of prison.

I kept going to the chapel, too, as much to break up the boredom as to half-heartedly hope to find something greater. There were times when outside speakers came, and one, in particular, stood out. He was a large man covered in tattoos – a world apart from the slight figure of Father John, yet they both spoke with the same voice.

"Without love, a man's heart turns to dust in the desert, draining away his life," the visitor said, striding up and down. Sometimes he glanced piercingly at individuals, forcing them to follow his pendulous movement.

"I had felt it, the hatred within, burning me up. It gave me the force to match my opponents. It gave me the means to control an empire, up and down this country, dealing out death wherever I reached my hand."

His words echoed throughout the chapel. Captivating a hall full of prisoners was a challenge and one he succeeded in. There was none of the customary talking and whispering: everyone was silent.

"Men feared me. Those who didn't, I obliterated. I felt invincible, like nothing could ever bring me down."

He burst into laughter. "But it did brothers, it did."

"Within a year, I had lost everything – the sports cars, helicopter, houses, money, women. All gone."

By the end, he'd described how he 'found Christ' and gone on to become a prison speaker and youth camp leader. At this stage, a few pockets of talking resumed.

If only it were so easy to follow blindly – or, if not blindly, then with the ability to cast aside pressing questions. Like why humans and Earth were so unique out of trillions of planets. Or why a benevolent, all-powerful creator would allow such dark deeds to sweep across creation, unchecked and rising each year?

By the end of that service, I witnessed a drug handover: another prisoner loaded up with 'Golden Virginia' tobacco pouches swapping them for a bag of 'stuff'. Chapel was always one of the preferred locations for such deals.

***

I finally left Genesis on Summer Solstice. Only Ady bothered to say goodbye with his usual dark humour. "I'll see you on the other side," he smirked.

Shortly before this, something unexpected happened. My personal officer, a middle-aged man with close-cropped ginger hair called Phil, left some newly received mail. At the top was a mysterious, bulging brown envelope. "I'll be back in a few minutes," he said, "when your bags are packed."

Curious, I took out the envelope's contents, thinking it might be some new OU textbook. Instead, it was.... my *wing file!* Prisoners were never meant to see this, save if they put in a special 'Data Protection Act' request (when most of it got redacted), for it contained observations from wing staff about my 'behaviour'. There were even some loose slips corresponding to 'negative IEP incidents'.

I hesitated for only a few seconds – then quickly removed the slips from the file. My eyes scanned through passages that could not so easily be obliterated: -

'Threatening behaviour to staff...' (*apparently relating to an incident when I complained about outdoor exercise being cancelled*)
'Wants to be taken to Lowdham Grange, recommend against it....' (*written by the lovely Eve*)
'Intel received about potential drug use...' (*sounded like some fake allegation from Craig that resulted in a negative 'piss test' the next day*)

I sensed the door about to open and quickly shoved the file – minus the negative slips – back into its envelope.

Phil appeared and glanced down. "My mistake," he said, taking back the envelope. "Shouldn't have given you that. Ready now?"

I would never know whether it was a mistake or some kind of favour. Perhaps amongst all the brief interactions we had together – including two games of chess – a note of mercy resounded in his heart, strong enough to go against some of his colleagues. Or perhaps it really had just been a silly mistake.

I was taken to 'Houseblock One, D Wing' and put into a double cell.

It seemed like the typical British prison wing: noisy and chaotic. Within minutes I lodged a transfer request to Lowdham Grange and applied for a job. It was unclear how long I would be at Dovegate, and being lumbered with a double cell meant finding ways to spend as much time out of it as possible. My cellmate (number 10) was in his early twenties but had the attitude of a boy still in his early teens – the unruly, vandalising kind.

Only a week passed before a voice on the in-cell intercom blared.

"Jackley, Reception is coming for ya!"

It was barely 6:00 am.

"Why are they coming?" I asked.

"Court or Release."

Of course, it could be neither – what they meant was my transfer to Lowdham Grange was happening. But so soon? Still, having just been ejected prematurely from sleep, there was no harm in pretending a dream had come true. So, I bagged up my belongings and happily told anyone who asked that I was being released.

"It's a court appearance, Jackley," a screw said irritably at Reception after I repeated the dream a fourth time.

"I don't have any court..."

"You're due up at Shrewsbury Crown Court," he growled.

That made no sense, but they insisted there was a 'production order' with my name on it.

On the transit van, the summer countryside spread its reminder of a beauty I had missed for so long. Through the glass porthole of the prison transport, I saw people strolling on the streets, their faces glowing with freedom. Could something incredible be waiting ahead: a case of confused identity, an ambush by sympathetic parties? Such a fleeting hope, as small as a star, and yet...

The van cruised up to the court after about two hours, and instead of going into an underground parking lot or sealed-off area, it just stopped on the street.

Could this be... my mind rushed as the door opened.

But I was handcuffed – or rather triple-handcuffed with both hands, the right one linked to a guard.

They took me down into the court's 'dungeon', leaving me alone in a holding cell. In that bare space, my hopes and worries buzzed around like bees.

"Your barrister's here," one of the guards announced.

I entered a room where a man and woman stood.

"You look different from when I last saw you," the barrister said.

"I'm completely in the dark," a voice like Homer Simpson replied. "I've never seen you before."

And so, the chance that might have seen me walk free crumbled to dust. The mystery unravelled: they thought I was somebody else called Mark Mason. Before prison, I had used the alias 'Mason', but how that could have resulted in me going to court was baffling.

Then I learned that this guy entered the court late. The hearing was about his bail, which one of the guards said was granted.

Back in the holding cell, I couldn't take it anymore. I called out in agony.

A female guard flung back the hatch. "What's going on? What's happening? Are you okay?"

"Tell me," I cried, "please... what would have happened... if I had gone up as Mark Mason."

She sighed. "Well, you would have been brought back here."

Perhaps she could see the tears edging my eyes, for her voice became gentle. "Your court papers show that you are doing thirteen years, anyway."

Is that so? I thought. *Is that really the case?*

"We'll take you back to Dovegate soon."

When the door closed, I looked at the wall. Fists clenched, I slipped from the bench and folded to the ground. Back to being a corpse, ready for its rotting catacomb. Back to the nightmare.

A single guard led me out, handcuffed as before.

He took a different route, obscure and unwatched. We came to a single door that led to the outside parking lot, where he waited for his colleague.

Electricity surged through my spine. Here it was again: the opportunity for *Freedom*, only a door away! A sharp elbow, a rapid kick, a bit of confident persuasion – just those handcuffs between me and the outside – a bit of metal, held by an average man, waiting to be broken. And then?

'*I will run, I will run, I will keep on running....*'

Such was the vow when contemplating an opportunity for freedom.

But no. I stood there, held captive, unwilling to take a chance. The journey back felt like a punishment for such stupidity and cowardice. A hot, airless van, taunting me with visions of what could have been; young people bronzed by the sun, grass as tall as my waist, trees, sunshine, rivers, smiles, laughter, Freedom...

All gone.

I hardly noticed someone else in one of the other cubicles. Only when looking twice did I realise it was a girl, barely out of her teens. She held her head low, black hair falling across her face.

Scrawled around me, I saw different graffiti:

'*Laura Carlson of Wolves going to HMP Foston Hall.*'

'*Riding HMP like Queen B.*'

How many girls and women had been sitting here to traverse a similar landscape of mental anguish and turmoil – their worlds and families torn away, their thoughts cycling around shame and self-hatred?

No matter how hard I tried, I couldn't forget that day. Only on one other occasion had a similar opportunity arisen – in New York when ICE agents led me out onto the Streets, their van waiting on a curb near the detention centre.

Now it had happened again – a case of mistaken identity – an incredible chance, thrown to me like a pair of keys.

I could have told them I was Mark Mason. And if that did not work, I could have used the slightest force and escaped through the single door to freedom.

What prevented me?

The fear of failure, of getting captured and facing the consequences? The fact that I would be destined to run endlessly and eschew contact with the remaining people I owed allegiance to – principally, my mother?

Still, I was torn asunder by my failure. Twenty-five, with the prospect of more than four years to spend inside prison - assuming the system did not ensnare me as it had done to others.

The ensuing days in Dovegate did nothing to help. One afternoon my cellmate returned from his 'education class' early and, just as I was in the middle of writing, started to rearrange TV cables and displaced my paperwork. There was only one small table, but the TV took priority.

I sighed. "Can't you read a book or something until 4:30?"

That was the time he was meant to return from his class.

"Nah mate," he replied. "Why should I?"

This guy had only *two months* left. He would be out before this summer even ended.

I hit the cell button, which in Dovegate connected to an intercom system. "What's the problem?" a voice crackled.

"I need to get out of here!"

To my surprise, a woman officer came a few minutes later, who opened the door and let me wander around the wing to 'cool off'.

I did a few circuits around the landings, breathing slowly, and soon realised a few other inmates were out – the so-called 'wing cleaners'. Like the ones at Garth, they spent a few minutes cleaning and the rest of the time chatting and playing cards. One immediately started making loud comments.

"Boys, we gotta fruit-a-loop on the prowl!" He stood there on the landing outside his cell door, two others beside him.

The fact I had not socialised much and had come from the Therapeutic Community – a place branded by mainstream prisoners for nonces and informers – did not help my status.

"You looking for something to suck, mate?"

The woman officer heard the taunts but did not say anything. She just told me to return to my cell.

I went back to trying to read *Lord of the Rings*, doing my best to ignore the TV's blare. But, as time crept closer to 4 pm, thoughts shifted to Association: once the cell door was open, they'd be waiting.

I had the anger and strength to at least put up a fight, despite the gym access at Dovegate being a fraction of Parkhurst's – yet where would this path lead?

Not to Lowdham Grange, not to a successful re-categorisation, but to more months and years in the lower levels of hell. Just after I had almost escaped it.

Unlock came, and I braced myself. The women officer appeared just as I put my book down.

"I've found a place on another wing for you," she said.

I looked at her. She was mid-thirty, short and edging towards 'plump', with dark blonde hair. There was something in her tone that I struggled to understand.

I packed my belongings and followed her out of the wing. Behind, hostile eyes watched.

She didn't go far – it was a wing on the same House Block. But, right then, it could have been a different prison.

I followed her to a large empty cell.

"Hopefully, you should find this better," she said, pausing at the doorway.

Again, that look in her gaze. I didn't recognise it then – the last such look had been in Chris's eyes. Only later, alone in the new cell, did it dawn on me: the officer *liked* me. Her slight smile, her almost shy voice... and I had barely said 'thank you'.

What if...?

The thought evaporated as soon as it arose. *No,* I told myself, *that could never happen.*

Chapter 13: Lowdham

'The real criminals in this society are not all the people who populate the prisons across the state, but those who have stolen the wealth of the world from everyone else.'

Angela Davis

There is a group of prisoners who wielded tremendous power when outside. They had led international drug conspiracies, been members of powerful gangs, owned huge mansions and yachts. Like British society itself, they existed in a bubble, away from the harshness experienced by others. HMP Lowdham Grange was one of the few closed prisons that catered for this class, run by the same company as Dovegate.

I arrived there on the 11th of June 2011, after a three-hour journey. It was based outside the city of Nottingham, not far from Nottingham Forest, and built by Serco in 1998.

The screws seemed better – even those at Reception, who tended to be worse in any prison because their attitude prevented them from working on the wings. Suddenly, items that had been sent to me but held back by other prisons were allowed in my possession: clothing, stationery and even the harmonica that had caused so much uproar at Dovegate. I was led through open grounds to the Induction Wing, immediately discovering an exercise yard with pull-up bars, sit-up benches and dip bars. Inside was a well-equipped exercise room, and the cells were large, with windows that could actually open. I was paired with someone named Barry, who had just been transferred from Wandsworth.

The rumours about Lowdham Grange were not myths. There only barely-paying jobs, a canteen list that featured items I could not even remember from supermarkets outside, and the servery food was excellent.

Only one thing bothered me. When being transferred, I was handcuffed, just as it had been when travelling to and from Parkhurst. The friendly young G4S guard (perhaps related to Phil at HMP Dovegate) came over with my security file – which was meant to be secret – and showed me a few entries.

'Attempted to escape from Court/US Marshals custody.'

'Intelligence received – may have planned to escape from Hereford Court in 2009.'

My mind flashed back to HMP Gloucester and the chess-playing prisoner. He had grassed. And with such entries in my file, I would never get to open prison.

"You should get it removed," my new cellmate (#11) said.

"How?" I asked.

"No idea," he said. "But if it were me, I'd be straight onto my barrister."

Barry said he was serving a ten-year sentence for a multi-million-pound drug conspiracy – or, in his words, "a complete setup". He had a family outside, and because the cells were all fitted with phones, he spent many hours talking to them in a thick Cockney accent.

I only made one call to my mother. Usually, I avoided describing what life was like inside, but this time I went through some of the prison's positives, hoping it would cheer her up.

"You think this place is good, then?" Barry asked afterwards.

"Yes, it's brilliant."

"Certainly a damned sight better than Wandsworth, but I

thought they'd have the cells open more."

"Surely you had more bang up in Wandsworth?" I asked.

"Mate, my door was always open. I worked as an orderly, see. Only lock-up was at night."

He acted pretty jovial, but got agitated when I started playing the harmonica.

"Oh, need a bit of practice there, mate." It had only been a few chords.

With the long unlock, open exercise yard and pleasant cellmate, my two weeks on the Induction Wing passed quickly. I was moved to J Wing, on 'House Block 3', designated for 'Enhanced Only' prisoners of 'excellent behaviour'. Removing the negative IEP slips in my wing file at Dovegate had apparently paid dividends.

Most J Wing cells were single, and there was no daily lock-up. The exercise yard constantly opened from 8 am to 8 pm, instead of the puny thirty minutes I was used to elsewhere. On the downside, it meant having to interact with prisoners more. One, who might have been a double for Arnold Schwarzenegger, quizzed me on where I had been, what I had done, and whom I knew. Nobody was the answer, and his evil grin gave me second thoughts about being so honest. But I soon encountered a pleasant handful, such as Ricky – a slight man in his fifties with greying hair and a tanned face. He was part of a gypsy family and had a few other relatives in the same prison – including, to my surprise, the Schwarzenegger (his nephew). Ricky called me 'Loxley', an allusion to the actual name of Robin Hood.

Well-connected prisoners could access information about others, and that is how Ricky knew about my background. I went from being regarded suspiciously to being casually accepted, with one even helping me in the gym. Everyone called him 'Jock' because of his Scottish heritage; he almost matched the Schwarzenegger in shape.

Another thing I discovered was an active chaplaincy, which

held regular weekday meetings. The prison governor – or 'director' – was said to be a practising Christian who could be seen attending services. He was the first governor I met, aside from the one at Hewell.

"I like to know who is coming into my prison," he told a group of us in the newly built Education Block, saying how many opportunities Lowdham Grange offered.

"You can all do well here," he concluded, "and move forward with your sentences. We're not here to punish you but to see that you are kept in custody and hopefully won't return."

I wondered what Ady would make of his speech.

And yet such governors held tremendous power in determining what the regime would be like. A change in governors was always noticed, for better or worse.

**

Ricky used to sit in the yard, in a patch of shade, with a pile of paperwork beside his chair. He told me he was writing a book.

"What's it about?"

"My life," he smiled.

"You know, I never asked what you were in prison for."

"No, you didn't. And I liked you because of that. But I'll tell you now: I took the fall for someone else, Loxley. We were implicated in burgling Lord Rothschild's mansions."

Lord Rothschild was part of a British banking family worth £400 billion. He owned an extensive portfolio in property, banking, and oil.

"Nobody got hurt. But you know what it's like – the law is there to protect the rich and their property. I'm doing more time than the average rapist."

We spoke about the disparity in sentences, of how those who deliberately targeted people often received less time than those who simply targeted property.

"The system is bent, Loxley. I know that; you know that."

I asked if he got away with anything from the mansions.

"The Old Bill said it was some antiques. The kind of thing that old man might glance upon once in his life, maybe, just sitting there…" he trailed off. "But might as well have been the Crown Jewels for how the police got riled up – helicopters, Land Rovers full of armed cops, you name it. Burgle thousands of council homes, and you'd have none of that – but a Rothschild mansion!"

I almost remarked this was probably due to the items being of higher value, but then realised that burgling a poor person's home, where they actually lived and had all their worldly possessions, was actually far worse than taking items from a rich man's mansion that he barely saw and rarely visited. The law, of course, saw otherwise.

"How'd they get you?"

I had a feeling he already knew, but I told him anyway.

"Why ever didn't you just buy a gun in England?"

I sighed. "Because I didn't know anyone here. I was not in criminal circles. I didn't see myself as a criminal."

"Neither of us are criminals, Loxley. Look at the bent judges and lords, the banks and corporations, people who screw over everyone else who don't dare to stand up to it; these are the real criminals."

Ricky was one of the few who understood what I sought to represent and my chosen mission. For that reason, I opened up to him. Nor was I afraid to ask him questions, like what he had done before prison and what it meant to be a gypsy or 'traveller'.

"It depends where you are," he said. "My family travel around, like the rest, but it's not the same – we can't move about like we used to. We are shunned, even when trying to do decent jobs."

To be a traveller with no fixed home was something I saw in a romantic light – a life of no borders, being connected closely to nature, and always finding new opportunities.

"Those times are in the past," he remarked sadly. "Most chose to live in the same place and put comfort before tradition. There're few true travellers left anymore. And those who cause problems have messed it up for everyone else."

Ricky told me that getting a job was easy, and the prison also ran a dedicated session for Open University students that could be attended twice a week. I applied straightaway, and soon discovered a classroom of eight computers, overseen by a relaxed officer who spent most of her time elsewhere.

In the same education building was a large room where eight prisoners were hunched over like bridges on padded matts. A grey-haired lady with a youthful face saw me staring through the door, and after hearing of my interest, said that I could apply to attend the class every week. She also handed over a little booklet that explained the therapeutic aspects of yoga. Apparently it had a proven track record in helping issues around poor mental health and drug addiction, to say nothing of improving overall fitness. Despite these benefits, the public sector prisons had almost entirely phased out yoga classes across England, as ordered by the new right-wing government, and the private estate would soon follow in their footsteps.

Another change was being allocated an Offender Supervisor. These were dedicated officers who worked with prisoners to achieve their 'sentence plan' targets, but until now, I hardly spoke with any of those previously assigned to me. Not much was on my sentence plan besides attending some Victim Awareness course, which Steph Lloyd – my new Offender Supervisor – enrolled me on. She was a short woman in her thirties with a freckled face and brown hair held back in a ponytail. To my surprise, she was also friendly, even expressing interest in my OU course. When she noted that it would be unlikely that I get downgraded to Category C this year, I was pleased to be remaining at Lowdham. After that was a long phone conference with my probation officer – the third one allocated – who referenced being put on 'MAPPA Tier 4' and having to go to 'a hostel' upon release. It seemed too distant to worry about, but I was annoyed to be put on the same tier as serial murderers and rapists. Even prolific repeat offenders were not usually placed so high.

These assessments and reports by probation officials were ones that no prisoner had any input into; indeed, the bulk of them were often kept secret. They were weaving stories based on second-hand accounts, having never met the people they were writing about or, in some cases, for only a tiny fraction of time. These stories made the difference between release and continued imprisonment, time in the community, being recalled to custody, returning to one's family home, or being confined in a hostel.

It was why people like Ricky chose to spend the entire period of their sentences in prison. Typically, those subject to 'determinate' (set) sentences could be released at the halfway point (subject to good behavior in custody), as was the case with me – whilst still subject to probation supervision. Previous governments had tinkered with this split, with it formerly being two-thirds[7], but judges took account of the change by increasing sentence lengths.[8] What they had not taken into account, however, was how some offences resulted in more punitive conditions even after release, albeit I did not fully understand the actual implications until further down the line.

Descriptions of probation hostels were comparable to drug-infested rat holes filled with sex offenders. Those who had been returned to custody after being on license spoke of nightmare scenarios in which the smallest unfounded allegation, or the missing of one probation appointment, caused them to be 'recalled'. But to spend the *entirety* of one's sentence in custody out of choice! Being outside was surely worth any number of restrictions and inconveniences.

"Wait till you get out there," Ricky noted. "You've never been through it. You don't realise how much you have to deal with out there. Housing, work, bills – here, we have all that covered. And

---

7 As of 2022, it was changed back again to two-thirds, for certain types of 'violent' offences, including robbery.
8 The subsequent two-thirds addition appears to not have resulted in total sentences being reduced to reflect that more time is spent in custody.

no games with probation either."

He took a sip from a big porcelain mug. Another thing about Lowdham Grange was that prisoners could have proper crockery and cutlery.

I looked at the paper pad in his lap and asked what he'd been writing about.

His tanned face, heavily lined by time, shone. "One thing I always remember, Loxley, was this beautiful clock. No – clock isn't the right word. It was a masterpiece of time. It had some mahogany, a bit of silver, and the carvings – whoever made them carvings was a magician. They kept me entranced for hours. I put that clock on my caravan mantelpiece – can you imagine it, Loxley? Kept it there for months until the chiming messed with the missus's head. But I still see it each time I wake up. Strange, don't you think?"

I nodded, unsure how to respond. He showed me a bit of handwriting that seemed to describe, yes, a clock, but the sentences were muddled.

"This looks good," I said. "You could improve it, though. I find my writing improved when I did a lot of reading – you start to take in how sentences should flow, things like that."

"Read!" he exclaimed. "All this you see here, this is me, self-taught. Nobody ever taught me to read or to write."

"But you must have read to be able to write?"

"Oh, well, maybe I read a little. But I don't haggle around with books, Loxley. My words come from the world."

Again, I just nodded. Sometimes it was hard to know how to respond to Ricky.

Two other inmates came onto the yard, smoking. Whenever a female officer walked along the perimeter of the exercise yard fence, they attempted to solicit conversation – some more successfully than others.

"That one I shagged back in Bedford was hot as fuck," the shorter of the two remarked to his mate.

Relationships between staff and prisoners did, of course, happen. In the private estate there were also more female officers, and training appeared not as stringent as in public prisons. Essentially anyone could become a screw – they did not even need many GCSEs to get accepted. In public prisons, many had formerly served in the military, whilst others had been rejected as police officers. The latter were often more vindictive, for they enjoyed exercising power. But in places like Dovegate and Lowdham, officers came from a broader range of backgrounds – not to mention a plethora of different shapes and sizes. I wondered how some could be expected to defend themselves if assaulted, whilst a few female officers might have found a career in modelling. None were quite as stunning as Ms James back in Hewell, though.

***

The 19th of August marked 'thirty-nine months in Hell'. Perhaps it represented a turning point – a little interlude in the darkness. I had finally found a good prison, with plenty of gym, access to outdoors and decent conditions. It was just as Joe had described. With a bit of asking around, I found that he was here, on one of the '*super*-enhanced' wings. They were alleged to have even bigger cells, with a quieter environment and daily access to a special gym, so I applied to move over.

Prisoners here were unlike others. Their confidence and assertiveness differed from other establishments' unstable and broken characters. Was it the conditions themselves or the backgrounds of the prisoners? Most were serving long sentences of around ten years for financially orientated offences, usually involving drug conspiracies, and many had made a success of their criminal exploits. Others were part of large crime networks or families; their roles may have been relatively low, but they seemed well taken care of.

As for myself, I had no wealthy relatives or connections to

send in money to buy clothes from the prison catalogues, gym supplements, or any of the other 'luxuries' available at Lowdham. Only through working could I get money, and within three weeks of arriving, I was offered a position in the 'upholstery workshop'.

It turned out to be a huge warehouse, with rows of machines and long tables where around sixty worked in specialist roles. Some joined the wooden frames of sofas and chairs with huge industrial staplers; others cut and fitted leather onto items before they were packaged and boxed for posting. Commission-based pay was added to a basic weekly salary, with some earning around £50 a week – a fortune by prison standards – though half went into their 'savings' accounts, which could not be touched until they were released.

My first session was spent learning how to use the stapling equipment correctly: essentially, a high-powered gun. Beside me, with his own stapler, a man was doing life for several counts of manslaughter and GBH.

Perhaps the most surprising thing was the total lack of incidents. Nobody wanted to cause trouble: they had decent jobs and were allowed to earn a good wage. It was an example of how even the most 'violent' of inmates could be trusted in a place where, if they had a mind to, they could cause serious damage.

Yet was it *really* surprising? Unlike the depiction of the British tabloids, these men had come to prison more through circumstance than from character. Save from the greater number of tattoos and fitness levels; the workshop could have been mistaken for any other outside.

Society fostered an embedded caucus who did nothing but pore over a prisoner's (or indeed former prisoner's) offence, no matter how exceptional or historic. This group subscribed to a philosophy that nobody could change; that criminality is somehow embedded, and saw all those who broke the law as bearing some indelible stain like the mark of Cain. One mistake, one act of unparalleled stupidity, and that's it: your life is over, regardless of what you did after or even what you did before the offence occurred. You were your crime; nothing else. This was the mentality that crept into the mainstream, encouraged by an irresponsible press and lack of awareness of what really happened in prisons.

To be allowed education sessions, gym access, healthy food and things like yoga was looked upon as scandalous. No matter that such things acted as constructive benefits to physical and mental wellbeing – the foundations of a law abiding life - as well as paths to self-improvement. No matter that, irrespective of how decent Lowdham Grange was then, all these 'perks' were mere distractions to the cold reality of imprisonment, in a place that no sane person would want to be.

Nobody wanted to be here, yet it was the best that could be offered. Our punishment was the deprivation of liberty, as maintained by law, but society now wanted more.

Chapter 14: Millionaire's Row

One of the library books had a directory of literary agents and publishers filled with scribbles – a fair amount from Ricky. He smiled when I mentioned it.

"We're not the only writers here, Loxley. We got at least two Dickens's to compete with on Millionaire's Row."

"Why not go over there?"

"I'm settled here, and over theresome people think they are better than everyone else."

So-called Millionaire's Row supposedly had more multi-millionaires than the average British town. One, it was rumoured, even held a fair chunk of shares in Serco. I took a small degree of comfort in knowing the system was not so wholly corrupted as to issue 'Get Out of Jail Free' cards to the rich. But whilst you couldn't bribe the courts, you *could* do second best by paying for the best legal representatives in a system where the quality of one's barrister could make the difference between nine years and fourteen. There was no enigma over why they charged vastly different rates.

"I would end up being... mischievous there," Ricky continued, chuckling.

One of his tricks, he told me, was to smoke the bags of peppermint tea that could be purchased from the canteen.

"Smells just like weed," he grinned. "Some nights, I just sit by the crack in my door and puff that stuff out, Loxley. It sure gets the screws riled up trying to find out who is getting high."

Getting (real) drugs into prison constituted a major business that some had created entire enterprises around. In other prisons, the primary substance of interest was heroin – of which its legal substitute, methadone, could be prescribed and traded. I had seen them all through my sentence: their eyes hollow as their soul retreated into itself, spending nearly all their time in-cell. For some, their addiction had begun before entering the prison gates. For others, it was a virtual escape that removed them from the boredom and heartache of imprisonment. The standard means of getting drugs was from visits, of which a package could be secreted via a kiss or other discrete method. This way always brought risk, for the Visits Hall was watched closely, with random strip searches of prisoners afterwards. Some were caught, while others made it back to the wings with drugs 'plugged' up their bum. There were other routes of drugs into prison: parcels thrown over the walls, cleverly placing items in canteen orders via an outside supplier, and through screws themselves. With salaries as low as £16,000 a year, a few thousand on top of that was worth the risk for some.

Ironically, the lightest of all drugs – cannabis – carried the highest risk. A piss test would show up to a month after smoking, whereas other substances dissipated more rapidly. Indeed, at that time, some were not visible in tests at all – 'spice' being a prominent example.

For most at Lowdham, it simply wasn't worth it. If you were caught with drugs, the best scenario would be a few weeks in Segregation. At worst, you'd find yourself moved to another prison. It was the same with fights – not to say they didn't happen, simply that people generally settled their differences in their cells, away from the screws and cameras. It almost happened to me once.

Two inmates were before me in the dinner cue, laughing away as if they had just left a spa. In front of them, a gap opened up.

"You going to move forward, or you just letting me go in front?" I said irritably.

The tallest of the two, heavily covered in tattoos, swung around.

"Who you talking to?"

"You," I said, returning the hostile gaze.

"Yeah? What cell you in? I'll talk to you later."

I gave him my location, then pushed past.

An hour went by as I waited for him to appear, with my dinner plate sitting on the desk cold. I was about to start eating it when his face framed the door slit.

He came in, and I stood.

"You want to fight?" he said.

My body tensed, ready. "Sure, I don't mind."

"Some people have got good things to say about you. Maybe I annoyed you at the hot plate? But I'd be careful how you talk to people in the future. Outside, I was a cage fighter."

"Yeah? I was a boxer."

It was only partly true: I had just gone to the boxing club a few times at Worcester University, covering the footwork technique more than anything else.

"Cool. You want to draw a line under this, or fight?"

"Up to you," I shrugged.

He held out his hand, and I shook it.

Later I saw Ricky, who just laughed.

"What's so funny?"

"Four of them were up here about you, Loxley," he replied.

"What do you mean?"

"Oh, some guy you insulted at the servery? He and his friends wanted to know about you. Think they would have had a bit on their minds if I hadn't spoken to them."

Little did I know then, Ricky was a senior Johnson Family member, labelled 'Britain's Number One Crime Family'. His favour counted for a lot. However, he'd been a bit excessive with the 'good words'. The next day, I received several polite nods and attempts at friendly conversation. Apparently, Ricky had said I was a 'world-famous bank robber who spent time in US penitentiaries and other countries'. He had also said, for reasons unknown, that I was 'sitting on millions'. The first bit may have been partly true, but the second had no substance whatsoever.

I wasn't sure whether he believed this, but prisoners held a common assumption that most people had only been sentenced for some of their crimes, rather than all of them.

No doubt, without Ricky's input, I would have gone to Segregation for fighting – or, at best, to medical for treatment of injuries. Indeed, what happened next would never have taken place.

It was around Tuesday or Wednesday, as I stapled up the back of another sofa, that the supervising officer received a call.

Would I like to go to P Wing? They were inviting me to Millionaire's Row!

I immediately said yes and packed my belongings in the evening. Ricky came to say farewell.

"Perhaps I'll see you over there?" I said.

"Maybe, Loxley, maybe."

***

Somehow, the cells on P Wing were even bigger. Next door was Russell Tate, convicted of a multi-million-pound drug conspiracy and owner of various luxury properties in Essex. He was a jovial, hyperactive man who rapidly walked around the exercise yard daily for hours.

"I've heard you are quiet," he greeted me. "You need anything – canteen, stuff for your cell?"

The question surprised me. "No, I'm fine, thanks."

Further down, on the same landing, was a man said to have controlled all of the drug flow from above Manchester.

The majority had Essex and London accents, having spent many years in criminal endeavours and building up money and contacts. With like-minded companions and comfortable conditions, they may have been doing similar sentence lengths to mine, but I doubted if the *qualitative* length could be the same.

Did any of them experience a journey up and down the UK or find themselves sent to Segregation? Had any of them been put on suicide watch, punched by guards, or subjected to bullying? Perhaps. But, looking at their designer clothes and hearing their confident, jovial conversations, it was unlikely. The very physical fabric of P wing made the difference apparent, with huge cells adorned with thick curtains, PlayStations and huge stereos. Most of them were also wing workers or orderlies.

Joe was one of the latter. After returning from his job at the staff bistro, he caught up with me in the evening.

"Pie-Guy! What took you so long?"

I grimaced at the annoying nickname acquired from HMP Hewell's 'pie night' episode, and hoped Joe didn't spread it around P Wing. At least he was interested in my description of journeying around England's prisons.

"Bloody hell," he exclaimed. "Did you get on an OU course yet?"

"I'm due to start my third module in a few weeks."

"What are you studying?"

"Next module is Environmental Science."

"Interesting. We'll catch up another time, okay?"

Later I saw him sitting at the head of a table playing cards with a group who looked like they were meeting in a pub.

I may have been on 'Hell Level 1', but it was still prison. The only difference was time could pass more endurably – of which gym was so important. Alongside the main prison gym, the super-enhanced wings also had their own special one, meaning I could potentially complete nine sessions a week: five on weekday evenings and four on the weekends. Even a special weekly afternoon session to undertake a 'gym trainer' qualification could be applied to, which I duly did and received swift approval to undertake. It was like the course I had done at Parkhurst but with real PE textbooks rather than black and white photocopied pages stapled together. However, returning to the upholstery workshop one week later, I received a surprise.

On the table where I usually worked, there were no spaces. A very large, bald inmate was in my place.

"I've got your job now," he said, hardly looking at me.

I went to the supervisor, and he just blinked. "Your place has been filled," he told me, going against his earlier promise that participating in the gym course wouldn't be an issue. "But I have just heard there is a vacancy in the DHL shop, and I can sort that out for you if you want?"

The DHL shop was rumoured to be one of the best jobs in the prison, where canteen goods got packaged up.

"Okay, that sounds good," I said quickly.

Within minutes of returning to P Wing, Russell came up to me.

"So, you're going to work in the canteen," he smiled.

I had not told anyone about my new job.

"Yeah."

"Can you pick my orders when they come through? I like to get the best fruit and veg; if not, I end up getting bruised shit. I'll make it worth your while."

I didn't understand what he meant about picking things, but the request sounded harmless.

"Sure, I'll try."

DHL managed the prison's canteen contract. Products arrived by crate and were stacked on shelves, ready to be 'bagged' for prisoners' orders. The job simply entailed reading a printed list from each canteen order and picking out items from the shelves to be sealed in a plastic bag.

Unfortunately, most of the time involved doing nothing. There were six other workers, who sat around together chatting about subjects. Turnover was high because almost all fell for the temptation of stealing. One thought he could empty a box of cornflakes and fill it with tins of tuna instead – not realising that the DHL staff could tell the weight difference. He was quickly dismissed. Another stuffed so many items into his underwear that he got taken aside even before any hands felt around his crotch. Others took to eating items in the workshop itself, notwithstanding being cameras everywhere. Many discreetly chomped on things as they sat around, hiding the wrappers in toilet paper.

Friday was the only day we could officially eat things in the workplace – the leftover fruit and veg, usually battered and bruised, unless pieces had been discreetly 'reserved' (hidden behind other items) beforehand. Russell's request wasn't difficult or risky: he just wanted me to pick out better quality fruit and vegetables from his existing order. Most of the others had similar requests from people on their wings. He thanked me when his bag arrived, appearing in my cell a few minutes later with a Cadbury's Chocolate Nut Bar (£1 each).

"Heard you like these," he smiled.

He could have known that only through Ricky, yet he never left P Wing.

As I continued at DHL, I began to take a few risks. Unlike other inmates, who favoured chocolate, my first preference was olives. They came in small re-sealable packets, and I used to quickly open one before pouring the contents into one of the prison-issue workshop mugs. That way, I could sit down, 'sipping' at my 'tea' when the staff checked nobody was eating anything.

"Why the hell are you eating those?" one prisoner asked when he looked into my mug.

"They are nice. Do you want one?"

"Eww!"

***

One day, Joe approached me under the pretence of making an arrangement like Russell's.

"You should be careful," he said once the door was pulled to.

"What do you mean?"

"Your writing. The stuff you get published."

I guessed he was referring to an article I had published in *Inside Time.*

"You're criticising the system and letting them know what you think. I agree with you; most of us do, but when it comes to what matters, none of them will care if you get fucked up. If you want to stay here, I wouldn't be writing up articles for newspapers."

I nodded. "You're right, but I have to speak my mind. Besides, the last article was about Dovegate – not Lowdham Grange."

"It's the same company that runs both," he observed. "What exactly is it you want from your sentence?"

"Just to get released," I replied.

"So, focus on that rather than writing critical articles. It's already annoyed some of the screws – they were talking about you in the bistro today."

"Great," I sighed.

"Yes, and it will get worse. They don't like prisoners who seem more intelligent than them - not if you haven't got any clout on the outside. And you should be careful in what you say to people, too – your neighbour, for instance."

I wasn't sure what he meant, but nodded.

"What do you want for picking my canteen?"

"It's okay; you don't need to give me anything."

He smiled. "That's why I like you. You've got balls – not many here would rob a bank by themselves – and you've got manners. But I don't accept freebies."

He left the cell, then shouted back to me from the staircase.

"Pie-Guy! The nutty one, right?"

It took a few seconds to understand his meaning.

"Yes, Cadbury's Nut Chocolate."

Joe may have been right, yet writing was not just a form of ritual or therapy; it was also a duty. The public did not know what really happened in prisons since the media presented a skewed and biased picture. Moreover, I had recently encountered someone whilst in the Education block who offered me a place on the 'Creative Writing class'. His name was Tim Watson, and he resembled an elderly schoolteacher – short of stature, with a pair of spectacles balanced at the end of his nose. He planned to retire as a proofreader and kindly reviewed some of my written pieces. Thanks to his guidance, I recognised incorrect placement of commas and poor sentence structure – techniques not usually taught in most schools and universities. And he wasn't afraid to be critical, asking me if one story I spent days refining was "a dinner I had prepared for the bin".

Thus, my week got split between doing OU and creative writing sessions, together with the necessary boredom of working at DHL. Tim used to bring copies of various writing magazines to read, some of which I brought to work. He even arranged with the *New Writer* to allow prisoners free entry into their 'prose/poetry' competition.

With Tim's help, I submitted a dozen pieces to various competitions and awards, as well as the Koestler Trust. When the awards list was released months later, Lowdham came top for the most awarded prison, - not as a result of having more talented inmates, but because it gave them the opportunities and freedom to submit entries.

Nonetheless, subtle changes began trickling down from the Ministry of Justice's instructions. Yoga classes stopped, there were more random prisoner searches, and the staff became less friendly. It culminated, months later, in Tim himself being dismissed and the creative writing classes ending. He never got to see my writing getting accepted into magazines like Sarasvati and Dawntreader or winning £120 from the Koestler Trust for my short stories.

Seeing one's work in print is an immense boost to self-esteem. It forms a tangible link to being a contributing member of society;

of impacting others positively. Such things can only help to reduce reoffending and the negative thoughts that go with it, yet the Ministry of Justice barely acknowledged the power of writing.

There is a power in pen and paper that imbues survival. It was a gateway to another world, a catharsis to deeply buried traumas, and a journey of exploration without walls or frontiers. The removal of this outlet, by stopping creative writing sessions, created a deep chasm that would undoubtedly end up ricocheting onto wider society.

Certainly, the stated purpose of prison was as a punishment – to be deprived of one's liberty – and yet alongside this, supposedly balancing it like the very scales of justice, was the intention to rehabilitate. So, the question arises: what exactly is rehabilitation? I had asked this multiple times throughout my sentence, and for the first time, I accepted that it was possible in prison. Thoughts of escape were no longer present; I just wanted to re-enter society and start afresh as a law-abiding citizen.

Even so, mistakes were made that could never be undone. The Victim Awareness Course I attended clarified the 'ripple effect' of crimes and how actions could last long after they occurred. Thinking back to the witness statements in my trial bundle, I remembered the people who were hurt far beyond my intentions. This had included threatening a betting shop manager with a knife when they couldn't open the safe. To say nothing of the fear and distress of being confronted by someone masked, appearing to wield a gun. Thinking of such things, shame and disbelief surged within. *Who was that person?* Could someone be so blinded by a mission and goal as to overlook their actions in getting there? Could they sacrifice their good nature and kindness in the name of something greater? History was replete with ayes. And many examples were mass murder, forced relocation and destruction – by people who thought they were on the road to creating a 'better world'. I had chosen the sinuous and misleading road of good intentions, which led me into hell – both physically and morally.

For perhaps the first time, I looked around and saw myself as one of them – a prisoner, not a courageous rebel or simple lawbreaker, but someone who had inflicted harm upon others.

Rehabilitation was restoration, but it was also about change. Like every lifeform that exists, human beings are complex patterns and processes. Akin to rivers, their minds may remain the same, but within these are thoughts, emotions, hormones, and endlessly changing interactions of chemicals that even the most materialistic scientists cannot confidently claim to represent the sum of who we are. Are you the same person as five years ago, ten, or more?

But as far as society was concerned, the person who had robbed banks was the same who sat in a prison cell, writing short stories, years later. Yes, I still held to certain notions. I could not let them know that I saw myself as living in a tyranny, imprisoned by the minions of a corrupt, oppressive regime. It was called a democracy but might as well have been a dictatorship, for the masses were enslaved to the capitalist system, coerced to scrape a living through the material acquisition of lies. That was money – just a representation of wealth based on nothing. I could not tell them I *sought* to change the course ahead – one of greater environmental devastation, human suffering, inequality, and mindless waste. That I *aimed* to stand up in order to end tyranny and oppression; to give hope and opportunity to the masses so long denied.

Faceless corporations, oppressive governments – these were the powers that shaped our Earth. They would make it into a burning wasteland to uphold their luxurious lifestyles. Those who Stood Up to it would be marginalised, imprisoned, tortured, and executed. Those who dared to speak out may find themselves leading a fringe of rebellion, yet it would be merely a revolt of words and inconvenience to the status quo. By the time the masses realised how far things had gone – when the greed of the elite truly impacted their lives – it would be too late. No number of riots or overthrowing of regimes could change the situation then. The damage would already have been done in the shape of an irreversible environmental catastrophe.

And those who had caused the most harm would face the consequences last, shielded from the impacts, perhaps even finding a way to live within their own self-contained Millionaires' Rows.

Yet the courts would never see this. Even as their very foundations became redundant, their primary concern was the kind of justice handed down by the rich and powerful.

I regretted my actions insofar as they had been taken hastily, without concern for the individuals working in banks and bookmakers. There were better ways which did not involve causing harm to people. I had been stupid, and I deserved prison for the damage that I had caused. My only contention was to be judged in a manner that matched my lawful culpability level, as opposed to being cast into the same category as those who intentionally sought to cause harm, in full knowledge of that harm, to others.

Chapter 15: Legal Eagle

From a journey that had begun at HMP Dovegate in writing to a new solicitor, I now took the next step. A psychiatrist called Dr Gallapathie came to visit, undertaking a short evaluation to assess, firstly, if I had Asperger's Syndrome and, secondly, to what extent it impacted my offences.

His report, sent a month later by the solicitor, made passing reference to having Asperger's Syndrome' and the likelihood that it may have had an impact on the offences, whilst phasing into descriptions of 'mild depression' and 'alcohol dependency'. No mention of the doctors and mental health workers I had seen since childhood had been included, all of whom were itemised for him.

The solicitor said it was insufficient to justify an appeal, affirming that my sentence could be substituted for an IPP, which contradicted their previous advice.

For a few weeks, I wasn't sure what to do. Lowdham had a well-stocked library with many legal textbooks, so I began to peruse them rather than take out the usual fantasy or sci-fi novel. They all pointed towards a sentence reduction if all mitigating factors in my case were considered. Not only would that be closer to the case of Naidoo, noted by my barrister, but it would match with countless others.

The issue was over culpability, of which the sentencing guidelines had four different tiers. Judge Cavell had placed me on the highest possible tier: the intention to cause harm. The one below that was being reckless as to whether harm was caused, or more accurately:

"Is reckless as to whether harm is caused, that is, where the offender appreciates at least some harm would be caused but proceeds giving no thought to the consequences even though the extent of the risk would be obvious to most people."

Clearly, this was the correct level I should have been sentenced. Although I'd extensively planned offences, I never intended to cause harm to individuals. Where harm was caused, I only truly appreciated it after reading witness statements. Never, at the time of offending, did I grasp the real emotional impacts my offences would have. What better evidence could there be than the diary entries I had made at the time? There was now proof of a condition, raised even before I was sentenced yet not brought to the court's attention, that in all previous cases had been recognised as having some bearing on culpability.

The only option left was to do it myself, so I wrote to the Court of Appeal asking for the necessary paperwork. The library at least provided access to the relevant material. Moreover, there was even a 'legal session' that could be booked, where computers were available for typing and printing legal material. All this was overseen by the prison's librarian, George Sainsbury. He was an eccentric man with a mop of brown hair, which many joked was a wig. If treated respectfully, he would go on the internet to source legal articles, and rumours suggested he even bought many of the library's books himself.

Mr Sainsbury provided guidance on completing the court forms, which also required copies of the 'grounds for appeal', the psychiatric evaluation, and other things.

But I knew, with the present evaluation, the chances of success were slimmer than they should have been. If I was rich, like all my peers on P wing, I could have paid for the best possible report - one where, instead of skimming over relevant areas, they were elucidated with clarity.

All that remained was to seal the documents into a fat

envelope and hand it into the wing office to be posted. Only mail marked with 'Legal – Rule 39 Correspondence' could be sealed; otherwise, you had to leave the envelope open. Every prison contained an entire department that ploughed through incoming and outgoing correspondence, thwarting anything from escape attempts (like Brian at Parkhurst) to planned assaults or suicides.

A risk remained, albeit slim, that the time I spent in custody 'as an appellant' would not be counted towards my sentence. It was a draconian procedure used to deter appeals with no merit, so I pushed it aside and tried not to dwell on the appeal's overall prospects.

***

Just before Christmas, Ricky had a change of heart and moved over to P wing. His first week was defined by - in his words - 'inducting visitors to the prison'. The wing always got chosen as a place to bring the many groups who visited Lowdham, and he took exception to them seeing a 'false image of what prison is really like'. To that end, he wandered around the exercise yard, discreetly flinging up wads of wet toilet paper, which stuck to the walls like a paintball target range.

On one occasion, a batch of would-be prison officers arrived, many of them looking like they'd just left college. Ricky scuttled into his cell, and soon half the wing smelt of cannabis.

On the exercise yard, one of the trainees came marching up to me.

I was not feeling talkative, but his wide eyes were locked on mine.

"Hello, how are you?"

"Fine, thanks, how about you?"

The round face crinkled into a smile. We could have met under a bus shelter. "Very well, thank you. How are you finding it here?"

I began to speak, but he launched into a long cough.

"Do you want some water?" I asked.

"Oh..."

I thought he would say yes, but after a long hesitation, he just shook his head and asked me a question I needed him to repeat.

"Is the weed good here?"

I never knew whether it was a joke, a trap, or a genuine question.

"Never tried it," I said, before making an excuse about needing to use the toilet.

What would the young officer be like in a few years? It wasn't hard to imagine. Most screws were tight-knit, cementing ranks in an 'us and them' mentality that judged inmates without knowing them. It is in human nature to judge, but fair judgement takes account of a person's actions and all the circumstances surrounding those actions. All too often, judging was done based on incomplete or tainted information.

Around this time, Amanda arrived – a man who wanted to be recognised as a woman and transferred to a female prison. (S)he had undoubtedly been moved to the wing because she would have been ruthlessly bullied elsewhere. But Amanda's behaviour was enough to cause a stir even amongst the millionaires – with blatant 'flirting' and requests that made some turn red in embarrassment or rage. Russell initially welcomed Amanda onto the wing, but his amicability ended when (s)he asked him for "cocoa butter scented with penis". Likewise, (s)he had requested medication – rumoured to be given to people who practised gay sex – from another inmate who frequently visited healthcare. He fumed about this for weeks after, telling people if (s)he approached him again, the consequences would be far from pretty. But Ricky loved it and spent a fair amount of time encouraging Amanda to make requests to various staff and inmates.

Over time, Amanda's presence was less noticed – (s)he sometimes would not appear for several days. Nevertheless, there was always some rumour about what (s)he had done, including – on one occasion – walking around the wing in a 'dress' that (s)he had made. It could not have been stranger: a sizeable black inmate strutting around a prison wing of the nation's top gangsters in a custom dress. If a visitor arrived then, they would have also caught the reek of Ricky's 'cannabis' and the sight of a wall peppered with blobs of dried toilet paper. They might well have concluded it was a place for people awaiting transfer to an asylum.

***

Ricky had spent all of his eight-year determinate sentence inside prison, mainly at Lowdham, and in January he was going to leave a free man.

"I hate goodbyes," he said. "So tomorrow I am just leaving – don't bother coming down to see me off."

"All right."

"And I don't write no letters either, but I hope your appeal goes well. Even if it doesn't, you can do your sentence. Just don't let the system beat you down, or anyone else for that matter."

We hugged.

The next day, early in the morning, I heard Ricky shouting "farewell" to a handful of prisoners – including me, "Loxley".

I felt his absence keenly, but time passed a little easier when my MP3 player arrived – it had been ordered weeks previously in one of the catalogues. The only problem was I had no music to download onto it. I mentioned this to Joe, who asked what kind of music I liked.

It was difficult to answer because my taste was so diverse.

"Oh, you can just see what I have then," he said, pointing to his cell. Like at Hewell, he had heavy curtains, shelves with stacks of CDs and books, plus an open wardrobe full of clothes.

"Take a look through some of these songs," he said, showing me how to use the large stereo. "Anything you like, just write down. I've got to go and play this poker game now; no need to rush."

It was an honour to be left there alone. Pictures of his family were on the walls: two young boys and a woman, whom I assumed to be his wife and children. Beside these were some pictures of an elderly couple smiling before a backdrop of trees.

I wondered what they would be going through – to have their husband, father and son committed to prison. From what he told me before, it was also his first time in custody, although he had managed to make millions of pounds from drugs before entering the gates. For his first offence, he was given a fourteen-year sentence.

I browsed through the songs, pausing at a few classic rock and pop bands. There were too many to choose from, though; he seemed to have thousands stored on his stereo.

"How's it going?" he asked upon returning to the cell.

"Yeah, good... I have written some down, but there's so much. Anything like this kind of music is good. How do I get it onto the MP3?"

He showed me, but it quickly became apparent that all the music would take many hours to download. "Don't worry, I'll download it for you," he said. "It will give me something to do tonight."

"Are you sure?"

"Of course, no problem. I'll have it ready for you in the morning."

I wasn't used to such gestures and would have found an excuse to refuse it if anyone else had offered. But I'd known Joe since Hewell and regarded him with respect and trust. Nor had he ever let me down: his advice had proven invaluable, and the next day he stuck to his word by returning my MP3, filled with music.

Thanks to this little music trinket, I found it easier to focus in the gym. Boosted by creatine, I was up to the same weights I had been amazed to see others do back at HMPs Garth and Parkhurst.

As for Amanda, (s)he had just received a disciplinary sanction, kept locked up in the mornings. Nobody knew why, but there was plenty of speculation. The most common theory was that (s)he had "offered a blowjob" to a certain screw.

I found it hard to believe how s(he) could ever be accepted to a female prison, and, even if (s)he was, the kind of experience that would result. A couple at Lowdham had 'girlfriends' in the female estate, including one at the DHL workshop. He always described the conditions conveyed to him by letter, which sounded far from pleasant.

***

As another year crept over the horizon, I wrote down some 'New Year's Resolutions':-

> *Category C: The Verne [a 'semi-open' prison near Devon]*
> *Finish books*
> *Finalise appeal*
> *Depending on the above, prepare for release (money, housing, funding, employment)*
> *Save over £350*
> *Get published in three other magazines*
> *Improve strength and fitness*
> *Regular yoga*
> *Less swearing*
> *Improve communication skills and be more sociable*
> *Finish U116 [OU Module] and sign up for a new course*
> *Learn Spanish or French or both*
> *And lastly, Remember...*

By the last, I was thinking of the days before, those of unrestricted freedom and opportunity – particularly when travelling the world. Some places would still be there, insights that could never be forgotten.

I remembered. Even in the darkness of prison, I saw the outspread canvas of stars in the Australian desert. I remembered the majesty, the beauty, the mystery.

I could still see bats curving across a red sky near Khao Yai, lost and alone in the Jungle.

I had not forgotten the leaping dolphins in the waves of Blue Haven Beach, the rising morning mists of Goshen, the concave links of Sydney Opera House and the stirring music within.

I remembered the Kaikoura Mountains, Cadaques, Chefchaouen, Mount Gambier, Levuka, and the garden of my childhood.

For all its positives, Lowdham Grange was still prison. Every night I was locked in a cell with bars on the window. Society – the world itself – was 'beyond': unreachable, save through writing and dreams. Between the bars, I could see a field edged by trees, at first covered with a dusting of snow and now showing the first signs of Spring. It looked so peaceful, devoid of the noise and tension of the prison behind me. My cell, #33, sat right next to the snooker table, which meant every single moment of being unlocked – if not off the wing – I would hear the clicking of cue on ball, an exclamation of dismay or triumph, the squeak of trainers as a player positioned themselves... a curse, a shout, the slick pocketing of a ball. It was all interspersed by loud talking, whistling, sighing and laughter. Sometimes an errant ball leapt up and made a frantic bid for freedom, cracking and bouncing as it rolled hopefully away, only to be brought back to the table. I wondered, if the shiny sphere was gifted with speech, whether it would scream.

***

In early March, a letter came from the Court of Appeal. All this time I had been bracing for it. I frantically unfurled the sheet of paper, then stared.

A single judge had rejected my grounds.

And yet, it wasn't over. The British Justice system allowed for appeals against a sentence and conviction. In both cases, there were two stages: the filing of the appeal paperwork, which in general had to be done within twenty-eight days of sentencing or conviction and, after that, a decision by the Court of Appeal. In the first stage, a single judge would consider the paperwork and decide whether an appeal was likely to succeed. If he said no, an appellant could still proceed to the 'full court', which consisted of three judges. They sometimes decided there and then about whether to uphold the appeal – to reduce a sentence, overturn a conviction, or reject it. More often, it required a full hearing, so there would be three stages.

But it was effectively the end once the 'full court' decided. So many people had gone to the Court of Appeal and lost, but they did not give up. There was something else… a so-called 'Criminal Cases Review Commission' ('CCRC'), but in reality – as discovered later – this was nothing but a lottery gamble that only bothered referring cases back to the Court of Appeal that were 'high profile'. There were prisoners on P Wing submitting paperwork to the CCRC, and none had the slightest chance. Still, that didn't stop them from paying hundreds of thousands of pounds to legal counsel. I guessed even grasping at a straw was better than simply doing nothing.

Already my appeal was heading in the wrong direction. Maybe I had just got unlucky with the single judge, who might have taken an auditioning part for that outstanding member of the judiciary in Pink Floyd's *The Trial*. Many judges clothed their sadism towards people under the panoply of law, ruthlessly handing down judgements that reinforced injustice rather than doing the opposite.

But what if it got to the full court and was *still* knocked back? What if all the evidence was dismissed and the law itself – as set down by the Sentencing Guidelines Council and previous cases – just discarded? The question was asked, then quickly pushed aside. The courts were bound by the laws, procedures and precedents set down for them.

Nonetheless, the law's imbedded ruthlessness could bestow injustice as easily as it did justice. Like the chains it used to bind its former slaves, its cold embrace spoke only of Order and Constancy; of Necessity and Hierarchy. All had their place, and woe to them who stepped outside of their allotted roles. It was the voice of Javert condemning Valjean from Les Misérables; of the thousands of hard judges who sent children on boats to

Australia and others to their deaths for petty crimes. Ultimately, the system had not changed much since those days. If anything, I thought, it had become worse.

People were condemned to spend long years in prison, which could be better for society if they spent the time contributing with community service. And, when leaving prison, they would forever bear the isolating mark of 'criminal'. Those receiving over four years crossed a permanent divide of exponentially greater punishment: unlike those doing less, their convictions *never* became 'spent', which meant they always had to disclose their offences when asked. Any media outlet could broadcast the offences long after a person left prison, to be easily seen and discovered by anyone who made a casual internet search.

My first stage appeal knock-back was not aided by turning twenty-six a few days later – another reminder of time and youth fading away. Still, that birthday was okay. I spent hours sitting on the yard in the sunshine with grapes, cheese, and chocolate – all purchased from the more expansive canteen list of Lowdham, with an agreed day off from the DHL workshop. I even found someone who played chess, a relatively new arrival called Kenneth Noye. I didn't know it then, but he had allegedly handled gold from the biggest gold heist in British history and then been convicted of murder for a road rage incident. Despite being quite old – I estimated in his late fifties – he had a muscular, tanned body that spoke of years in prison gyms. I was astonished when, at one stage, he commenced doing some pull-ups, exceeding the reps that people half his age could do. None could beat me, though, fifteen reps of twenty sets in wide and close grip positions, with twenty reps in proper form if done stand-alone.

"You need to put some weight on," Ken observed.

"Yeah, but I can't – I eat and eat, but nothing happens."

He laughed. "Well, wait till you get past thirty – you have to watch it then. But I meant weight plates; they've got some at the gym."

It was a good point, and subsequently, I added weighted pull-ups to gym sessions.

Alongside three good chess games, that birthday was marked by a need to smoke a joint. They had given me a drug test last month, and before that five months ago; it seemed to be done in three to six-monthly intervals. Of course, it was still a risk, but one I felt like taking. A few inmates smoked weed on P Wing, one of whom – Pat – was known to Joe as reliable. So, I approached him and asked for enough to fill a single joint.

"No problem," Pat said in a heavy Yorkshire accent. "I'll get it for you now."

Pat could best be described as being in a state of extreme obesity, and I knew nothing about him save that he was serving a long sentence for – yes, drug dealing.

He came to my cell fifteen minutes later and handed over a plastic package about the same size as a 20p coin.

"Me and Ashley are going to have a little smoke on the yard in a bit if you want to join us," he said.

There was safety in numbers. "Okay, that sounds good. How much do you want for this?"

"Well, Joe put in a good word for you, so just an ounce of burn will do."

He meant an ounce of Golden Virginia ('GV') tobacco – the standard prison currency – which cost about £8 then.

I joined him and his friend on the yard. We wandered off to a corner, out of sight from the CCTV camera, and lit up. Only two other inmates were in the yard – one was working out, the other walking around. Both didn't seem to be a cause of concern, so I inhaled without too much worry – only to immediately cough.

"Haha," Pat said, "pretty strong, eh? When was the last time you had a puff?"

"Erm, a few months ago," I said.

"I heard you smoked a bit with the old traveller," Ashley said.

He was short, roughly my age, with short brown hair.

I wasn't sure whether to tell them about Ricky's peppermint trick, so just shrugged.

"You don't talk to many people, do you?"

"He's okay," Pat said, smiling. "That's the best way to do your bird – keep yourself to yourself."

"How long are you doing?" Ashley asked.

"Thirteen years."

I could tell he was about to ask, "what for" but Pat spoke again. "Pretty long for a spate of robberies. You were a university student, weren't you, with a clean record? And you used a toy gun?"

"That's right." I guessed he had heard the story from Joe.

Ashley raised his eyebrows. "I thought you were in for fraud or drugs or something. What kind of robberies?"

Pat shoved his shoulder. "What? You've never heard about our friend, Robin Hood, here? Haha, it's a right laugh!"

He commenced giving an outline of my story.

"Fucking hell, man," Ashley exclaimed, holding up his fist. He wanted me to bump mine against it – the gesture was quite common in prison – so I did.

The weed started to take effect: a gradual sliding of reality, or whatever we normally call reality. The evening became brighter; new sounds came to my perception. I also worried that a screw would come onto the yard and catch a whiff. Still, that may not have caused much concern after Ricky's peppermint puffing.

"I'm going to head back inside now," I drawled.

"Yeah, us too," Pat said, stubbing his joint on the wall and pocketing the remnant.

"Nice chattin' to ya," Ashley added.

Thus ended my twenty-sixth birthday, as I slipped into a sea of dreams and inner peace that only 'the herb' could provide.

Chapter 16: Summertime

Spring moved to summer in the only closed prison I would describe as genuinely humane and decent. A marathon contest on the large AstroTurf football pitch raised £1600 for a local children's hospital, with each prisoner securing 'sponsors' from others. I took part, lapping the pitch seventy-five times for the half marathon and putting £32 towards the pot. It was a mere month away from the UK prison system being managed by one of history's most disingenuous and destructive ministers. The media had already paved the road to his rule: no story of prisoners raising money for charity would ever be covered; instead, prisons were 'holiday camps' filled with irredeemable reprobates who deserved as much punishment as possible.

The prospect of leaving Lowdham Grange began to fill me with dread. When Steph Lloyd, my offender supervisor, came up to me smiling and said I had been made 'Cat C' during the yearly categorisation review meeting, I almost asked her to rethink the decision. It meant a transfer was imminent. Some prisoners spoke of how, after making C Category, they got into a serious incident to be 'upgraded' to 'B' again, but that entailed huge risks – including the prospect of being moved elsewhere anyway. Moreover, if I could ever obtain the much-vaunted status of 'D' and get to an open prison, I had to first move through 'C'. The only exception were orderlies, who could 'frog leap' from Lowdham Grange to an open prison.

So, of all prisons, I applied for HMP The Verne, which was in Dorset and rumoured to have good conditions. It was even classed as 'semi-open' because prisoners had full access to the grounds.

The location meant I could receive visits from my mother – who, again, was writing regularly about coming to see me.

I told Joe about my new status, and he just nodded.

"You're not going to stay here?"

"No, how can I? They'll never make me an orderly when there's millionaires lined up for a job. Anyway, I've put in for The Verne."

"Hmm, I know someone there. He tells me it's all right. But… I think you are going to miss this prison, Pie-Guy. No place beats Lowdham Grange, apart from 'D' cat."

Whether it was the desire for company or something more, I had become a regular attendee of the chapel and Tuesday Bible Study sessions. They were overseen by a man called David. He had a mop of blonde-white hair and came in with his wife, Susan. Together, they launched into sudden bursts of song, guitar playing, and 'talking tongues' while I played the Bongo drums. At other times they led ponderous discussions on sections of the Bible.

It was a small group of about six people, with the occasional person coming and going. In many cases, I suppose they were just curious or wanted a break from their usual regime. Another thing that made it unique were the monthly visits of a Christian group in Nottingham, who described themselves as 'Faith Healers'. I wasn't sure what to expect when I first put my name forward to meet them. I entered a small room adjoining the chapel, where three elderly people laid their hands on my shoulders and head, saying blessings. It felt awkward and unusual because the only physical contact in prison was generally confined to being strip-searched by guards or getting into fights with prisoners. But after a minute, their presence warmed and imbued safety; like, in some abstract way, I was part of a family. To be surrounded by compassion in an environment of animosity and condemnation felt like finding a waterfall of crystal water in an arid plain.

Christmas and Easter were special occasions, thanks to David and his Christian group. Alongside the official chaplain, he also received support from the prison governor, who had met me with a small group when I arrived.

Sometimes, in the dark of night and with the deeper uncertainty of what lay ahead, I prayed to God. It may sound strange for someone who previously focused so ardently on escape at the beginning of their sentence, but I did not ask for immediate release. I simply asked to be judged based on the level of culpability that was lawful and fair.

It was also perhaps strange that I wrote so often of God in a personal way. But then again, perhaps not. I continued going to Bible Study every Tuesday, and some of what arose in those sessions changed me. I still saw God as part of the Universe, with the beauty of existence as magnificent as any creator. But I also believed, and desperately hoped, that there was a possibility of higher intelligence, that is, of God, actually caring for individual human lives. So bright a notion could not be dismissed lightly, especially in times of despair and need.

When thrown into the bare concrete cell in The Hole of an American prison, I did not cry out to the sky or sea but to God.

When facing animosity and torment at Dovegate, I did not call upon the atoms around me for a change of environment but to God.

Yes, it was God I always turned to in times of greatest darkness. There was no proof of His existence, nor any evidence that He had intervened. Yet I could not deny that a Light had come to me in America – making me persevere when giving up seemed the easiest option. And in England, at turning points that may have led to worse conditions, I had been 'rescued' by individuals with the light of kindness, understanding and compassion in their eyes. Was this the work of God or some random coalescence of chance?

I dared not debate it, instead placing trust in the possibility that there was not just the materialistic interaction of energy and matter or even the immense beauty that arose from such things, but instead a Force – a Plan – a Being – whose purpose was good.

***

In June, I heard news from the Court of Appeal. At first, I was told the hearing 'was adjourned', with no reason given, but then two days later, I asked the librarian, George Sainsbury, to look on the internet. He was not in a good mood – it sometimes happened for no reason – and he occasionally boomed at them to leave the library when he took a disliking to them. In my case, he kept me waiting around, spending time in his office flicking through a book with 'Ancient Greece' written across its cover. Just when I was about to return to the wing, he called my name.

"They want another psychiatric assessment," he said.

And that was all I'd get: it would take another two weeks for the formal decision to arrive by letter, by which time a family relative had sent in a cutting from a newspaper. It reported on the hearing negatively, making out that I was 'claiming' to have Asperger's Syndrome in an 'attempt' to reduce the sentence.

Would they have been satisfied if the sentence had been twenty years? Forty years? Life…? Just what did they think such time would accomplish? If they sought punishment, why not just advocate execution or lifelong exile?

The only thing that dampened my frustration was realising I wasn't alone. Some inmates did not even know when they would be released due to receiving so-called 'indeterminate' sentences. One IPP prisoner from DHL was dragged off the wing – accused of stealing canteen items – after he refused to relocate. A group of officers stormed onto the wing and took him away in handcuffs. Not only would he find himself in worse conditions, but the incident would also be used against him at probation to keep him longer in prison. Such was the added uncertainty and punishments that some faced.

At least the court had not rejected the appeal outright. They wanted another report by a psychiatrist and a 'representation order' so that I could instruct a lawyer to argue my case. It was far from a failure, but the uncertainty it created was immense.

I sometimes wondered what would happen for all the others who had ongoing appeals – whether against their sentence or conviction. And, even when they were released from prison, would they only go on to reoffend? I guessed those at Lowdham had a much better chance of not returning than many of those I had met in other prisons. Here, people could complete qualifications, win prizes, earn money to help them restart their lives on release, and build up their self-esteem and skills. There was none of the jagged bitterness and alienation from being barked at by your second name or slotted into a machine where your prison number was the first thing of reference.

Having a job, accommodation and family stability was essential to successfully reintegrating into society, but there was also a deeper level. Goals, aspirations, endeavours, targets, dreams, values... these were the underlying components of a person's character and behaviour. To change those was to truly address offending, but that was the hardest thing of all. Moreover, the goals and values of modern society only encouraged crime – most of which was defined by acquisitive acts or simply the abuse of power over others.

Was it really any surprise that crime is highest in places of greatest inequality, where the goals (money, influence, power) are highlighted above all others yet hardest to reach – thus forcing people to commit offences? And yet was not the greater crime a system that conditions and subjugates people to follow such artificial, destructive goals?

People did not see Earth's curvature until leaving the atmosphere or seeing photos from space. Similarly, they would not truly realise the nature of the society and system they lived in – and were shaped by – unless they stepped outside its borders with eyes wide open. I could write as much as I liked; nothing would change that. Perhaps faint realisations passed across a person's awareness occasionally – in the rebellious state of youth or after some shock – but they would soon settle back into their allotted positions.

Prisoners were conditioned to pursue the same goals, although they had taken different routes to achieve them. The drive for material acquisition, 'to get rich or die trying', would not just vanish when they left the prison gates.

***

Ken Noye was on a roll. For five games running, he had beaten me at chess. Later, he showed me a book he had been reading from the library.

"It's full of gambits that all the champions use," he noted. "A couple of them will change your gameplay entirely."

I flicked through the pages, glancing at the diagrams of chess boards and vague arrows with bafflement.

"Interesting," I said, handing it back. He put the book under his chair (another unique addition to Lowdham was the plastic chairs they kept stocked for use beside the exercise yard doors).

"You're a pretty intelligent guy. How did you end up in prison?"

The question was annoying because I had already touched upon it before. "Just through being stupid," I replied.

Where could I possibly begin? Ricky had understood, perhaps, but only because he'd stood slightly apart from the system. Ken had been a gangster, but still part of integrated criminal circles that moved alongside the regular flows of wealth, just as London's best cocaine dealers had customers who frequented the Palace of Westminster.

Ken just smiled and nodded. He was usually quiet with others, much like me. I wondered if society would ever accept him again or if he would spend the remainder of his productive years inside prisons.

"It takes a man to suffer ignorance and smile – be yourself, no matter what they say..."

The words of Sting's "Englishman in New York" drifted from the window of a nearby cell, touching upon the stirring irony of how most around me hid behind masks of confidence and a flawed criminal fraternity. Some gazed in Amanda's direction when (s)he came out onto the yard, and I wondered how many harboured desire behind their masks of disgust. Pat and Ashley strolled out too, heading for the same corner we had smoked a joint on my birthday. They nodded, friendly and accepting of my presence. Yet when I first arrived, their glances had been nothing but hostile. It was more masks, suppressing the natural curiosity that humans have from birth.

Nobody showed their true selves. Did they even remember who they had been before entering prison – before taking the route of crime? Behind the masks, there had to be something that could not be removed. But society fashioned and refashioned how people saw themselves; how they behaved; what they did, and in doing so, buried the truth of people's characters.

Prison had the same power hierarchies that could be found beyond the walls. Everyone had a place, played the games they needed to play, and the system always won... whilst you went by its rules, at least.

"You want another game?"

I looked at Ken, topless in his chair facing the sun, and shook my head. A little bee alighted on the edge of his cup, which he let crawl onto his fingertip and then fly away into the sky. A slight smile spread across his face.

To the press, he was a vicious murderer and remorseless gangster.

To me, he was just an old man who had as much chance of reoffending as the bee reaching the moon.

It was the last summer day I would remember in Lowdham. Two weeks of intermittent drizzle followed, with a slip under my door confirming the transfer to HMP The Verne. Even as I packed my belongings – which now filled two large prison bags – I felt a change in the world outside. The trees were fading to shades of orange and brown, the field beyond the prison walls was low with grass, and thin swathes of cloud sketched the sky.

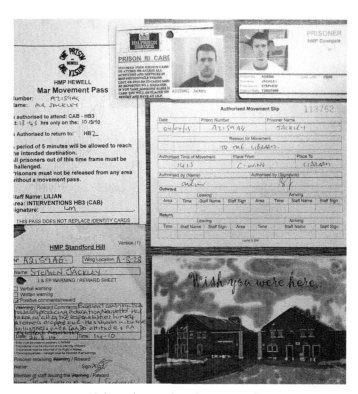

Various prison cards and movement slips

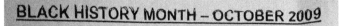

BLACK HISTORY MONTH – OCTOBER 2009

One of the many African tribes; there were hundreds with their own language and culture.

Beginning of the African Slave trade: centuries of oppression.

"*I have a dream… my four little children will one day not be judged by the color of their skin but by the content of their character.*"

Ministry of JUSTICE

HMP Hewell
Hewell Lane
REDDITCH
Worcestershire
B97 6QS

Tel: 01527 785000
Fax: 01527 785001

Mr Jackley
AD9556
House Block 2

12 October 2009

Dear Mr Jackley

Re: Poster competition - Black History Month

I am pleased to inform you that your poster entry came first in the competition.

You have won a credit of £10 to go into your pinphone account arrangements will be made for this to take place as soon as possible, hopefully this week.

The standard of entry was extremely good but yours was chosen for its informative content. The poster will be displayed around the prison across all 3 sites.

Thank you for your efforts

Black History Month competition

Parkhurst

Note: Available Spend Cannot Be Manually Amended

Prison canteen sheet

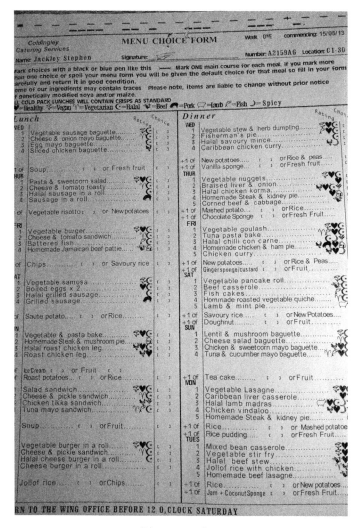

Coldingley
Catering Services

Name: Jackley Stephen   Signature: Number: A2159AG   Location: C1-30

Mark choices with a black or blue pen like this ▬ Mark ONE main course for each meal. If you mark more than one choice or spoil your menu form you will be given the default choice for that meal so fill in your form carefully and return it in good condition.
Some of our ingredients may contain traces. Please note, items are liable to change without prior notice if genetically modified soya and/or maize.
ALL COLD PACK LUNCHES WILL CONTAIN CRISPS AS STANDARD

♥=Healthy ✿=Vegan Ⓥ=Vegetarian Ⓒ=Halal ◆=Beef 🐷=Pork 🐑=Lamb ✎=Fish ᴐ=Spicy

Lunch	Rating	Choice	Dinner	Rating	Choice
WED			**WED**		
1 Vegetable sausage baguette.			1 Vegetable stew & herb dumpling.		
2 Cheese & onion mayo baguette.			2 Fisherman's pie.		
3 Egg mayo baguette.			3 Halal savoury mince.		
4 Sliced chicken baguette.			4 Caribbean chicken curry.		
+1 of Soup ( ) or Fresh fruit ( )			+1 of New potatoes. ( ) or Rice & peas.		
			+1 of Vanilla sponge. ( ) or Fresh fruit.		
THUR			**THUR**		
1 Pasta & sweetcorn salad.			1 Vegetable nuggets.		
2 Cheese & tomato toasty.			2 Braised liver & onion.		
3 Halal sausage in a roll.			3 Halal chicken korma.		
4 Sausage in a roll.			4 Homemade Steak & kidney pie.		
			5 Corned beef & cabbage.		
+of Vegetable risotto ( ) or New potatoes			+1 of Mashed potato. ( ) or Rice.		
			+1 of Chocolate Sponge ( ) or Fresh Fruit.		
FRI			**FRI**		
1 Vegetable burger.			1 Vegetable goulash.		
2 Cheese & tomato sandwich.			2 Tuna pasta bake.		
3 Battered fish.			3 Halal chilli con carne.		
4 Homemade Jamaican beef pattie.			4 Homemade chicken & ham pie.		
			5 Chicken curry.		
+of Chips. ( ) or Savoury rice ( )			+1 of New potatoes. ( ) or Rice & Peas.		
			+1 of Ginger sponge/custard ( ) or Fruit.		
SAT			**SAT**		
1 Vegetable samosa.			1 Vegetable pancake roll.		
2 Boiled eggs x 2.			2 Beef casserole.		
3 Halal grilled sausage.			3 Fish cakes.		
4 Grilled sausage.			4 Hommade roasted vegetable quiche.		
			5 Lamb & mint pie.		
+of Saute potato. ( ) or Rice.			+1 of Savoury rice. ( ) or New Potatoes.		
			+1 of Doughnut. ( ) or Fruit.		
SUN			**SUN**		
1 Vegetable & pasta bake.			1 Lentil & mushroom baguette.		
2 Homemade Steak & mushroom pie.			2 Cheese salad baguette.		
3 Halal roast chicken leg.			3 Chicken & sweetcorn mayo baguette.		
4 Roast chicken leg.			4 Tuna & cucumber mayo baguette.		
+f Ice Cream ( ) or Fruit ( )					
Roast potatoes. ( ) or Rice.			+1 of Tea cake. ( ) or Fruit.		
MON			**MON**		
Salad sandwich.			1 Vegetable Lasagne.		
Cheese & pickle sandwich.			2 Caribbean liver casserole.		
Chicken tikka sandwich.			3 Halal lamb madras.		
Tuna mayo sandwich.			4 Chicken vindaloo.		
			5 Homemade Steak & kidney pie.		
Soup. ( ) or Fruit.			+1 of Rice. ( ) or Mashed potatoe		
			+1 of Rice pudding. ( ) or Fresh Fruit.		
TUES			**TUES**		
Vegetable burger in a roll.			1 Mixed bean casserole.		
Cheese & pickle sandwich.			2 Vegetable stir fry.		
Halal cheese burger in a roll.			3 Halal beef stew.		
Cheese burger in a roll.			4 Jollof rice with chicken.		
			5 Homemade beef lasagne.		
Jollof rice. ( ) or Chips.			+1 of Rice. ( ) or New potatoes.		
			+1 of Jam + Coconut Sponge ( ) or Fresh Fruit.		

Prison menu sheet

192

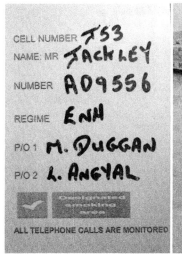

CELL NUMBER **J53**
NAME: MR **JACKLEY**
NUMBER **AO9556**
REGIME **ENH**
P/O 1 **M. DUGGAN**
P/O 2 **L. ANGYAL**

Designated smoking area

ALL TELEPHONE CALLS ARE MONITORED

Prisoner cell door card and photo of author at 26
to prove completion of bricklaying course

Bringing service to life
serco

To: Mr Jackley   A4101CL   5P

From: C Whyler

OS: Steph Lloyd

Copy: Duty Manager Office
        Core Record

Date: 14th September 2012

NOTIFICATION OF PROGRESSIVE TRANSFER

Dear Mr Jackley,

A transfer to HMP The Verne has been arranged for you in the week commencing Monday 17th September 2012. This is a progressive move for you.

This progressive move is in accordance with your sentence planning needs and therefore you have been allocated to a suitable establishment reflective of your security status.

Your Offender Supervisor will explore any concerns you may have in relation to this progressive transfer.

A refusal to transfer will initiate a review of your IEP status with a withdrawal of your enhanced status. This status will remain the same until your transfer is facilitated.

Most Cat C and Cat D prisoners leave HMP Lowdham Grange and successfully progress with their sentences and work in a positive manner towards open conditions and resettlement. I hope that our position is clear and leaves you with clarity as to what you can expect. Your anticipated cooperation under the Responsible Prisoner Compact is appreciated.

We wish you well in the future and thank you for your contribution to the regime here at HMP Lowdham Grange.

C Whyler
OMU Manager

Lowdham Grange 'progressive' transfer letter –
note the veiled threats if such a 'progression' is declined

ALLOCATION CRITERIA CHECKLIST
HMP THE VERNE

PRISONER NAME JACKLEY   NUMBER A 2159 AG

	Compliant	Non-Compliant	Remarks
Must be 25 years of age or over	☑	☐	
Must have at least 9 months left to serve	☑	☐	
Progressive life sentence moves	N/A	☐	
Must have no history of escape or attempt escape from prison custody in last 10 years	☐	☑	PLANNED TO ESCAPE F COURT 2009, HEREFO ATTEMPTED ESCAPO U.S. MARSHALL'S VA
Must have no history of racism	☐	☐	2 x FAKED SEIZURES GET TO O/HOSPITA FOUND IN POSSESS
Must have no significant history of prison drug trafficking or dealing in past 5 years	☐	☐	A PRISON HAT + INGREDIANTS THAT
If sex offender on present or previous sentences, must have completed SOTP if required	☐	☐	MAKE AN EXPLOS
Must not require methadone detoxification	☐	☐	
Must not require intensive psychiatric intervention	☐	☐	
Must not be assessed as "high risk" on cell-sharing risk assessment in last three months	☑	☐	

(NOT KNOWN)

COMPLIANT WITH ESTABLISHMENT CRITERIA   YES / NO

RECEPTION OFFICER SIGNATURE AND NAME REQUIRED BELOW

Signed _____ Name CREW-DON Date 20/9/12.

REFER TO GOVERNOR   YES / NO

ASSESSMENT – Head of Operations / Duty Governor

To Seg Unit pending full security file.

Signed _____ Name M Date 23.09.12.

DECISION GOVERNOR OPERATIONAL GRADE E AND ABOVE

Prison security notes upon arrival
at HMP The Verne (obtained after release)

195

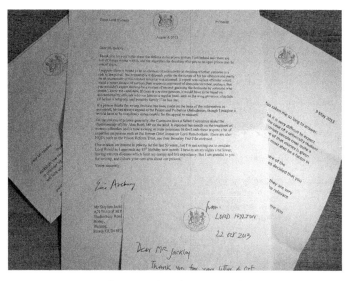

Some letters received from House of Lords

DP/JAC/010413   30 April 2013

Prisons reform

Further to your letter dated 1 April, which was addressed to Oliver Letwin MP, I am writing to inform you that following your relocation to HMP Guy's Marsh in the North Dorset constituency, I am now your Member of Parliament.

I read your letter and proposal with interest. I agree with much of what you say about the importance of rehabilitative programmes to tackle reoffending rates. As you are aware, the Government is undertaking reforms to see fewer offenders returning to the system, as part of the so-called 'rehabilitation revolution', under which the Prime Minister called on charities, companies and voluntary organisations to help offenders reform by providing drugs treatment, education and skills training on a 'payment by results' basis. Whilst the Prime Minister acknowledged there would be some high-risk offenders for whom it would not be appropriate, he insisted this approach should be the norm rather than the exception.

I hope you agree these proposals represent a radical sea-change not only in practical terms but in the overall outlook towards the prison and rehabilitation culture, which is much needed. I would of course be happy to pass on your personal comments to the Prisons Minister, Jeremy Wright MP, including your concerns at the problem of overcrowding, and I will be in touch as soon as I have his response to hand.

Thank you for taking the time to contact me.

---

14 May 2013

Dear Mr Jackley

Thank you very much for your letter of 25th April. I appreciate you taking the time and trouble to update me. I am still awaiting the response from the Rt. Hon Chris Grayling MP. If he feels this matter should be dealt with by the Home Secretary he will, of course, forward the correspondence to her office. I will send you the response when it is received.

With every good wish

The Rt. Hon Michael Gove MP
Secretary of State for Education

Some letters from MPs

In the High Court of Justice
Queen's Bench Division
Administrative Court

CO Ref:

CO/5773/2013

In the matter of an application for Judicial Review

The Queen on the application of

STEPHEN JACKLEY

versus SECRETARY OF STATE FOR JUSTICE

NOTIFICATION of the Judge's decision (CPR Part 54.11, 54.12)

Following consideration of the documents lodged by the Claimant, and the Acknowledgment of service filed by the Defendant

Order by HHJ McKenna sitting as a Judge of the high Court

Permission is hereby granted

Observations. It is at least arguable on the facts of this case that the Defendant acted unlawfully in failing to facilitate access to and use of IT facilities given the passage of time since the request was first made

Case management directions

- The defendant and any other person served with the claim form who wishes to contest the claim or support it on additional grounds must file and serve detailed grounds for contesting the claim or supporting it on additional grounds and any written evidence, within 35 days after service of this order.
- Any reply and any application by the claimant to lodge further evidence must be lodged within 21 days of the service of detailed grounds for contesting the claim.
- The claimant must file and serve a trial bundle not less than 4 weeks before the date of the hearing of the judicial review.
- The claimant must file and serve a skeleton argument not less than 14 days before the date of the hearing of the judicial review.
- The defendant and any interested party must file and serve a skeleton argument not less than 7 days before the date of the hearing of the judicial review.
- The defendant must file an agreed bundle of authorities, not less than 3 days before the date of the hearing of the judicial review.

Permission granted for judicial review –
access to ICT for legal purposes case

One is vexed by the prevention to cultivate acorns for later planting. As a long-term prisoner who has never been incarcerated before and who genuinely needs to be in/should be in open conditions I am being given no means whatsoever to re-establish contact with the natural world or regain a normative existence. You have previously ruled out tree planting and a small-scale ant farm, so I really hoped that cultivating acorn seeds (as a step for later planting by others) would be allowed.

I have noted elsewhere the apparent prejudice towards native birdlife and now it appears there is a repugnance towards trees. Such an outlook is worrying.

Mr Jackley

Your comments have been noted — As an establishment we endeavour to keep prisoners who are interested in the 'nature' wildlife interested through our horticulture work party. Could I suggest you make enquires to join the team. Otherwise I'm sure there is a wide selection of books in our library that maybe of interest to you.

Coldingley complaint train – no contact with natural world

Some officers lacked humour!

I am not extrinsically a marine creature. However there appears to be a predominance of puddles, occuring across every space of this edifice. I see puddles in walkways, on the yard, in hall ways, even living areas. Such hazards need to be marked, mopped and/or absorbed.

Of course, these puddles would not occur had you allowed grass to grow in native soil in appropriate areas instead of erecting a multi-layered parking lot maze where the cars are all clumped and in actual fact people.

(Plants would do the same job of absorbing.)

Signed ~~~~~   Date 24.05.2013

DEAR MR JACKLEY,
I HAVE FOUND DESIPHERING YOUR COMPLAINT VERY DIFFICULT. THE ISSUES OF PUDDLES IN WALKWAYS ETC SHOULD BE BROUGHT TO THE ATTENTION OF YOUR WING STAFF IN THE FIRST INSTANCE OR TO THE RESIDENTIAL GOVERNOR IF REQUIRED.

YOUR SOLUTION TO THESE ISSUES APPEARS QUITE BEZARR, AS PUTTING SOIL/GRASS IN CORRIDORS OR WALKWAYS IS UNHEARD OF. AGAIN, I'M NOT QUITE SURE WHAT A MULTI-LAYERED CARPARK & CLUMPED OR CLAMPED CARS HAS TO DO WITH ANYTHING. (PERHAPS I HAVE MISSED YOUR POINT SOMEHOW).

Who art will save us from the puddles?

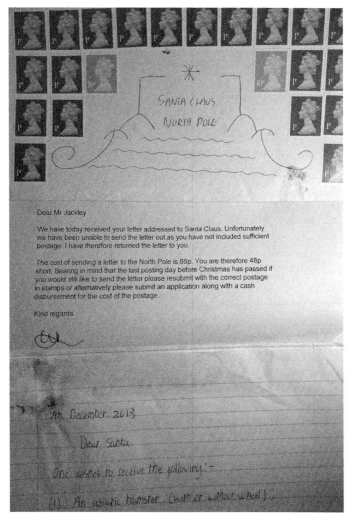

Dear Mr Jackley

We have today received your letter addressed to Santa Claus. Unfortunately we have been unable to send the letter out as you have not included sufficient postage. I have therefore returned the letter to you.

The cost of sending a letter to the North Pole is 88p. You are therefore 48p short. Bearing in mind that the last posting day before Christmas has passed if you would still like to send the letter please resubmit with the correct postage in stamps or alternatively please submit an application along with a cash disbursement for the cost of the postage.

Kind regards

The drawing on the envelope reads:
SANTA CLAUS
NORTH POLE

The handwritten letter reads:
4th December 2013

Dear Santa

One wishes to receive the following:–

(1) An asiatic hamster (with or without wheel),

A letter to Santa

Ministry of
JUSTICE

National Offender
Management Service

Eoin McLennan-Murray
Governor
HMP Coldingley
Bisley
WOKING
Surrey GU24 9EX
Tel: 01483 344300
Fax: 01483 344377
Email : Eoin.McLennan-Murray@hmps.gsi.gov.uk

Confidential
Mr Stephen Jackley A2159AG
E Wing
HMP Coldingley

29 October 2013

Dear Stephen

Thank you for your note of 20 October concerning information that you say Security have on you and have disclosed, and also the potential remand time you want to claim from your time in custody in the USA.

I will make my own enquiries with Security to see what it is you say they have done, and if any errors have occurred then I would seek to put them right.

In relation to the remand time, I have checked to see whether my authority extends to allowing you this remand time. However, regrettably it does not, and attached with this note are extracts from Prison Service Instruction 13/2013 Sentence Calculation – Determinate Sentenced Prisoners. I would draw your attention to Para 7.9.2 which makes it clear that it has to be the sentencing judge who presided over your UK offences who then decides whether the time you spent after sentence in the USA can count as remand time towards your current sentence.

I have not checked your warrants, but it would appear that the sentencing judge made no recommendation and your only course of action now is to either write to him personally or get your solicitor to raise the issue with him to see whether, retrospectively, he would allow your USA time to be counted towards your current sentence.

Appendix C of the attachment sets out what remand time can count towards a sentence and the last bullet point refers to your circumstances.

When we spoke about this matter I did say that if it was something I had discretion on then I would use it, but clearly I have no discretion in this matter and it is down to the sentencing judge.

Within the next week or so when I am on walkabout I will pick you up and we can have a further chat.

Yours sincerely

Eoin McLennan-Murray
Governor

A letter from Coldingley's governor regarding security file comments and failure to have time spent awaiting deportation back to UK in custody discounted from sentence

- *Section 149 ('the Public Sector Equality Duty')*: Public authorities like the Defendant have a positive obligation to promote equality of opportunity and eliminate forms of discrimination. This includes removing or minimising disadvantages suffered by people who have a protected characteristic and taking steps to meet the needs of people who share a protected characteristic that are different from the needs of persons who do not have a protected characteristic.

- *Section 119*: Outlines the remedies available to a court, whether of an equitable (injunctive) or common law (damages) nature.

The Case Law

36. Prevention of access to the law reports severely curtails the Claimants ability to review and cite relevant cases, but they are able to draw the court's attention to some authorities, as noted below.

37. The Claimant's are unaware of any challenges against the blanket application of the 'less than 4 year rule' of the current HDC policy. However, there are several cases under the old HDC policy that demonstrate how a decision should be properly undertaken.

38. In *R (PA) v Governor of Lewes Prison (2011) QBD (Admin)* the court considered the application of a prisoner ('PA') serving over 4 years who was refused HDC. The defendant accepted that PA passed the first two 'exceptional circumstances' criteria for HDC (as outlined at para 23 herein) but deemed that his social phobia did not constitute an infirmity.

39. The court held that the term 'infirm' was not a medical one but rather a description used by laymen to describe the consequences of a condition from which a person might suffer. On that basis, 'infirmity' was held to be a value judgment and accordingly the refusal of HDC for PA was within the defendant's lawful discretion.

40. Although the reason for refusal differs from the case of the Claimants (where indeed no adequate reasons or consideration has been given at all), this case shows how HDC decisions should be carefully undertaken. It also shows how the Defendant's policies should be intended to provide guidance in the exercise of administrative discretion.

10

A page from a trial bundle. Such bundles could often go into several hundred pages.

Part III: TWILIGHT ZONE

"Do you understand, sir, do you understand what it means when you have absolutely nowhere to turn?" Marmeladov's question came suddenly into his mind "for every man must have somewhere to turn..."

'Crime and Punishment', Dostoevsky

Chapter 17: The Verne

If tomorrow could be read like a map
What route to take, what road to travel?
Would the destination be better
Or the trip less real?
If tomorrow could be read like a map
Would we even start the journey at all?

On the 19th September, marking exactly 52 months in prison, I departed Lowdham Grange. After 4 hours on motorways, the van stopped off at HMP Gloucester. It was just as I remembered, right to the rusting window bars, smashed lights, and reek of excrement. I had to share a cell with a chain-smoker, although most of his smoke escaped through the broken window, which was occasionally patrolled by a manky, obese pigeon - somehow fitting through the bars.

I attempted to be positive and elicit conversation. "You feed the pigeons here?"

"Ya wart?" he grimaced.

I repeated the question.

"Wart ya sayin? Nart pig in 'ere."

Maybe it was my accent.

The next day, when the G4S van took a turning along the Portland coast, I caught a glimpse of the sea: an expense of green and blue, flecked with white waves. It was like seeing a close relative after years of estrangement, my heart leapt at the joy of being so close.

HMP The Verne jutted off from the Dorset coastline, on the isle of Portland – a former citadel built by Napoleonic Prisoners of War in the 19th Century. And now, after going through a tunnel, the van pulled into a gatehouse, bordered on each side by a white wall. I stepped out into fresh air – legs shaky with disuse and eyes squinting in the daylight– and walked into Reception.

Two other prisoners came with me from Gloucester. We were greeted by an orderly, who started talking about plenty of jobs, even opportunities to get 'Release on Temporary License' ('ROTL') to do work outside prison.

Before I could grasp what he was saying, a gruff voice called. "Mr Jackley!"

Two screws towered over me.

"I'm afraid we're going to have to take you to Segregation," one said.

The other prisoners and orderly just stared as the screws marched me away.

It was about my 'escape history' - all those reports about attempting to escape from US Marshals custody and planning to escape from court – yet, surely, they would have known all this before I came? I was simply told that "the matter will be investigated".

Like at my arrival in HMP Hewell, they took away my clothing in place of the first patchy blue and yellow 'escape risk' uniform I had known when starting the sentence. All the property I had at Lowdham Grange – from paperwork to my MP3 player – was bagged up and kept at Reception.

It was back to prison-issue writing paper and blue flexi-pens as I turned to writing for comfort. The cell was small, barren and cold, so I grabbed the yellow blanket on the bed and wrapped it around me. Within minutes a hostile voice framed the cell door window, demanding that I remove the blanket.

I sighed.

The prospect of being returned to Lowdham wasn't so bad, apart from enduring another long journey and 'restarting' there. But I could also be sent somewhere else, and if The Verne would not accept me, where would? With such 'escape' comments on file, how could I ever reach open prison?

Two days passed – ones where I put in a formal complaint and asked to see the Governor. I did not expect him to appear, but was proven wrong when the cell door opened after lunch.

"Mr Jackley?"

Before me stood a tall man, wearing a smart suit, who looked like a university graduate in his 20s.

"I'm Mr Lucas, the governing governor," he said. "You asked to see me."

I told him about the letter of acceptance, sent to HMP Lowdham Grange, that had been signed in his name.

"Yes, I can see why you are upset," he said pleasantly. "We need to be very careful with who we take on. You are not the only prisoner to arrive here and be sent back to their original establishment."

"But I have never escaped or attempted to escape. There's just allegations, all unproven. Okay, the US Marshals incident was something, but that was many years ago, in a different country, serving a different sentence. And if you are so careful about people who have allegations of trying to escape, why accept me in the first place?"

He looked at me in silence for a few seconds.

"I'm a reasonable person. If I let you stay, you have to promise that you will behave, not try to escape, and won't cause any problems."

I affirmed to him all these things.

"Very well. I will get you moved to the main prison by the end of the day."

We shook hands and he left. To say I was surprised by such an exchange would be an understatement: governors were usually aloof - if seen at all - and weren't known to be helpful.

Yet the young governor kept his word. Within two hours, they unlocked the gates of Segregation and brusquely told me to go to the Induction Wing.

Always before, I had been escorted from one location to another, but in The Verne prisoners were able to roam around by themselves. There were no gates between wings, and an even larger expanse of grounds could be accessed throughout the day. For the first time, the prison gardens really could be seen and enjoyed by inmates themselves.

When finding the wing, another surprise came. No bars on the windows! Even the doors were left permanently unlocked, although there was a privacy lock that could be engaged, and each wing had a main door that was locked at night.

The only downside was no in-cell sanitation - just a communal washing area, shared by around thirty others. The cells were also in corridors, with prisoners able to associate until midnight.

***

To feel grass beneath my feet and wind through trees – after over four years, these things rushed upon me with awe. I could have stopped at every flower and gazed upon its buds for an hour, or just lay on the ground watching clouds until the day ended. Even though the prison's full grounds were only open for a limited time, every minute was bliss.

However, I had to contend with others. The Verne held around 300 prisoners, all of them sauntering around in groups and pairs, with several eyeing me suspiciously. It was nothing new, but coupled with the piss smelling communal washroom – having spent years with a sink and toilet in my own cell (including a shower for the last two prisons) – I felt uncomfortable. Moreover, there was something that made me stand out, above that of having no acquaintances.

The Verne's acceptance criteria essentially consisted of three things: being 'C' category, having no escape history, and not being convicted of a sex offence. Most of the time, when sex offenders arrived, they were marched to Segregation upon arrival. Thus, when the orderly saw me being led away by guards, it had given rise to a suspicion that I might have been convicted of a sex offence. Not knowing anyone else at the prison, and being naturally quiet, did not help. Even when I explained what happened to some inmates, many found it hard to believe that someone put into Segregation for an 'escape history' could then just be let out again.

When I first heard the word 'nonce' being thrown in my direction, I assumed it was aimed at someone else. And when I heard it again, a few days later, I just ignored it. The correct course would have been to challenge whoever said it.

Yet I assumed people were reasonable, and, after realising their error, would apologise. Moreover, I remembered my sworn promise to Mr Lucas. It had been sealed by a handshake, and I'd be breaching my word if I got into a fight barely days later just for the sake of a few idiots words, which they would sooner or later realise were wrong anyway. Not only that, but any negative incidents could risk impeding the appeal, and *nothing* could be allowed to interfere with that.

Before leaving Lowdham, I'd made contact with a barrister through the 'direct representation' scheme, which foregoes the need for a solicitor. Her name was Flo Kraus, and she previously represented Ronnie Biggs – a famous train robber. The next step was to find a psychiatrist who could undertake an assessment ordered by the Court of Appeal. The first one that Flo thought of – Dr Simon Cohen-Baron – was rejected as being 'too expensive', even though he was a prominent expert.

Needless to say, such an issue wouldn't be an issue for my former peers on Millionaire's Row.

Some of them would surely be coming to The Verne, since it was the UK's only 'semi-open' Category C establishment. There were eight wings, all linked together by a single passageway.

Being located on a coastal promontory, at the top of a hill, strong winds blew through, which grew colder as winter encroached. Soon venturing outside entailed wrapping up in multiple layers and relying on the heavy prison-issue 'donkey jackets'.

The irony for long-term prisoners who are used to 'lock up' is that such time tends to pass faster than when given the choice of leaving one's cell. Because socialisation was hard, my options were limited. There was a gym, but it was far less accessible than at Lowdham Grange, as well as being much smaller.

Another thing about The Verne was the food. It may have been a result of cutbacks, but the portions were the smallest I had ever received - barely enough for the average adult. Within days of arriving, I longed for earlier meal times and tripled the quantities of canteen purchases. However, without a job, this would not be sustainable, and the average wage of £12 a week represented one third of what I had received at Lowdham.

A sizable number of prisoners were of different nationalities. Walking around, you could easily hear conversations in Spanish, French and a variety of other languages. These were the nicest, but generally did not mix with others outside of their circle. As for the screws, they could have come from HMP Parkhurst's Induction Wing. Gone were the days of being called by my first name, and one in particular took a disliking to me. His name was Officer Smallwood, part of the 'Security Team', and perhaps he felt over-ruled by the governor's decision. I had first encountered him in Segregation, when he wordlessly inspected the cell. He stood over six feet, with a bald head and fat black eyebrows. He was the sort of man who could have been in his early 30s or late 40s: no discernible lines marked his face, not even around his eyes.

On our second meeting, he called me into a small office and ordered me to sit.

An open envelope and card lay on the desk in front of him, which he pushed forwards.

I immediately recognised my mother's handwriting and my first thought was that she had written something 'bad'. She'd occasionally done this before, making allusions to escape as a kind of joke, but it had never been remarked upon before.

A pair of pliers lay next to the envelope. Smallwood had evidently used them to pick the card apart: a little bird she had drawn now sung headless, whilst a cat sitting on-top of a fence had been deprived of its tail. Like many of those she had sent before, it was hand-made and consisted of paper being glued to an old postcard.

"What's the problem?" I asked.

Smallwood scowled. "What do you think the problem is?"

If an alarm bell had not rung in my head before, it was now blaring. A sadist faced me – the kind I had first learned to deal with the hard way in America.

My tone went from annoyed to entirely neutral, almost robotic. "I've no idea what the problem is, officer."

The scowl remained. He sat in silence for a few seconds, eyes unwavering. "We don't allow glued cards or pictures here. Tell whoever sent this in to not do it again."

I couldn't resist commenting that such cards were allowed at all the other prisons, including supposedly higher security 'B' Category ones.

Smallwood's eyes bulged. "We have rules here for a reason, Jackley. This mail could have concealed drugs. And I don't care what other prisons do. You got a problem with that?"

I shook my head, observing him like a scientist might look upon a newly discovered species.

"Right, take your mail."

I picked up the mangled card, then walked to the door.

"Another thing," Smallwood said just as I turned the handle.

I paused, expecting him to interject some other reclamation, but instead he demanded that I sit down again.

"I've read your file from day one of your sentence," he said, once I was seated. "Any more issues, and you'll be dealing with me - personally."

***

Three horses sometimes appeared on the prison's upper field, part of a rehabilitation programme for qualifying inmates. The eyes of the noble animals spoke of something far different from the hostility and shallow mindedness usually projected around me. They used to group together in their paddock, making occasional whinnies in the cold air, as prisoners passed by in their own little groups.

The governor, Mr Lucas, also used to occasionally walk around with his black Labrador, pausing to speak with anyone he came across. One evening he called to me.

"How are you getting on?"

I wasn't quite sure how to answer, because the truth would have sounded ungrateful, so I just told him everything was fine.

"Good to hear," he replied.

The Labrador looked up at me, and I bent down to pat it.

Later a pair of prisoners mentioned how they would have liked to 'boot' the placid dog, with another adding something about using poison. I passed them quickly.

The novelty of increased freedom at The Verne wore off fast, although I thought that moving to a new wing might help. Every night a group used to drag a table outside my cell and sit there playing dominoes. It went on till midnight (the official time prisoners were meant to be in their cells – or 'rooms', as staff called them), with some taking great delight in slamming their dominos down at maximum force. Then followed the booming beats of a neighbour's stereo.

Until I could get ear plugs from healthcare, and with my MP3 player from Lowdham 'not allowed', I was averaging four hours sleep per night.

Fortunately, it didn't take more than a few days to move.

Initially it meant sharing a cell on the new wing ('A1'), as there was a waiting list for the singles, but my cellmate (#12) seemed quite decent. He was a man in his 20s, doing 6 years for drugs. Like me, he was also into fitness. *Unlike* me, he managed to get a job as a gym orderly – although quite how he managed that, despite being at the prison for a short while, I could only guess.

Around this time I managed to speak with the prison chaplain, Bill Cave. He reminded me of Father John – slight build, with a calm voice that could deliver powerful sermons. We talked about my appeal and he mentioned that he knew Flo Kraus.

"We had mutual interest over the same individuals," he noted. "She is one of the best."

Bill went on to offer sending an email to Flo's clerk to see if a video link could be set up to discuss the appeal, which I gladly accepted.

"I can also let you know about any Exeter-based psychiatrists," he said.

"That would be great," I told the chaplain.

A few days after meeting Bill, I was told to see my 'Offender Supervisor' at 9:00am.

The person before me looked in her late 30s, slightly overweight, with a large mass of curly brown hair. She started off the conversation with a barked order to "sit".

Her tone, rigid posture and hostile eyes took me aback. *Maybe she is Smallwood's sister*, I wondered.

She then said that there'd been a recent 'MAPPA meeting', which had not resulted in my 'risk' being reduced, despite all the courses I had attended and excellent custodial behaviour.

"You've done absolutely nothing to reduce your risk," she affirmed, when I made the mistake of arguing. "All you've done," she continued, "is hide away in private prisons under a flimsy diagnosis of Asperger's Syndrome."

She had polluted the MAPPA meeting with these unsubstantiated opinions, piling more negativity onto something that was already heavily weighted against me.

"Well, how should I reduce my risk then?"

"I'm looking into that," she said ominously. "It might mean doing proper offending behaviour programmes that address your issues."

Such 'programmes' were notorious, being held in different prisons across the country – usually bad ones. The typical format was a group of prisoners talking, similar to the Dovegate Therapeutic Community sessions.

Part of me felt like asking how she regarded repeat offenders on their 6th prison sentence. What would be her proposal to reduce *their* 'risk'? I suppose it didn't matter: under her definitions, 'risk' for such offenders was usually low anyway.

Lowering my 'risk to the public' was relevant because I was placed on 'high' and, under the 'MAPPA' structure, also put on the top tier of management. This would cause problems getting release on temporary license ('ROTL') to do work outside the prison and moving to Open Conditions, which I reminded her.

"Of course," she said. "You won't be going to Open Conditions or getting ROTL until you reduce your risk. But I would question your suitability for either, at any point in your sentence, even if your risk is reduced."

She sipped her cup slowly.

"Why?"

She slammed the cup down and glared. "I don't have to explain myself to you."

I left the office in deep worry. One's character, one's very identity, can be viewed from many perspectives. It could be shrouded by thick mist, the true details kept hidden – made ugly or beautiful according to the eyes of the beholder. And so easily could a prisoner become like a lost ruin in the Scottish wilderness, known only by the reports that are written. They become something else, constructed from words and half-formed perceptions - a citadel made monstrous by stereotypes, inaccuracy and general fallacy. The life before one's crime and the circumstances that led to it are sketched as a background so hazy that it hardly exists at all. Through these reports, a person's real identity and character become lost, even hijacked. A life becomes a story, and the authors can write whatever they want.

My own citadel rose up from the mists of prison life. First I was an 'escape risk', which had some initial truth in it, but the label stuck long after it ceased to apply. Then 'extremist' was stuck on, and this got grasped by all those who delighted in portraying darkness. Such fearful attributes were woven into a description of being dangerous and a 'high risk' to the public, until my real identity became completely smothered. Prison and probation officials used their evocative terms like bricks to build a new citadel of identity, following the stereotypical blueprint of 'the criminal'. What else could explain how someone could undertake a spree of robbing banks and bookmakers? How could someone sentenced to 13 years' imprisonment – with no former criminal background or part of a 'gang' - be otherwise regarded? Of course, anything other than 'dangerous', 'extremist' and 'violent' was beyond imagining.

That I might have made a terrible mistake, having no previous convictions and being hardly out of my teens at the time the offences occurred, didn't matter. Likewise, the prospect that I might have sought to do good was something the report writers never entertained. The only wholly accurate statement in my 'OASys' – of having a very low likelihood of reoffending – was determined exclusively by a mathematical algorithm that could not be manipulated. A robot would have presented a much fairer and truthful account than the humans who loved to squeeze me into their warped categorisations. But of course, once something bad was written, it provided the foundations for the next brick to be laid.

After meeting Benson, I almost ran to the chapel, desperate to speak with someone able to treat me like a human. Bill stood there, hovering over a row of candles, and I explained to him what happened.

"It sounds... not very nice," he said. "It might help if you speak with your solicitor about these things. Can you make a call on the wing?"

I shook my head. "They only just gave me my PIN code, so I wasn't able to transfer any credit onto it."

"In that case, I may be able to arrange a phone call from here. I'll need to get approval first, though. Wait here, I'll be back shortly."

He left the office, leaving me alone.

All around, there were shelves of books – ranging from religious items used for Sunday services to 'classics' you would find in a library.

Sitting there, in silence, my anxiety subsided. When Bill came back ten minutes later, I could breathe more freely.

"Well," he said, "the deputy governor has blocked me from making a phone call."

He commenced rigorously typing on a computer.

"I've just sent an email to Flo's clerk. I'm not sure when he will reply, but I've asked him to contact you. Is that okay?"

I nodded. "Thank you."

"It's fine. In the meantime, try to be calm. Being angry and upset will get you nowhere."

His intervention made a big difference. Telling a long-term prisoner they would never get ROTL or Open Conditions was akin to saying their sentence was being extended by several years. Such things were not only critical bridges to final release, but in many respects a lightening of what would otherwise be a much heavier sentence.

At least the new wing was more 'civilised' than the last. A few inmates even engaged me in friendly conversation, rather than barking questions at me suspiciously. During a hair cut, the 'wing barber', called Kramer Craft, told me he knew Russell Tate when I mentioned coming from Lowdham Grange.

"I tried to get there myself," he said, "but kept getting sent back to local prisons for court confiscation hearings."

"Yes, I've been moved around a lot too," I told him.

Kramer was also a 'Listener'. Even though I knew most took the position for its perks, the status made me a little more open with him. I asked what the job was like.

"Nothing special," he remarked. "This prison doesn't give you anything for being a Listener, unlike others."

It turned out he was serving a 13-year determinate sentence for his first offence (a drug conspiracy). This broad similarity, along with his generally friendly demeanour, saw us talk for longer than the time it took to cut my hair.

After mentioning my appeal and potential problems with probation, he spoke about "being involved with various legal proceedings" – going on to describe how he was suing the prison for a defective TV.

I laughed.

"You think I'm joking? No, I'll show you all the paperwork later."

Sure enough, Kramer was embroiled in a County Court case about being charged too much for a broken TV. I scanned through his paperwork with mixed humour and awe, which consisted of various formal complaints and their accompanying, typically antagonistic prison official answers, along with more complicated court forms that I had never seen before.

"You did all this yourself?" I asked, noting the use of complex words and well-constructed sentences. With his broad Essex accent replete with Cockney slang, he did not previously strike me as someone who could write so well.

"I've had a bit of help from a former solicitor. Kevin Steele – you know him?"

I shook my head. "Oh, I'll introduce you. Decent geezer. Looks like a nonce, but he's doing bird for a multi-million pound fraud case. Used to represent Lady Diana."

Never before had I contemplated that civil proceedings against the Prison Service could be realistically commenced without the backing of an expert solicitor, but Kramer had succeeded in getting actual court hearings – with one being due next week. I didn't think he could win, but inconveniencing officials must have been a kind of victory in itself.

Kramer shared the kind of rebellious spirit that saw me through the hell of American prisons and through many English ones. He could fight against the system, yet not by smashing windows or assaulting screws. Nor was his rebellion limited to court proceedings – it extended to the kind of mischievous games like Ricky did in Lowdham Grange.

Shortly before I arrived there had been a HM Inspectorate visit to The Verne. With another inmate, Kramer organised an alarm to go off on C wing – resulting in screws from across the prison running there. Then, when they piled onto that wing, Kramer would hit an alarm on A wing. Being spread so far apart, this resulted in screws constantly running between the wings. Many were overweight, so it must have made quite an interesting spectacle for the inspectors.

Officer Smallwood had also featured in Kramer's attack scope, in the form of multiple complaints – many containing various Latin phrases. It reached a point where Governor Lucas responded with his own lines of Latin.

"I don't understand why they haven't transferred you," I remarked.

"I've got a medical hold." This was connected to yet another court case. "But even if they did transfer me, I wouldn't care."

Having a companion put an end to the negativity and hostility I had formerly experienced. Moreover, Kramer – being similar in age – shared an interest in gym and running. The Verne, while lacking in accessible gym facilities, boasted ample opportunities for running. On weekends we ran around the field and wider grounds, and in the evenings, when not cutting hair, he joined me in running up and down the outside association area between the wings.

***

I had applied to work on the gardens department in every prison. Now - in the very one I was almost carted away for being an escape risk – I found myself standing on fresh Earth with a spade in one hand.

A frigid wind blew across my brow, as cold rain began to fall. In the few moments when sun shone, I relished the chance to touch plants and pick herbs at will, with birds singing around. Occasionally guards would stroll past me as they went to different parts of the prison, including Deborah Benson. Despite our previous meeting, I waved my hand and said hello; she acted like I wasn't there.

Days of cold mist and drizzle, interspersed with icy winds, filled subsequent weeks. There was nothing to do, apart from dig. And dig I did – to the point of drawing stares from the other workers.

To avoid 4 ½ days of increasingly bitter cold, I requested undertaking a 'Radio Production' course. Only a handful were doing it, all of whom were decent. We soon got stuck into making recordings and editing them using specialist software. The final task was to produce a small piece for the prison's radio station, linked into the 'National Prison Radio' recorded up in London.

My Offender Supervisor showed little interest in such endeavours. When I next met her she noted "you have so many negative entries that they practically ooze from your prison file."

How this had happened was a mystery, but such entries could be recorded without a prisoner's knowledge. Maybe I'd spoken a bit too rudely to some screws – like the male gym officer who refused me access one weekend, despite there being only three others using the facility. Or maybe she was just exaggerating. In either case, I wasn't that bothered. What mattered was moving into a single cell after six weeks of sharing a small double.

It was right at the end of the corridor, so quiet. The previous occupant got put on 'Basic' and therefore reassigned to my double cell. I felt awkward taking his cell, but he did not express any negativity about it. Indeed, he even asked if I would like him to clean it out – it was already pretty spotless, save for a copy of the Koran that lay on top of the highest shelf, which he offered to let me read. Even though I had read through a copy years ago in Orange County Jail (USA), it made a nice change from the usual legal textbooks I'd been ploughing through. One of these, Ashworth's Sentencing Guidelines, consolidated all the research undertaken at Lowdham Grange. And despite the wisdom of 'hoping for the best and expecting the worse', not a day passed when I did not think about the appeal. It was also a subject raised by my mother when she wrote, with references to preparing my bedroom and washing my clothes. In many ways she existed in her own world, but I couldn't bring myself to directly point out that, as much as I hoped it would not happen, there could be several more years in prison.

These subjects were best broached on a visit, with one booked for early February, because that was the only time my godparents could drive her to The Verne from Devon.

Before the visit with my mother, another one kept me on edge for days. A psychiatrist had finally been found cheap enough for the Legal Aid Commission: Dr Suleman. He came on 6th December. I met him in the main visits hall, among other inmates and staff: with his brown suit, briefcase and glasses, he easily stood apart.

After introducing himself, he began to ask a series of extremely sensitive questions – delving into my childhood and relationships. To talk about such things, in the presence of others sat at adjacent tables, was very difficult. But I tried nonetheless; the option of scheduling another visit to be done in private would have only incurred more delay. Speaking low, I tried to answer his questions to the best of my ability.

Then the visit was cut short barely an hour after he arrived. The doctor looked up, only halfway through his list of questions, and told the guard he needed more time. It was only 4pm.

"Maximum time for visits is an hour and a half," came the response.

I almost observed how they started the visits session late, by about twenty minutes, but knew it was pointless.

Afterwards, on mentioning what had happened to Kramer, he handed me a copy of the Prison Service Instruction covering legal and medical and legal visits. It said they were meant to take place privately, out of hearing of both staff and inmates. Also, there was not meant to be any cut off time for such visits. Now, because of their disregard of procedures, Dr Suleman would have to visit again to finish his report. Might that mean more problems getting funding?

That The Verne may have jeopardised or delayed my appeal made me furious, and I put in a formal complaint.

"Welcome to the complaints team, Stevie," Kramer said. "And why stop at one? You should write a letter to Lucas."

His TV case had been heard a few weeks earlier, and unsurprisingly he had lost. However, he recounted a conversation between the district judge and the prison's solicitor, who sought costs.

"Costs?" the old judge said. "But this is the small claims track. And Mr Craft is a serving prisoner. I'm not awarding costs!"

"But, your honour, this claim was completely unnecessary and a waste of the court's time."

"That's for me to decide. No costs for the Defendant. Case dismissed."

I thought Kramer would be happy with that outcome, but he was talking about appealing it. "No, they have got me proper wound up now. Smallwood had the nerve to threaten me again."

He related how Smallwood had come to his cell and removed some 'excess' property. In retaliation, Kramer had managed to flood the staff office downstairs.

"However did you do that?" I asked, incredulous.

"The showers on this landing were cordoned off for repair

last week – didn't you see? Well, I just climbed over with Harvey and we wedged the water knobs. The whole floor was flooded out by the end of the weekend, they never bothered checking, and it leaked through downstairs, right onto their poxy filing cabinets!"

I laughed, wishing it had been where Deborah Benson kept all her 'MAPPA' paperwork.

Harvey was based in a cell further down on Kramer's landing, but recently it had been blockaded and padlocked. I asked what happened.

"Got shipped out. Suspected of conspiring to import drugs from overseas."

"What? Doing that from his cell?"

Later, away from any ears. Kramer mentioned how a guy was storing around 15 'blowers' (mobile phones) in a table he had specially hollowed out. Kramer went on to explain how people were paid a weekly 'rent' for storing phones, although in most cases these were used to have private conversations with relatives.

"By the way, you hear about that new cunt prisons minister?"

I shook my head.

"Grayling. He's gonna cut Legal Aid."

There had been a fleeting period with Ken Clarke, but it now seemed one of the writer's in 'Inside Time' was right about the new one.. '*A Conservative attack dog who will use prisoners as toys to further his political ambitions,*' the article had said of Grayling. He was known for views that made his predecessor seem almost benevolent in comparison, but at this stage I couldn't see how much damage he could really do. Prisons were part of the civil service, which was separate from the political system, after all.

***

Things might have continued tolerably for me at The Verne were it not for the decision of a certain deputy governor to turn 'A1' wing into a 'resettlement unit'. It required all who were not on ROTL or prison orderlies to depart. The reason given was so that those on ROTL could be in a 'positive environment', away from 'any pressures they may get to bring items in'. That such prisoners were already quite privileged, and were checked each time they re-entered the prison for items, was irrelevant to the governor. She stood out with her short auburn hair and short skirts, with tights and a blouse that had a plunging neckline. When she came onto the wing, which 'coincidentally' had her office on the ground floor, it usually pre-empted a barked order at an inmate.

Despite her negative attitude, I attempted to reason with her – putting in an application, explaining how I had settled and how moving onto a new wing, with a diagnosis of Asperger's Syndrome, would incur immense stress. Her response simply re-stated the 'logic' she had used to make A1 wing into a 'resettlement unit'. Besides, she noted, I would still get a single cell.

The consequences of not leaving were outlined by a guard as "first, a warning; then, if you still refuse, an adjudication". So I packed my belongings yet again and prepared for another move. It did not have to come until after Christmas, at least.

The radio production I had done with three others got broadcast, which drew some compliments from the chaplain, Bill. We talked a little about religion, too, but he was more inclined to discuss the Russian writer Dostoevsky, recommending I read 'Crime and Punishment'.

"You are, in some ways, reminiscent of Raskalnikov."

I didn't understand what he meant until months later.

For Christmas Day, Kramer attempted making a 'cake' for himself and others on the wing. A few took a look at the gloopy, brown mess and made some excuse about eating too much earlier in the day.

I risked trying a slice, however, and it wasn't too bad.

Compared to the other Christmases spent in prison, The Verne's was the most sociable. A handful of prisoners exchanged gifts and pleasantries, reminding me a little of my time in New York. Even some of the 'dog screws' were a tad more human.

Yet, even when Dr Suleman visited again on the 27th

December, much sooner than I thought he would, a sense of foreboding grew. I couldn't know what he would write, only that a decision on my appeal could be made very shortly.

Of all wings they chose to relocate me to, it turned out to be 'C' – the first place I had been housed after segregation. Nobody else from A1 went there. At the same time, Kramer was transferred to another prison in order to attend yet another of his confiscation court hearings.

Now, once more, alone: no running partner; nobody to speak to on association, and very little to do. When not working on the gardens, I studied and trained. It didn't take long for a recommencement of the brainless 'nonce' taunts I had received when first arriving, including from an inmate on my landing who bore an uncanny resemblance to textbook pictures of Neanderthals.

It couldn't just be left to continue and draw in others. One evening, in the shadows between wings, I stepped up to him, demanding to know what his problem was.

He just strode on with two prisoners beside him, throwing a "fuck off" over his shoulder.

I had left it too late. The correct course would have been to challenge such people when the bullying first started. Instead, I'd retreated into a bubble on another wing, found security in the friendship with another, and concentrated on more important things like the appeal. Now, with nobody else in the prison to back me up, the bullies cemented ranks. Like all cowards, they only threw their verbal assaults when in a group.

Even though the Neanderthal was sometimes alone in his cell, important considerations held me back from retaliating: first and foremost, I worried about any consequences on my appeal. An incident of violence on my prison record would essentially make the unbroken record of good behaviour count for nothing. Secondly, I could not forget the promise to Mr Lucas, 'not to cause trouble'. Thirdly, despite what others liked to write about me, I was not a violent person. Settling the matter by civilised discussion would have been the most preferred way.

I cast aside the option of telling staff, refusing to become a 'grass'. Such a standard was perhaps naïve, but I maintained it. I did not even mention the behaviour to the chaplain.

Perhaps the resulting despondency was solely down to the bullying and negative conditions, or it might have just been the mounting uncertainty over my appeal. One thing was sure: remaining at The Verne would result in zero progress. I would not be getting ROTL or Open Conditions with Deborah Benson as my Offender Supervisor.

Nor did I get much sleep: every night someone shouted, as well as my neighbour's assortment of bangs and scrapes. Ear plugs had minimum effect at dampening this racket. Some inmates were able to sleep most of the day, perhaps from having 'wing jobs', resulting in them being up all night – a problem that wasn't present on the previous wing.

On 3rd February I got sick of it and put in a strongly worded application requesting relocation. The response was from the auburn haired resettlement governor herself:-

'You will not be moving.'

Nothing else was written.

It caused enough frustration to draw me to the wing office, where I hoped to catch at least one decent screw on duty.

But their blank, smirking faces summarised how far I would get.

I went back to my landing and almost tripped over the Neanderthal hanging outside his cell, who had deliberately put his foot out.

I stared at him, on the verge of confrontation. It would have been so easy... yet, again, I held myself back.

In the cell I listened to the vibrating bass of an inmate's stereo, strong enough to cause the letters on my desk to bounce – none of which gave positive news.

An intense feeling of entrapment overcame me. There didn't seem to be anything for me at The Verne; only set-backs, hostility from officers, and now the insidious element of bullying – which could only get worse before it got better.

I grabbed a pen and paper, then wrote something that represented a sure-fire Way Out.

Five minutes later, I slammed the note down on the screw's desk and stormed back to the cell.

It didn't take long to bag all my belongings.

Screws could move fast when they wanted to, and on this occasion I was presented with the pleasure of Smallwood's face.

Chapter 18: Starred Up

*'It is easier to destroy the Light within than
defeat the darkness that surrounds.'*

From the film, 'Nightwatch'

It took just one day to leave HMP The Verne and be moved to nearby HMP Dorchester. The note I had penned may have been hasty, but it was tragically simple in its effectiveness. It had simply said, due to being under various pressures, that I presented an escape risk. Any mention of the 'e word' was enough to galvanise the sludgy prison mechanisms into swift action, not least for someone with my record.

If I had not left The Verne through a simple note, it would have been through a fight or some other act that would have jeopardised the appeal and directly contravened my promise to Mr Lucas.

So it was another change, as certain as a waning candle brought deeper darkness. Back to the conditions I started with - in yellow and blue 'E-man' clothing. The new prison was another Victorian-era Category 'B' local establishment, located close to the centre of Dorchester. Like similar 'holding' prisons, the inmates were predominantly in their 20s and doing shorter sentences. They walked around the concrete exercise yard in the usual anti-clockwise direction, their pasty faces prematurely wasted by drugs. As an e-man, it meant having to be escorted everywhere, with officers eyeing my every action. I exercised nonetheless, if only to catch some fresh air. Anyone walking into that prison for the first time would have smelt the miasma of sweat, piss, decay and fear. But, after a few days, I forgot it even existed.

For sixteen months I had been given a respite in Lowdham Grange, followed by a tentative taste of freedom in The Verne. Now I faced the dungeon-like conditions I thought had been left behind. To be given the chance to wander freely outside, with unlocked doors and unbarred windows, only to be sent to a place like Dorchester...

Which was better: to endure in a better environment with hostile characters, or to suffer in a bad environment with neutral ones? Despite the stress and sleeplessness, there might have been another way out of The Verne's situation. If I had waited a bit longer, maybe speaking to Bill Cave, or health care...

Could haves, would haves, should haves. Again they taunted me, and again I pushed them away.

With little to do but write, my single pad of lined A4 paper quickly ran out, so I saved the last few sheets for 'emergency use' and using the back of application forms to maintain a semblance of a diary. Every prison wing had a rack of such forms nailed to a wall – along with complaints forms, next to a yellow 'complaints' box, and an assortment of other forms for each element of the prison bureaucracy.

On the 4th day an officer called Mr Boley appeared, from the 'OCA' (Offender Categorisation and Allocation department) and confirmed that a transfer back to Lowdham Grange was possible - provided I was 'B' Category, off the 'e list', and well behaved.

However, as things stood, I did not even know what Category I was. As for being 'Enhanced' IEP level, this had apparently been taken away when I left The Verne. How they could justify that, simply by me writing a note saying I could present an escape risk, was baffling. I told Mr Boley as much.

He just shrugged. "And what's this thing about wanting to see the IMB?"

He meant the Independent Monitoring Board, who I had applied to see.

"I've come from a semi-open C category prison where I worked on the gardens. I could have escaped there if I wanted to. Instead I forewarned them that it may be best for me to go to closed conditions to prevent that. But to be made an e-man *after* coming to closed conditions.... It's crazy."

"I'd say a prisoner writing a note saying they are an escape risk could be described the same. Anyway, I'll do what I can to get you sent back to Lowdham Grange."

Later, remembering Bill Cave's recommendation at The Verne, I obtained a copy of *Crime and Punishment* from the library.

I was instantly hooked. The book described a well-intentioned university student called Raskalnikov who took the road of crime, envisioning doing great deeds. Now I understood why Bill had drawn his comparison.

Raskalnikov killed in the name of a theory, a dream, whose actions were born out of good intentions.

I robbed for the same.

If the ends meant the preservation of Earth and continuance of humanity then surely any deed was justified? Would The Law prefer that the entire world perish for the sake of making the lives of a handful comfortable?

It seemed, the greater the goal, the more things could be justified in reaching it. If the desire to reach that goal was honest and committed, who could draw a line in the sand and stubbornly declaim: '*Go No Further*'?

***

They removed me from the E-List after a week. It marked a return to the usual routine that I knew from HMP Gloucester. Here, the 19th Century wings towered up 5 tiers, no doubt creating a landmark for Dorchester's skyline. I never heard any Cathedral bells, however, and the chapel inside the prison was even bleaker than Gloucester's. The only colour was a stained glass cross, covered with bars, and a small plastic plant on the corner of the altar. On Sunday, a single row sat at the front half-heartedly singing hymns, with a sprinkling of groups chatting amongst themselves at the back.

Within less than a year the whole prison population would actually be leaving, because the place would be shut. An 'urban explorer' wrote afterwards:-

'The tiny cells are a real eye-opener. And description of grim is all too true. Damp & blackspot litter the cold, stone block walls, the only heating source is a pipe running down one side of the cell. The metal framed bunk-beds have an air of torture about their features, and in the corner, a stainless steel toilet with nothing but a curtain to divide you from your cellmate. A brief, comical moment of panic sets in as we shut the cell door behind us only to find the all the handles removed, an all too real-to-life experience! The whole wing feels very claustrophobic, with cages all around you and just enough room for one person on the walkways.'[9]

This captures only a portion of what Dorchester was actually like. Throw 300 men into the mix, all kept against their will, with multiple psychological issues, and you start getting closer to the truth. On reflection, I thought it much better than Gloucester and Garth. But, compared to Lowdham Grange and the semi-open environment of The Verne, it seemed like going back 100 years.

Aside from returning to the usual survival mix of in-cell exercises, I flew through the thickness of Dostoevsky's 'Crime and Punishment'. Fate must have been weaving a thread of heightened irony, for a passage of synchronicity passed: *'We sometimes encounter people, even perfect strangers, who begin to interest us at first*

---

9   https://www.theurbanexplorer.co.uk/dorchester-prison-dorset/

sight, somehow suddenly, all at once, before a word has been spoken.'

The door then clankily unlocked, revealing a tall screw who held a bag of clothing. "Jackley, you're getting company," he announced.

"Someone decent, hopefully," I said half to myself, sighing.

"He's come straight from the YO estate," the screw chuffed. "Maybe he'll calm down with a long termer like you."

With that comment, someone appeared at the entrance: scrawny, with short blonde hair. He looked 16.

The kid stared back at me, then grabbed the bag held by the screw and threw it into a corner of the cell.

"Oi!" the screw cried.

"Fuck off!"

"You've just earned yourself another negative entry," the screw grinned, slamming the door.

My new cellmate (#13) just screamed a curse at the cold metal.

I put a hand to my brow and closed my eyes - so much for 'encounters with interesting people'! I looked at the kid again, who was pulling out some grey tracksuit bottoms from the plastic bag.

He threw back a glance.

"What ya looking at?"

I almost laughed. He had a bit of sinewy muscle, but was about as threatening as a riled-up gnome.

"Where did you come from?" I asked.

He said a line of curses – I couldn't tell if they were directed at me, the screw, or something else.

"Feltham," he finally said. "You?"

"The Verne."

"Yeah? What you in for then?"

His tone was starting to annoy. I removed my glasses and put them on top of Dostoevsky. "Armed robbery. You?"

He paused, looking me up and down. "What you rob?"

"Banks and bookmakers."

Again a pause. "How long you get?"

"13 years."

"Sheeeet," he drawled. "Yeah, well I'm in for a knife offence. Some mug cunt made the mistake of crossing me and my mates. Got 2 ½ years for it, but doing another year cos' of some fucked up shit in the other prison."

He threw the clothes onto the bottom bunk. "Wait, you're not using this, right?"

I shook my head, removing a towel I had put there so he could fit some sheets to it.

"This prison's shit," he said. "Been here long?"

"About a week. Just got taken off the e-list."

He blinked, appearing not to know what that word meant, but refraining from asking.

"How old are you?"

He glowered at me with renewed hostility. "What's it to you?"

"Just curious," I said.

To my astonishment, he launched a wild kick at the metal toilet and sink unit, hard enough to leave a dent. "You better not be a fucking nonce," he hissed. "Last one I came across got cut up so bad he ended up in hospital."

My fists tensed. Then I looked at him again. Something thawed in me – a feeling of pity, at seeing his youth. Would I be any different, in his shoes...?

It so happened, amongst my legal paperwork I had been going through, that there was a newspaper cutting talking about my last appeal hearing. I wearily took this out and handed it over. "Not that I have to explain myself to you, but that might set your mind at ease."

He took the paper, but handed it back seconds later. Whether he couldn't read, was just satisfied with the first few lines, or simply reassured by my demeanour, I was unsure.

"Sorry, man."

He sat down on the bed.

Apologies were rare in prison, even when they were warranted.

"I'm 19," he said quietly.

We didn't talk for a while after that. I went back to Dostoevsky, and he went back to – well, nothing. He just lay on the bottom bunk, eyes shut.

***

Raskalnikov's theory was easily transferable to prisoners. The main justifications for crime rested in Comparison, Denial, Circumstance and Altruism. For Comparison, some people argued that there were others doing similar or worse offences, but not being punished for it; the actions of the rich and powerful, even of entire governments, sometimes went on to cause immense harm, yet they would never face the hammer of a judge. For Denial, it was a simple case of saying that they had not done anything wrong in the first place. Circumstance was more common, where an offence was attributed to have arisen from poverty, social exclusion, abuse and similar things. Altruism was the rarest – the one I found affinity with – where someone justifies an offence by saying it leads to long-term benefits; that any negatives in the crime are outweighed by the positives that would result from it.

In reality, many prisoners' justifications contained a little of each. The most common references were not being guilty in the first place, or being punished for something that was really quite minor and even inevitable. Few, however, acted as individual,s but as part of as a group – perhaps fitting the definition of a 'criminal subculture'.

Perhaps my new cellmate was within this latter category. After lock-up, he told me his name was Jay and that he'd actually been sentenced as part of a gang, two of whom had 'knifed' someone. He denied being involved in the actual stabbing, saying that his mere presence at the time was enough to get him sentenced. Whether true or not, I knew that such things happened under the law of 'conspiracy'.

I was curious how he ended up in a gang, and his response reminded me of others.

"I've been in and out of care homes my entire life, man. Didn't really have much of a family, just my mum and brothers. My mates took their place; I would have died for them. Still would. We did some crazy shit, and that night we just went on a bender and some crank guy came along. I can't even remember why my two mates stabbed him – we were so fucking drunk."

"So you weren't sentenced before this offence?"

"Nah, not to prison," he replied. "Just had a few cautions for vandalism and disorderly behaviour, or whatever they call it. I once set fire to a police car, too, but I was only around 11 then."

"Why'd you do that?"

"Fucking hate the pigs man. Police, screws, anyone in authority. Its 'cos of what happened... you know, when I was a kid."

I didn't ask him to elaborate.

"What about you? I've never met a bank robber before. No offence or anything, but I wouldn't peg you for one."

I laughed. "So what would you 'peg' me for?"

"I dunno... fraud, I guess, or drugs. You look kinda smart, with the glasses and all."

"Not smart enough to avoid getting caught," I corrected him.

How to explain to him my real route into crime? Instead I just settled on the easy 'getting involved in drugs' and 'needing money' story.

He asked the usual questions - what drugs I took, which prisons I had been in; then it reached the point where I didn't want to lie about being in America. Maybe I should have, for the resulting barrage of queries. Half-robotically, I answered them – watching the sparkle in his eyes as I described the journey through America's finest.

"It's like a fucking movie, man," he quipped.

I yawned.

"You know... that newspaper thing you showed me, I never got taught to read so well. I could tell you weren't a nonce without reading it all. Fucking stupid thing for me to say, I know, but that's me!"

"Hmm. There's one thing I don't get. You're 19 – so should be in a young offender's institute. Right? I don't actually know the age limit, but I think you're the youngest prisoner I've met."

"Nah, you're right. You normally gotta be 21 to get to prisons like this. I just got Starred Up."

"You were started up, like... set up?"

"No, no... *Starred Up*! It's where people under 21 get sent from YOs to adult prisons, innit."

"Oh," I said. "Because you misbehave or something?"

"Exactly," he replied. "Although in my case, I did more than misbehave. I punched a fucking governor's face in."

He went on to say that the governor in question was a "queer" who was "making nonce moves".

"After they put me in Seg, I smashed the cell up, did dirty protests, anything to get out of that shit hole. Then I came here."

Such was my ignorance that I asked him to clarify what a dirty protest was, although I'd heard the term before from as long ago as Parkhurst. His subsequent description was sufficient to eradicate any former hunger I had been feeling after the paltry prison dinner.[10]

"I can't imagine doing that myself," I observed.

"Yeah? Well you need to spend a few months in Feltham then. There were other guys cutting themselves up just to try and get out of there. The week before they moved me, someone hung themselves."

Dirty protests, self-harm, suicide... such was the under-fabric of the fifth largest economy's criminal justice system. And the new Justice Secretary, Chris Grayling, would swiftly oversee a period in which these things doubled by the month.

Jay went quiet again, so I returned to reading Dostoevsky. Once more, I plunged into the world of my alter-ego protagonist.

---

10   A dirty protest was where a prisoner spread their own faeces around whilst being in cellular confinement, to resist attempts at restraint or just to express extreme discontent.

Raskalnikov saw that some of the most powerful and influential actors in human history have broken the law, even going on to determine what is illegal and legal themselves. Power, to all intents and purposes, was the greatest legitimising force on Earth. But in striving to achieve it, with the aim of doing good, he lost sight of the consequences and immediate impacts of his actions.

***

Something made me wake up in the middle of the night. It was not unusual for me – ever since the nightly cell moves at Southern State Correctional Facility in America. But this time it was different, for I heard a continuing muffled noise, almost like a mewing. For a moment I thought a cat sat outside the window - then I realised the sound came from directly below.

There was silence for a bit, then a sniff. It took me a few moments to realise that my cellmate had been crying.

I opened my mouth to speak, but no words came out. Best that he thought I didn't hear. To show weakness as a young man was bad enough; to do it in prison was even worse. And part of me felt angry. Not at his sadness, not at the fake bravado he had displayed earlier, but at the system.

Just 19 years old, with no previous prison sentence, he'd been sent to an adult prison of hardened criminals after 'punching a governor' in his previous establishment. Two years after leaving school, society had branded him unworthy to be amongst its ranks, instead throwing him into a system that would do the very opposite of making him a better man.

I would have liked to grab the judge that sentenced him and thrust the robed figure into one of these cells, to spend some time sampling the fare that he so enthusiastically dished out.

They'd never know, of course, these figures of authority who served an elite. From their upbringings to their ascent to the Bench and quiet weekends at their country homes, they could not even comprehend the roads walked by the likes of Jay. From care home to prison; from one kind of abuse and oppression to another.

I lay there, silently, as the dull glow of dawn approached and the chinking metal of patrolling screws began. Within the hour, cell doors were unlocked for 'exercise', giving me a chance for 30 minutes of fresh air. Jay came out too, but he sidled over to a pair of youngsters on the yard. I left him to it – finding a good spot in the early sun to do a few push-ups. Next to the exercise yard, behind a metal fence, was a small grassy area with strange rectangular stones – the gravestones of hanged inmates from long ago. Time was called, but I hovered about waiting for other prisoners to file onto the wing so I could get a few more precious minutes of fresh air. Jay did the same with someone else.

"You done time in America?" Jay's companion asked.

Here we go again...

That afternoon I was called to see the IMB – an elderly man and woman, whose after-shave and perfume could be smelt even before they entered the wing. They wanted to follow up on the form I had posted in their box (another special addition to each wing) about the E-list issue, but as this was now resolved, I instead spoke about my uncertainties around categorisation and IEP level.

"Ve vill look into zese tings," the man said. Whether he was of German decent, or just spoke with this accent, I didn't ask.

"But you realise," the woman added sternly, "that we cannot do much about them?"

I nodded. They could do nothing, but sometimes their mere enquiries were enough to speed up certain processes or, at least, get some answers.

When I got back to the cell, it was association time, and Jay had vanished. I assumed he'd gone off to socialise, which encouraged me to do a little of the same, playing two games of pool with an education orderly who told me he was "desperate for burn". I was desperate for something else - a paper and a pen – so I traded a half-ounce of GV for four A4 writing pads and two decent biros. These items could be obtained 'freely' through certain means (i.e. stolen from education) but I judged it a fair trade. An alarm went off when we exchanged the items in his cell, causing us to briefly look up at the sound of running boots on the metal walkways, but I was more concerned with getting my newly acquired treasure 'stashed' next to Dostoevsky.

A screw came to the door. "My cellmate still hasn't come back," I told him.

"Oh yeah? He doesn't have long then."

The screw passed to the next cell and went down to the end of the landing, then circled back. I scanned the wing, squinting up the five tiers, but could not see Jay.

"Can't wait any longer," the screw said, locking the door.

An hour passed. I looked over to Jay's bed and the bag he had put under his mattress, which had a few letters at the bottom. Near his pillow, something had been carved into the wall:-

Let It End.

Was that there before? I didn't think so.

Normally, I would have delighted in having a cell to myself, but Jay's absence made me worry. I hardly knew him, yet hoped he was okay. It took until morning to find out. Two screws came into the cell and grabbed his bag, noting that he had been "taken to Seg."

"What for?" I asked.

One of the screws – a fat man with a greased-down black hair – just said "none of your business."

But when he left, the other screw said it had arisen due to "assaulting a member of staff."

"How did that happen?"

The slammed door answered.

My eyes turned to '*Crime and Punishment*'. It was no use. I looked back at the empty bed.

Would he get sucked up by the system, to get more years subtracted from his life for bad behaviour in custody? Where would it end for him – release, only to be reconvicted again, because no other plausible route was available for 'such people'?

Of course, that was the 'default outcome'. The system and its tabloid lackeys would see Jay as nothing more than a number, another statistic; a hard example of heartless, stupid, irredeemable offenders who deserved nothing more than a jail cell. That was the one-dimensional lens that many 'law abiding citizens' had been duped into believing, even as their taxes subsidised the system's continuance on the backs of people like Jay.

But his own words, scrawled onto the wall beside his prison bed, spoke of something entirely different.

Let It End.

The person I had shared a cell with was not a heartless, irredeemable offender. He was a human being who'd taken the wrong path, being conditioned to fight against any authority figure he encountered, with a mentality only cemented by what he experienced inside.

He just wanted it to end.

Chapter 19: Dungeon Darkness

"Steal small and they throw you in jail; steal big and they make you king," Bob Dylan aptly said.

The clever criminals don't get caught. Only the stupid ones, or those hindered by greed, manage that – with very few exceptions. The con, the hustle, the game... it is what society unknowingly moves to. Those in the upper stratas are apt players, or rather those who hide in the shadows, cloaked in layers of wealth, power and influence. These hidden criminals will never see the inside of a prison. They will never face punishment or condemnation as handed out by a court of law. They are untouchables of an era orientated around capital – that dictator and director of human existence.

I received Dr Suleman's report after completing Crime and Punishment. Its dry passages skimmed over many things, yet it concluded that my crimes had indeed been motivated by the desire to do good: in his words, 'to save the Earth and its resources'. That was the truth. They had not been born out of malice or to enact harm upon individuals, yet I'd been sentenced under that presumption. It was now for the Court of Appeal to decide, but I felt confident they could not ignore the evidence.

Being alone, I could read, write, study and exercise without worrying about what someone else was doing. It was the mode of survival I learnt in America and which had been reinforced by most of my time in English prisons too. But places like Dorchester were short of space, with cells designated for single use now being used as doubles.

Sure enough, on 24th February, someone new came – the 14th cellmate of my sentence. He was an old man, well into his 60s - and he stood constantly within two feet of the TV screen, even when eating. Attempts at conversation were difficult – he was either deaf or pretending to be – but eventually I found out he was doing time for "breaking a restraint order". In other words, just a few months.

Then there was his farting. It was near-continuous and soon smothered the cell.

I coughed loudly. "Can't you aim your ass at the crack in the door when you feel the need to let loose gas?"

He grunted, kind enough to oblige. However, he still had to lie down at night, happily farting away. Then, about half an hour before morning unlock, he grabbed a roll and started layering the toilet seat with paper.

"You know they are going to unlock very shortly, right?" I told him.

In 'prison etiquette', you took a dump when your cell mate was outside, save for 'emergencies'. But this old man just proceeded to release his bowels right then.

As soon as the door opened, I headed for the nearest screw.

"I can't share a cell with this guy," I told him.

"Why not?"

"All night he farted, and he did a shit just minutes before unlock." The screw's chubby face burst into laughter.

"Well, we haven't got any free cells on this wing," he said, composing himself. "You'll just have to *lump it* and put in an app."

I watched the screw waddle off and proceeded to approach two others. Both gave varying mixtures of the same response.

Not until evening association, after enduring another eight hours of the old fart's presence, did I finally manage to find a sympathetic screw. Short and slim, in his 50s, with a military bearing, the name on his uniform read 'SO McAllistor'.

"I'm doing 13 years, this guy is getting out in a few months, and he is literally gassing the cell with his guts. Why am I getting cell mates like this?"

He took me aside.

"We don't have any single cells at the moment."

His accent was Scottish, which gave me hope. For some reason, all Scottish guards I had encountered were more friendly and helpful than their English counterparts.

"Is there nobody else I could share with?"

This was a bit of a gamble – it could result in having someone potentially even worse than the old man.

"There's no spaces on this wing," McAllistor said.

I sighed. "Best I go to the block[11] then."

"Why'd you want to do a daft thing like that? How long you been in – 4 years? In America too? You should know better by now. I'll tell ye what I'll do, it may be there is a space on another wing. If there is, I'll do my best to get you out of that cell. Okay? But it might not be immediate."

I thanked him.

"I'll also look into your transfer. I think Mr Bowley is sorting it?"

"Yes."

"I'll see what's possible," he finished.

When lock-up came, I bit my teeth, preparing for another night of farts and early morning shits, but McAllistor appeared and said a space was available. I swiftly packed and followed him through a series of gates to another wing, laid out exactly the same. He led me to a cell on the top landing and unlocked the door.

"Now I hope you can settle down for a bit until your transfer."

I thanked him again and heard the door lock.

---

11   Segregation

The cell was smaller than the previous, clearly intended for one person but part of the prison's notorious 'doubling up' procedure as a result of overcrowding. Even so, I was relieved not to find another old man. Instead my new cellmate (#15) looked in his late 20s, doing a 4-year sentence for burglary. Initially he seemed fine – at least, until he started snoring loudly. It was better than the smelly farts I had endured, yet Fate had not quite finished with her cruelty. Every single night, starting from around 3am, my cellmate tossed and turned forcefully, before switching on the TV.

Zapping of mind and body were the days that followed, each hour only adding to my baseline of frustration. On the 4th March, I was awoken, yet again, at the witching hour. The fragile bed made even slight movement cause a veritable earthquake in the whole frame. By choosing to sleep most of the day, it meant that at night my cellmate became fully active. Any attempt to make clear he had awoken me resulted in not even the smallest gesture – no apology, or even turning the TV volume down.

The next day, I spoke to SO McAllistor.

"You're booked on a bus to Portland," he told me. "It's leaving Thursday."

That was only four days away. Still, with barely any sleep, I found it hard to maintain energy to dilute the time with things that kept me strong: exercise, reading and writing. Indeed, I became forcibly synchronised with my cellmate's sleeping patterns – although he no longer maintained even the barest veneer of civility. Neither of us spoke to one another. When I attempted to break the torpid atmosphere, he either ignored me or gave one-syllable responses.

Try to picture, for just a moment, being in a 6 by 9 foot space, designed for one person, for 23 hours a day. Then imagine that other person with you refuses to speak and emanates complete disdain. One circumstance could be suffered; the other was akin to counting down the minutes like a ticking bomb moving inexorably closer to exploding.

As for the TV – he had sole control of it, flicking from channel to channel, before briefly pausing on some mindless celebrity fudge.

***

Thursday came - the day of my long awaited transfer. I was ready long before the door got unlocked.

The first screw had a vacant face with heavy bags under his eyes. I asked him when the Portland bus would be arriving.

"The what? Oh, the bus. Right. 'Lemme check'."

He went downstairs to the wing office, leaving me waiting around as other prisoners started streaming from their cells. When he appeared again, he started to plod off in another direction.

"Guv!" I cried.

"Oh, yes. Your transfer... yes. I've checked, and there's no transfer booked for you to go to Portland."

"There must be a mistake. Can you check again?"

"Well, hmm..."

"Please, it's really important."

"All right. Wait here."

More time passed, with inmates shouting, joking and laughing. But, gradually, a silence came over the wing.

Something built in the air; the kind of pressure that usually occurs before a fight. This time, however, the source was from me. My fists bunched, pulse racing, as sweat beaded my forehead.

I stormed up to the screw's office door and rapped loudly.

Another screw's face peered out. "What do you want?"

"I was just speaking to another officer, I think he's in there."

"He's on the phone."

"Oh... I'll just wait here then."

The screw nodded curtly, then slammed the door.

I stepped backwards – directly into the path of another inmate, who almost fell over.

"What the fu -"

One glimpse of my eyes cut him short.

"Mr Jackley?"

It was the first screw.

"I've just spoken to OCA. You are not going to Portland today, or tomorrow, because they don't accept prisoners serving over 10 years."

"But..."

He started to walk away.

A firm expectation had been broken, which in itself would have thrown me into a state of deep anxiety. On top of that, I now faced the prospect of more time in a cell where I'd spent the last three days counting down the hours to leave.

"Wait!" I called after the screw.

He just kept walking.

With the nights of sleepless stress tumbling every thought into chaos, only one option presented itself. I went back to the cell, with my nemesis on the bottom bunk giving his usual hateful glare, and chucked the few belongings I had taken out into the big plastic prison bags. I then dragged them down to the first floor landing.

"Going somewhere, Jackley?" another screw commented.

"Yeah. Segregation."

"Oh yes? What for?"

I ignored his sneering tone and just stood in front of the wing office. Lock-up was announced and prisoners filed back to their cells, with a few casting glances back at me.

"Jackley, get back to your cell!"

The screw continued circling round with the others, locking up doors. Then I caught a glimpse of someone walking across the centre-point that joined all wings: SO McAllistor.

"What's going on?"

"They cancelled the transfer. Portland only accepts prisoners serving under 10 years. I can't spend more time in that cell. It's better I go to Seg."

"I see," McAllistor said.

He unlocked the metal gate.

"What are you playing at?" he said in a low voice. "We've already talked about this. Portland was a mistake, but you will get transferred soon, to somewhere else – I'll see to that."

But no reassurances would see me going back to that cell.

"Okay. It's best I go to Segregation though, in the meantime."

McAllistor just shook his head. By now the other screws were marching in our direction.

"Jackley's refusing to lock up," the sneering one said.

"No, I just can't share a cell."

"And why's that?" another asked.

"If I do, my cell mate would get harmed."

"Ach, alright, alright," McAllistor interjected. "I'll sort this out."

I did not intend to harm my cellmate, yet they had a legal duty of care. When such threats of harm were issued, the only option was to relocate.

McAllistor unlocked the office door and called to the other screws to enter. "Jackley, stay there."

They chatted for a few minutes – the words barely audible.

When the door reopened, two of the scews marched off without saying a word. The other two, with McAllistor, just stared at me.

"You're going to a single cell on B wing," McAllistor said.

In other circumstances, I might have stepped forward and hugged the Scotsman. Instead all I could do was thank him, yet again, as the two other screws escorted me from the wing. Glancing back, his face was stern and yet without hostility - the same look I had glimpsed in SO Coleman's face at HMP Hewell, when she saved me from going to Segregation.

Down a flight of stairs and through another set of doors, I arrived on 'B1' wing. Into a cell – dirty, reeking of its previous occupant - yet it could have been a corner of paradise.

An hour later, I asked for some cleaning utensils.

"Sure, but you'll have to wait until tomorrow," came the response.

This didn't make any sense: evening association had not yet occurred.

The screw explained I'd been put on 'Basic' at the request of 'the governor', as well as receiving an adjudication (formal prison disciplinary charge).

The dark, dirty cell gave me solitude, but in gaining it I had lost my good prison record. Not only had I been put on 'Basic' – the lowest IEP status, which meant more lock-up, less visiting privileges, and a host of other curtailments – but I now faced my first ever adjudication. Under written prison procedures, it was not possible for a prisoner to be given a demotion in IEP status *and* a formal disciplinary charge for the same thing. Regardless, it had happened to me.

Then I realised that the simple refusal to share a cell – itself already meant for one person – might result in spending more *years* behind bars. Part of the appeal, albeit minor, rested on good custodial behaviour.

I stood there and slid against one of the walls.

Like a starving creature digging through a hole to reach food, I plunged into my bag for paper and pen. Angry words poured forth:-

With my last breath I vow to bring this corrupt, sadistic, evil factory of animosity to its knees. Hatred, real unadulterated loathing, boils in my veins against 'the system' – all those gutless parasites in black uniforms and suits whose only input into my life has been pain. Crushed and subjugated in disproportion to my mistakes, mentally crucified and abandoned in a wasteland of corrupted men, I will never forget it. Never. They've made an Ahab out of me; a man who'd make a canon of his heart just to destroy them. I'd damn them to the deepest levels of hell even if it meant me being marooned on its edges... and right now it seems I already am.

How many others felt these same emotions? How many, through unfair treatment, burned with resentment against the system that imprisoned them and, by extension, society itself? Most poignant of all, how many later crimes might be averted if the prison system instead fostered respect for one another, through fair treatment, as well as for the law?

Too many left the prison gates with my anger. They might succeed in keeping it hidden from authorities –playing the system well. But they remembered that years of their lives had been taken away; not for the sake of rehabilitation, but to enact a warped kind of punishment – the kind that severs their links to society and leads them to embrace negative attributes above positive values.

I saw it. I felt it. And I would never forget it.

I thought back to the proud words engraved on the blue porcelain steps of Dorchester's main entrance: '*Holding a key to a brighter future*'.

Whose future, exactly, were they thinking of?

I refused to accept any food until they allowed me to clean the cell. The light was smashed, there were streaks of blood on the walls, and marks that had the look and smell of drying piss decorated a corner. I guessed the previous occupant had 'kicked off' and got 'twisted up', which got confirmed by someone I spoke to on association through the cell door.

"He was a right nut case," the voice said. "You don't happen to have any burn?"

Feeling generous, I handed him a bit from my last reserve of Golden Virginia under the door.

"Is this segregation or something then?" I asked.

"No. You're on the medical unit. For people at risk of suicide and self-harm, mostly. Take it you're neither?"

"They moved me from another wing after I refused to share a cell."

He drifted off. Through the door crack, I saw he bordered on skeletal, in his thirties, with a maze of scars along twig-like arms.

As he passed, I also saw a uniform sat in a chair, gazing into the cell opposite mine. A cane stick, if slim enough to fit through the door gap, would have been able to poke him. There was something else, however, that might cause even more disturbance.

Amongst the tobacco I'd given away were some roll-up papers, and in my bag were a few peppermint teabags. Chuckling silently, I made one of Ricky's 'joints', then rolled up a bit of writing paper. I lit the 'joint' and puffed into the rolled-up paper, which wedged nicely into the door-crack. This would direct all the smell where I wanted it.

A trail of smoke drifted out. Three puffs, I reckoned, were enough.

The screw turned his head from side to side, sniffing. Then he got up and turned briefly towards my cell.

At that point I caught a glimpse of who he'd been 'guarding'. A prisoner sat hunched on his bed, arms covered in bandages, looking even younger than Jay.

The screw coughed, then sat down again.

I waited around ten minutes before lighting the 'joint' again, making four puffs instead of three.

Another puff and the game would have been over, because shortly after I retracted the rolled-up paper another screw appeared.

"You smell that?"

"Yes. Bit of whacky backy."

The other screw marched off, then two more began circling the wing and pausing at each cell. Most of the doors were open, but because I was on 'Basic' they had to unlock mine.

"How's things going, Mr Jackley?"

By this time I lay on the bed, pretending to read.

"Fine," I replied. "Wouldn't mind a chair though."

"Oh, you don't have one? I'll get one for you."

He disappeared, leaving his colleague standing there, glancing around the cell and sniffing.

The other screw returned with a chair.

"Thanks," I said.

"No problem. How are you finding things then?" he asked.

"Can't wait to get 'outta here."

They both laughed. "You're on a bus to Guys Marsh next week."

That was news to me. I wasn't sure whether to believe it given what happened with Portland.

"Great," I replied.

"We'll leave you to it then," the screw said, as both left and locked the door.

An hour later and another 'joint' smouldered at the ready – but I soon heard the distinctive sound of cells being searched, so flushed it away. By the time they reached the cell, and went through my property, all that they could find in the way of smoking were some remnants of tobacco. They were pretty thorough, doing a strip search and poring through my canteen items: a half-used peanut butter bottle, shower gel, can of Marvel and, of course, peppermint tea bags.

I waited for lock-up before lighting the next 'joint' and a new shift were on duty. As before, a screw sat outside the cell opposite, not realising that he would shortly be sampling a certain smell.

"Whaaaaaa!"

A cry came from next door - startling me enough to drop the 'joint' as the seated screw swivelled round.

"Davis! Are you smoking something in there?"

I quickly picked up the joint and stubbed it out.

"Meeee? Whaaaaaa! I want it, give it, I want it, give it…."

His repeated words drawled on for minutes before falling silent.

"Whoever is smoking cannabis here is going to be found out!" the screw yelled.

***

The next day I entered a small office about the adjudication. A senior officer sat behind a desk, his face expressionless.

I handed him a written statement, then said that I wanted the IMB to be present.

He didn't even look down at what I'd written.

"Well, we will have to postpone the hearing then."

"Can't you get them today?" I replied.

"No."

He slid the bit of paper back across the desk to me.

"But what about my transfer to Guys Marsh?"

"It won't be effected. Hearing's over, Jackley."

Back at the cell, I managed to get a brush and mop, spending my entire allotted time of 'association' (45 minutes) cleaning. I scoured the walls near the bed and desk, noticing a few lines of graffiti. One jumped out from the rest:-

'Let it End.'

Later, I asked the skeletal inmate to describe the person who had been in my cell.

"Oh, he was just a young'un. Proper caused a racket down here, let me tell you. Screws bent him up and took him here the day before you came. Think he got shipped out somewhere. A relative of yours?"

"No," I replied. "Just a friend."

What would become of him? I wondered again. *How long would the system beat him down, until there was nothing but a shade of bitterness, anger and wasted potential?*

If the threads of Fate chose a slightly different pattern, he would have been me. Without the tools of paper and pen for expression, we would have trodden the same path. Instead it was forms, letters, and a bit of peppermint tea that formed my current arsenal against the system – sitting deep in the heart of Dorchester's dungeon. For it was a dungeon: there were windows, but no natural light could penetrate, being so far down. It also resembled an asylum, with most having serious mental health issues that culminated in suicide attempts and self-harm. The inmate in the opposite cell was one example. The nurses gave him a lot of attention, but the screws just took turns silently keeping watch, night and day. All they cared about was *preventing* self-harm and suicide, not addressing the *causes* why someone would feel that way.

When the young suicidal prisoner needed to use the toilet they at least had the decency of letting him do so without being watched. However, on one occasion he tried to do something else – resulting in them piling into his cell and shouting 'Code Red' into their radios. Nurses followed, but within an hour it was back to the same constant observation.

I watched, anger bubbling. Another letter went out to the local MP, Oliver Letwin.

A few, like me, were on Basic and facing adjudications for bad behaviour. Apparently Segregation had been "full for weeks". Inmates across the prison were being paired up in cells designed for one, with an instruction coming directly from the Ministry of Justice that nobody should have a single cell.

There was even word that some of the double cells were being turned into triples.

Dorchester – every prison across the country – was built upon the principle of oppression and subjugation, for without these things it would not function. Every man is fettered, both physically and mentally, by a system that has judged them unworthy of freedom. Some have entered through mistakes, single blips of misconduct in an otherwise blameless life. For others it marks the end, or renewal, of a life spent outside of society's laws. In both cases, such conditions only harden and darken the spirit, forcing one to turn away from compassion, independence and honour. It breaks community and family ties, making widows of wives and orphans of children – all in the name of justice. These are not places built for reform, no matter how strong some politicians protest. They are the universities of crime, the holding pens for society's rejects – a sorry excuse for punishment, for there are better ways.

Cutbacks, overcrowding, curtailing the positive and more humane aspects of regimes: a new force was at the helm.

The last letters I received from Geoff and Chris – received at HMP The Verne – spoke of the same. Where before there were two hours on the exercise yard at Parkhurst on weekends, it was now down to the 'mandatory' 30 minutes. Geoff, at HMP The Mount, wrote of extended lock-downs due to staff shortages.

I replied to both of them, but never heard back.

A new era of penal history had begun, and my 27th birthday was just two days away.

Again, I found myself praying to God.

Where before all that mattered was the appeal, my thoughts turned to other things. My mother - who I had planned to visit only weeks before they transferred me from The Verne - was worrying. All I could write were assurances and half-truths. And as for those around me – people like Jay, and the young man on constant suicide watch in the cell opposite – how many are worrying for them, too?

Chapter 20: Marshlands

Arrival at HMP Guys Marsh was surprisingly pleasant. First, Reception staff said that I would be automatically placed on 'Standard' IEP level, therefore escaping the 'Basic' regime. Then, within moments of walking onto my assigned prison wing, Kramer Craft appeared. He'd gone to Peterborough Crown Court for his planned confiscation hearing and was returned to HMP The Verne three weeks later. However, within days of returning, he was placed on a G4S van on the grounds of 'population pressures'. Officer Smallwood had apparently been behind this, after Kramer initiated a "pre-action protocol letter" against him for the opening of legal 'Rule 39' correspondence.

I recounted my own journey – from The Verne to Dorchester – and he laughed about the peppermint game. Initially I was put in a double cell by myself, but luckily Kramer arranged to move in before anyone else could do so.

Guys Marsh was an intriguing establishment. Much like The Verne, prisoners could use the grounds between different wings on exercise and association. Unlike The Verne, locks were on the doors and bars on the windows, with extensive confinement. It was relatively new, having been built in 1960 as a borstal, and only changing to an adult prison in 1992. Based just outside of Shaftesbury in Dorset, many bore familiar South Western accents, with quite a few also coming from my native Devonshire.

The HM Prison Inspectorate would go on to say the prison was in 'crisis', with 'managers and staff losing all control'. Gangs operated openly, Spice and alcohol related violence were prolific, and prisoners were afraid to leave their cells for months at a time. The roots of that situation were already visible when I arrived and, had there not been the presence of Kramer, I might have experienced more of it first-hand.

Having a decent cellmate, capable of intelligent conversation and being polite, made all the difference. Kramer (cellmate #16) even went to the trouble of wrapping up a birthday present in some newspaper: two 'Lindt' chocolate bars. They melted luxuriously in my mouth, far outmatching the pleasure of the Cadbury's Nut Bars I had adored at Lowdham Grange.

We spoke about our respective legal battles and I helped Kramer with some writing, all the while conscious that my own appeal hearing was just around the corner.

Kramer had already generated a pile of complaints. "They've totally fucked me over," he remarked, "so I'm hardly going to make life easy for them."

His principal discontent stemmed from an on-going confiscation matter that had seen most of his assets seized by the Crown, even those that did not arise from criminal undertakings. Receiving a thirteen-year determinate sentence for a first offence certainly did not seem to accomplish much in the way of rehabilitation, save perhaps ticking the system's boxes of 'punishment' and 'deterrence'. The sentence had been handed down by a Cambridgeshire court for a drug conspiracy (cocaine, amphetamines and ecstasy) valued at £1.9 million.

Surely, in a liberal and democratic society, individuals had the choice on what they consumed? Certain outlawed drugs, such as cannabis, were proven to provide benefits and, at the very worse, had impacts comparable to tobacco and alcohol. Drugs such as cocaine, whilst man-made, also derived from plants that several cultures had used for thousands of years. The Ancient Mayans were documented to use coca leaves in ceremonies and day-to-day consumption. Even today, many South American people in Bolivia and Peru maintained this tradition by chewing the leaves, which helped sustain energy and alertness. Nor had Western countries overlooked the opportunities of these drugs – cannabis, opium and cocaine had all once been legal, even widely marketed. The British Empire profited immensely from the sale of opium to East Asian countries like China. Essentially this was history's largest drug dealing operation, undertaken by a government, which then used lethal force when China turned away shipments of the drug.

Dealers were simply suppliers meeting a demand. People turned to drugs for a reason: they were gap-fillers for broken lives in a fractured society. If people were happy and could pursue their dreams constructively, they wouldn't depend on drugs.

There was no better example of this than the microcosm of prison. The sky-rocketing demand for Spice arose not because of a sudden wave of hopeless addicts, but rather the prison structure itself. Nearly all of those at Guys Marsh were locked up without work or education. Gym consisted of three hour long sessions a week, crammed with other prisoners – if you were lucky enough to get on the list. As for evening art classes, yoga, and creative writing sessions, I may have been the only one who remembered them.

***

On 20th March, I was transferred to HMP Pentonville in preparation for the appeal. I didn't expect the journey to be a joy, and it wasn't: six hours in a cramped plastic box, mostly spent waiting outside the Reception.

The London prison was dirty, noisy, and full of unprofessional screws. It felt like being on a constantly malfunctioning conveyor belt. Despite leaving Guys Marsh prison in the early morning, I did not get allocated a cell at Pentonville until late evening. A tall Ukrainian inmate greeted me, but I hardly said anything with all my thoughts on the appeal. Even without the constant noise of shouting and slamming of doors and gates, I doubted if I would have gotten a minute's sleep.

I awoke zombified. More waiting followed in various holding rooms, then I was loaded onto a van bound for the High Court of Justice. Four others came with me, all with their own appeals. A mixture of buoyant and subdued conversation bounced between the cells. As the van wound its way through the congested London streets, I gazed out at pavements washed by sunshine – people moving freely as productive members of society. The van passed through a secure entrance-way of the court; its tall Gothic windows and elaborate masonry, built in the 1870s, towered on each side. To the holding cells I was led, along with the others. One blessing was having a cell each, so I brought my thoughts into some semblance of order without distraction. Pacing, breathing, poring through paperwork... two hours passed. Eventually my barrister, Flo Kraus, appeared.

"We don't have much time," she said, "I expect they will call you up very shortly."

I looked at her barrister's wig and dark robes, managing a smile.

"Did you get all the paperwork I sent you?"

Over the months, I must have sent her well over ten envelopes of different documents.

"Yes, thank you."

She looked perturbed.

"I was just given this," she said, handing me a document titled 'Skeleton Argument'.

"It's from the prosecution," she added. "He only gave it to me an hour ago. I'm sorry I could not get it to you sooner."

I flicked through the pages – far more than I expected.

"He is not a very pleasant man," Flo said.

I could only assume she referred to Gareth Walters, the CPS Prosecutor I had faced when being sentenced. Her words were an under-statement: four years ago, he submitted a series of misleading statements that bordered on outright lies. When I complained to my solicitor, he just told me nothing could be done.

"You only got this an hour ago?"

"Yes. He was meant to provide it at least 7 days before the hearing."

"So, is the court going to allow it?"

"I'm afraid so," she frowned. "Unfortunately, this kind of thing has happened before."

"But – can you – I don't know...."

I wasn't sure what to say; she was the barrister.

"Look, I have to go now. They will be calling you up soon. With the two reports and the other evidence you have a good chance."

I thanked her and watched her leave the cell, then turned back to Walters' Skeleton Argument.

The more I read, the angrier I became. Once again, he was submitting statements that were misleading. He twisted the findings of doctors and made baseless conclusions. Selectively picking out chunks of my diaries, he artfully placed them out of context in order to back his arguments. Not only that, but he threw in a few other things: that my behaviour in custody was only 'evidence of remorselessness and a dangerous personality'. References were made to 'manipulating prison officers with threats of escape' and 'making death threats' – drawing such assertions from reports made at HMP The Verne and Dorchester.

I frantically marked all the errors and inaccuracies and pressed the cell bell.

"I need to see my barrister," I said to a guard.

"But you've just seen her."

I tried to keep calm. "Yes, I know. Something else has come up. It's urgent."

As I waited, I made some written notes about some of the main points made by Walters, so that Flo could counter them.

The cell door opened – but she wasn't there.

Instead it was two guards, telling me to follow them. I grabbed my paperwork as they put me in handcuffs and led me up a twisting flight of stone stairs. *Are they taking me to Flo... or to the court room?*

"I really need to see my barrister," I told them again.

But they were silent, right to the point of opening a door and releasing my handcuffs.

Sure enough, it was a court room, bigger than any I had ever seen before. Flo stood there, as did Walters, who frowned up at me. I recognised his bearded face and large frame immediately. A few other people sat on benches above – I didn't recognise any, but it did not help having no glasses. In my haste, I'd left them in the holding cell.

I called down to Flo, who came close.

"The Skeleton Argument," I said, handing it over. "What he's written is totally wrong."

She took the document and walked back to her original position, then immediately a clerk called "all rise" as three robed figures swept into the court room.

I listened as Flo presented my appeal grounds. Her points were strong, seemingly incontestable. She finished and there was silence. For a moment I thought Walters would say nothing, but then he slowly rose.

Lies, conjecture and misdirection spewed from his mouth. I wanted to spring up and say something.

Two of the judges then started asking questions to Flo.

To my astonishment, she couldn't answer.

I raised my hand, then put it down. They were asking a critical question about the central appeal grounds, that of reduced culpability, which had come under most attack by Walters. There was an answer to it, right on the paper I had given her.

But she jumped to another issue, a secondary point in the appeal about increased punitively of sentence - something she had successfully argued for in another case.

At the end, the judges huddled together and announced that

a judgment would be made after a short adjournment. They left the court room, then reappeared five minutes later.

I sat, hardly trusting my ears, as they took a rambling course through their judgment. They started by describing my offences, then quoted passages from Dr Suleman's report. They spoke of how evidence existed of reduced culpability; how my Asperger's Syndrome had an impact on my emotional awareness. But then they veered into dismissing this, repeating phrases from Walter's Skeleton Argument.

At this point, I just phased out. My eyes drifted above them, to the seal above their bench: the emblem of the Crown; the motto I'd seen when being sentenced. By God and My Right. The curves in the unicorn's horn, which had so entranced me when Judge Cavell passed his 13 years, were just as I remembered.

Fate. Whatever they decided was already set; I could do nothing to change it.

Dimly, I became aware that it had not been a *complete* failure – they spoke of 'allowing' the appeal and 'reducing the sentence by one year', accepting the secondary ground that Flo had raised. But the main grounds for appeal, the very purpose for which it had been lodged, were dismissed.

Like a wraith, down the stone steps of hell, I was led back to the holding cell. Once there, all the paperwork slid from my arms onto the floor.

"Mr Jackley?" a voice called behind me.

I didn't move.

"Mr Jackley?"

Back to the nightmare, I walked to an adjoining room, and saw Flo.

"I'm sorry I couldn't answer some of their questions," she said.

I just stared.

"I realise this must be difficult for you."

She put a hand on my shoulder. "Stephen, I know this is hard, but…. I think it could have been worse. You got a year off your sentence – that's 6 months coming out earlier than you would have."

I shook my head, fighting back tears. "But the whole point of this appeal was around culpability. That man... that prosecutor... the stuff he said... How could he get away with dumping a skeleton argument on us less than one hour before the hearing? Did you see what I wrote on that – the notes I made? And there were things the court did not even consider, like the time I awaited deportation back to the UK. What about that? I can't understand how –"

Flo interrupted my rambling. "It's not something I agree with, the way that document was submitted and accepted. It wasn't fair, and it was against procedures. But the court has made its decision. The only way to change that is to go to the Criminal Cases Review Commission."

"How is that possible?"

"It's not easy," Flo said, removing her wig. "But I'll help you, if you decide to go that way. There are some grounds you could use."

She went on to mention a 'slip rule', which sounded promising.

"What about the Supreme Court?"

"You'd need a general point of wider public importance. But you may well have one."

She wrote something on a piece of paper and gave it to me. "It's worth trying," she added.

"Okay," I said. "Well... thank you."

She smiled, then gave me a hug.

"Take care of yourself, and feel free to write to me any time."

I could breathe again – just. I could walk forward, if only step by step. Even as I heard the others come back from their hearings, boasting of far more reduced sentences, there was a hope in my heart to carry on.

***

On entering Guys Marsh, it was around 10pm. They escorted me back to the cell I had shared with Kramer, who immediately asked how the appeal had gone. I waited for the screws to slam the door before answering.

"Got reduced to 12 years."

"Fantastic!"

"What...? No, it's a disaster." Solemnly, I recounted what happened.

"The amount of times I've seen people come back from that court with their sentences upheld... I think you had a result."

I just shook my head. "That prosecutor is evil."

"CPS prosecutors, yeah, I think that must be in their job description or something."

"But this one literally lied to the court."

Kramer then told me a similar story, where one prosecutor had 'suppressed evidence' in his trial. "Took it to the Court of Appeal, but they threw it out. At least you made it to a full hearing, and got a reduced sentence at the end."

Nothing he said changed my outlook. As tired as I was, I spent hours that night drafting grounds for going to the Supreme Court.

The next day, when making enquiries about using a computer to do legal work, I was met with a blank stare. "You can't do that here," a wing screw said.

"What?"

"You... cannot... use a computer... for legal work!" the screw repeated to me like a child.

At the B Category Lowdham Grange this was possible, yet in a lower security C Category establishment I was being told it couldn't be done.

"I really need to use a computer," I repeated.

The screw walked off.

If I had not declared war on the system when cast into Dorchester's dungeon, I declared it now. Sentencing Guidelines had been cast aside; crucial mitigation ignored; the principles of a fair hearing abused; and now I was prevented from effectively challenging it. *Henceforth*, I vowed, *every single minute of my custody will cost them as much as possible.* Not through fights and smashing up their property, but where it really hurt them: through paperwork; through the courts themselves – in any place where they would need to stand up and defend themselves. *And if justice was not possible for me, I would make sure it was within reach for others.*

Kramer and I made a pact. Like me, he wanted his incarceration to hurt the system as much as possible, whilst not impeding both our chances of being released. We both reached the conclusion that HMP Guys Marsh was nothing but a 'dead end'. Officially, there was a three month waiting period for any transfers, but Kramer had no intention of waiting that long. He bombarded them with complaints every day, as did I, about issues that ranged from the lack of work to the water temperature.

One day he noted there were no anti-slip tiles in the shower area.

"Yeah, I almost slipped up there yesterday."

And, sure enough, I indeed slipped the next day – requiring an ambulance to be called and resulting in a problem getting pain relief in the aftermath.

Kramer also had an accident: when walking up the stairs, boiling water spilled onto his ankles. This occurred because the prison did not have kettles in the cell, but instead required prisoners to collect hot water in jugs from a single dispenser on the wing.

With our conjoined complaints, coupled with pre-action protocol letters sent for our respective claims, the prison made an exception to its three-month transfer rule. We were told we would both be going to a prison in Surrey, HMP Coldingley.

However, just in case the prison changed its mind, Kramer acquired some Weetabix.

"You're 'gonna love this, Stevie," he beamed, wetting the brown cereal and mixing in a little coffee, then shaping it into blocks.

If anyone entered the cell then, it would have looked like someone had taken a series of shits on the floor.

"Now to decide where to put them – what do you reckon?"

"I wouldn't mind placing one in the application box," I said, "given that they never seem to respond to applications."

"Hahaha! But something's missing..."

He scooped up some sweetcorn from his dinner plate and imbedded it evenly on the brown lumps.

"There we go, that makes it look more authentic."

The next day we headed in separate directions – him to another spur, me to the screw's office. The 'poo' was in my pocket, and I only had a few seconds to get it into the application box. Stupidly, they left this unlocked in the mornings, so as soon as the screws were not looking I slipped in the 'poo' and strode away.

As I returned to the cell, I heard fragments of astonishment.

Kramer came back, red-faced and laughing.

"Did you do it?"

I nodded, laughing as well.

In the distance, we could still hear shouts of disgust. It became the talk of the entire wing.

If that weren't enough, we drew a massive picture of the nastiest screw on the cell door: belly hanging out, flies undone, with a speech bubble that read: *"Got any burn?"* Each time a screw opened the cell window flap to do their regular checks, they unwittingly framed the figure's face.

Such were our parting gifts to HMP Guys Marsh, as a new chapter of the prison journey ushered.

Chapter 21: Coldingley

When surrounded by the black swamp of man's worst
nature, what does it matter, when all is destined to
disintegrate, to move on? And who can say if each step
forward is for better or worse? Who can point to the
future's shrouded pen and say what words it forms?
All things pass... and some day all this will be but ashes –
brief echoes of a lost past.

The Supreme Court was created in 2009 as 'the final court of appeal in the UK for civil cases, and for criminal cases from England, Wales and Northern Ireland'. It was where cases of the highest importance were decided. Each one arrived through the work of a barrister, usually a QC (Queen's Council). Considering this, to think that they would give the barest consideration to a case brought by a self-representing prisoner – with hand-written grounds - was perhaps naive. Yet I had to try, and there were only 28 days after my hearing to send all the paperwork. By the time I left HMP Guys Marsh and arrived at HMP Coldingley, that meant just two weeks.

Coldingley, based twenty minutes from Woking in Surrey, was a 'C' Category training establishment housing 500 inmates. Most of the cells didn't have toilets; instead, each landing had a communal 'recess', which prisoners could access at night by pressing a button. It was a cued system, like I had experienced at HMP Gloucester, and entailed waiting hours at night to use the toilet. As a consequence, buckets were handed out on induction, with a sluice in the recess where they could be emptied. This so-called 'slopping out' had officially been declared obsolete by the Prison Service in 1996.

I had not given up trying to access a computer in order to present my grounds to the Supreme Court properly. However, it transpired that the prison only had two 'Access to Justice Laptops' and that neither could be used for typing or printing legal documents. Could Lowdham Grange be the only prison in the entire UK that allowed computers to be used for legal work? It didn't seem possible. My first complaint at Coldingley was about this issue, but with time running out I accepted the fact that my hand-written grounds had to be sent – albeit not before they had been carefully re-drafted. The last ground was about the failure to take into account my time spent awaiting deportation to the UK, supposedly mandatory under law. As I wrote:-

'Therefore, pursuant to Section 243 of the Criminal Justice Act 2003, the lower court was obliged to remit the time incurred.'

As I finished, someone knocked on the door. A sheet of paper got slid under.

"Take a look at this," Kramer's voice came through the door crack.

I picked up the paper and smiled - another complaint. I corrected a few spelling errors and made some suggested re-writes, then handed it back to him later. We delighted in finding phrases that would baffle the prison administration, including Latin terms. Needless to say, it did not exactly escalate our merit in the eyes of some officers.

Later, I got called up to explain an application I'd submitted.

'One requires access to the extensive compendium of Hawking's singularity theorems', it started.

A tall screw in his late 20s frowned. "Is this some kind of joke?"

I shook my head.

"Well, what do you want me to do with it?"

"I don't know."

"What do you think, Jackie?" he asked another officer.

"Education, maybe?"

"Seems the only place it could go," he added. "But, really, in future, just make applications that are about normal things."

"It would help if I could type up my legal work for the Supreme Court," I told him.

"Yes, another department is looking into that. They'll get back to you."

As it turned out, the complaint I submitted had been responded to by a manager, who wrote back that, under no circumstances, could computers be used for typing and printing legal materials. The words 'No' and 'Not allowed' had been underlined, twice.

I showed the response to Kramer.

"Typical mug off. You 'gonna appeal it?"

The complaints process comprised two tiers: an initial complaint form and, if the response to that did not resolve the issue, an appeal form. They were called 'Comp1' and 'Comp1A' forms. There was also a 'Comp2' form, reserved for matters of sensitivity about staff, and a 'Discrimination Incident Report Form' (DIRF).

Out of all the complaints we submitted, the responses were almost always dismissive. They never sought to provide a full resolution, or even recognise the issue raised. Comp1A's just reiterated the response in Comp1's. This is not to say that all complaints were pointless, for they could yield positive outcomes. On top of that, they cost the prison administration time and money.

After the internal complaints procedure, a prisoner could take their issue to the 'Prisons Ombudsman'. The problem with that was, due to a huge backlog, investigations by the Ombudsman could now take over a year. The days of things being investigated 'within

8 weeks' (the original target), with detailed reports being supplied at the end, were over. Kramer and a number of others told me they had been waiting from ten to fifteen months for responses. So, by the time an investigation was completed, the matter complained about was no longer relevant. And that fact alone was enough for the Ombudsman's office to rule against a prisoner!

The complaint system and the Prison Ombudsman had been setup in the wake of a report by a judge, Lord Woolf. Reflecting on the 1990 Strangeways Riots and subsequent wave of unrest, Woolf noted the need for:

> *'Improved standards of justice within prisons involving the giving of reasons to a prisoner for any decision which materially and adversely affects him; a grievance procedure and disciplinary proceedings which ensure that the governor deals with most matters under his present powers.'*

In 2015, he would go on to say that 'prisons are no better than 25 years ago' – after most of his recommendations had been torn apart following the tenure of Grayling. But even before Grayling's schemes were implemented, the complaints system and Ombudsman were poor shadows of what Woolf had originally intended them to be.

I fully expected the answer to my 'Comp1A' to be negative, with the next step having to be a judicial review. Finding information on how to do this at Coldingley's library was challenging, for legal books and reference material were not allowed to be loaned. It meant frantically making notes in the two 30-minute sessions provided each week – assuming there was enough staff to even facilitate a library visit. The majority of legal textbooks were also outdated, with others being more relevant to school pupils.

I was not alone in trying to represent myself. One guy on the induction wing was tasked with 'making representations' against his recall to prison, which he said came about due to a false allegation made by his girlfriend to his probation officer. A few were fighting their convictions, and others were making appeals against re-categorisation decisions. Whereas before they could have accessed Legal Aid for solicitors to assist them, they now had to do it themselves.

***

In order for a case to be heard by the Supreme Court, it must first be 'given permission' by the Court of Appeal. Within two weeks of lodging my grounds, I received a cryptic rejection from one of the very same judges who had heard my appeal, who merely stated that the appeal was 'successful' (i.e. on the basis of a one year subtraction for a secondary ground) and that 'no point of general public importance was raised'. He made no effort to deal with the points I had delved into – but it didn't surprise me. Which judge would want to give the green light to having one of their own decisions challenged, after all?

Now, only the Criminal Cases Review Commission (CCRC) could refer the case back to the Court of Appeal. This time, I was determined to be given reasonable means to research and present the case, which meant access to proper legal reference material and a computer to type up my grounds.

However, my 'Comp1A' was returned with a response that could have been written by the same person. It spurned me into submitting complaints and applications about other things – like Kramer, not caring if it would result in a transfer.

We were also discovering just how bad the sanitation system could be. Many times we had been kept waiting hours to use the toilet at night and, at least twice, there was a complete shut-down due to a system failure. Having to defecate in the same small space that one slept and ate in felt demeaning and unhealthy. Nor was there any means to wash afterwards, for the cells had no running water. Only after returning from the 30 minutes of exercise in the mornings did you realise how much the cells and wings stank of shit and piss, although the screws had the benefit of using air fresheners in their office.

Kramer thought there was a basis to commence a 'class action', and he started collecting details of who might be interested. Some were enthusiastic, others didn't want to risk 'getting noticed' by the prison officials - fearing it would jeopardise an upcoming recategorisation decision or even (in the case of IPP inmates) their release. Nonetheless, by the end of the week, Kramer amassed around a hundred names.

I wasn't sure what was worse about the sanitation system: having to sometimes defecate in my cell, or not knowing when the door would pop open after hitting the button to be let out. Sometimes it could be a few minutes, other times hours, depending on how many were in the cue. Just like at Gloucester, several also tried to extend their time unlocked as much as possible, talking to mates behind their doors. It was up to the staff to ensure the system wasn't abused in this way, but some didn't care.

Weekends were always the worse, for it meant being subject to a solid lock-up between 5pm to 9am. Not that week days were much better: without work or education, prisoners were also confined to their cells, although there were unlocks for exercise, lunch, association, dinner and the occasional gym session.

'E wing' was the only part of the prison with in-cell sanitation, but had a long waiting list in getting there. Nonetheless, I kept putting in applications and spoke with a male nurse at healthcare, who told me he would recommend a move. The Court of Appeal had accepted that I found prison conditions tougher by virtue of having Asperger's Syndrome and maybe for the first time the prison authorities had to take this into account.

In the meantime, I wrote to Lords, Ladies and Baronnesses, using a dated book in the library that provided details of all members of the House of Lords. I wasn't banking on a flurry of responses, but even if just one made enquiries with the Court of Appeal then it seemed worthwhile.

***

On the 7th May, the Government announced it would hold a referendum on the UK's membership of the European Union. Leaving the EU would mean breaking away from the European community, most countries of which had policies that were more enlightened than England, none more so than with regards to penal matters. The UK incarcerated more people than any other Western European nation, and its prison conditions had come under fire by the European Committee for the Prevention of Torture.

Chris Grayling – a strong opponent of the EU and human rights in general - no doubt delighted in this. His 'hard man' image targeted those who could not fight back and who were sweepingly misrepresented. Such Ministers, of course, were the 'good guys'; we were nothing more than scum. We already had too many privileges, it was argued. One newspaper regaled how prisoners were 'living in luxury', with 'reconvictions occurring because they didn't worry about getting sent back inside'. Clearly that columnist hadn't enjoyed a little stint in Coldingley, where he might have been given the luxury of sleeping and eating in a space the size of his broom cupboard, whilst defecating there in a bucket.

The only positive development was receiving responses from several Lords, Ladies and Baronesses. Some wrote at length, echoing the government rhetoric about the courts being independent and prisons being 'places of decency and ample opportunity'. Two said they had written to the Court of Appeal to ask why certain procedures had been set aside. Now that I'd been moved to his constituency, I also corresponded with Michael Gove MP. He wrote quite extensively and politely, seeming to have an interest in criminal justice matters. Little did I know, he would go on to succeed Grayling as Justice Secretary, overseeing a fleeting period of repair.

Whether because of the recommendation from healthcare, or perhaps more as a result of all the letters I received with official 'House of Lords' and 'House of Commons' seals, on 10th May they moved me over to 'E' wing. It had been built many years after the other prison wings, and boasted not only in-cell sanitation but also showers. Kramer managed to move over two days earlier than me, but had just been transferred to HMP Elmley for another confiscation hearing, so I ended up in his old cell. It felt lonely without him being around to talk to and train with. I couldn't discuss my ongoing legal matters with anyone else, even as the judicial review about the prison's refusal to use IT facilities for legal purpose was 'issued' (accepted for processing) by the High Court.

The wing also had its own exercise yard, smaller than the main prison's and overlooked by some trees behind the wall. I looked upon these with longing, feeling the gusts of Spring and seeing the vivid greens come to life. Not since the beginning of my sentence had I looked so ardently to release and freedom. Accessing a computer to represent myself effectively was important, but still paled into insignificance when asking the question of *how much longer?* 5 years had passed: one in America, four in the UK. Two remained – I was closer to the end than the beginning - but the light had receded far more than what it had been at Lowdham Grange. Perhaps it was more reflection than expectation: the thought of spending between the age of 22 to 28 in prison.

What would another two years really achieve, save from reinforcing the sense of bitterness, loss and separation from society?

The Court of Appeal had breached its own procedures by allowing the prosecutor's last minute Skeleton Argument and accepting it at face value. They had willingly allowed themselves to be misled, ignoring other crucial grounds. One year off a thirteen year sentence for a secondary ground that was then ridiculed in the British press – the whole thing was farcical.

Alongside taking my case to the CCRC, I also had a damages claim against Guys Marsh for the injury sustained there, which a solicitor now dealt with; Kramer's 'class action' against Coldingley's sanitation system that I had joined; and, lastly, the judicial review about denying access to IT for legal purposes. Every week now entailed dealing with correspondence from the courts and also my opponent, the Treasury Solicitor ('T-sol'). They were always the Prison Service's chosen representatives, since they acted as solicitors for most government departments, with a host of legal experts at their disposal – to say nothing of unlimited access to legal reference material and computers.

Legal issues aside, an Open University module needed completing. My OU tutor even made a visit to the prison to go over upcoming assignments, a nice lady called Jane Fowles.

"This is the first closed prison I have been to," she told me. "I don't think I have walked through so many locked doors and gates in the space of a few minutes before."

I laughed. "Yes, they are obsessed about security. Most prisons are. This one isn't too bad, although there are better ones."

I told her about Lowdham Grange and my problems with self-representation in the courts.

"That does seem quite illogical," she said, "making you write out complex legal grounds by hand and not giving you access to reference material."

Would people outside prison – even those half-brainwashed by the tabloids and lying Ministers, agree? More importantly, would the High Court?

It 'only' took a month to be given a job. They called it 'PICTA' – a training classroom that revolved around learning Cisco programming and some other ICT skills. I started by doing some courses on Microsoft's programmes – Word, Powerpoint and Excel. The irony, of being surrounded by computers when not allowed to use one for essential legal purposes, was not lost on me. Two instructors – Andy and George – were amicable, provided you did the work assigned and refrained from 'messing around'. Andy was fat, in his 40s, whilst George was an older Greek man about half Andy's size.

There were a few eccentric prisoners in PICTA. Manic Robby, in his 40s, could talk non-stop if you were not careful. Then there was Gohil, 'the lawyer', who had once been a partner in a top firm of solicitors, but was now doing a ten-year sentence for fraud and money laundering linked to a senior Nigerian politician (valued at over $40 million). It was something he adamantly denied and was in the process of overturning his conviction. When he discovered my own legal endeavours, we spoke at length.

"You should have been a barrister," he said, after I showed him the grounds for the judicial review.

"Too late for that now."

"Oh, but you could still apply to the Law Society to be admitted, after taking your exams. It's not like your offences involved fraud or deceit."

I shrugged. "What about you – can you be a solicitor again?"

"When I get this conviction overturned," he replied, pushing up his glasses, "of course I will practice the law again."

Many claimed innocence, but none were as vehement as Gohil. Most of the time he pored over piles of legal papers. He was also one of the two prisoners in Coldingley with an 'Access to Justice' laptop, although the device did not allow him to type or print documents. It was just intended for going through legal material – transcripts and the like. In Gohil's case, they'd been saved onto a remote drive by his solicitor.

"The whole thing rests on corruption," he said. "Police, the CPS – they are still out there, watching my every move."

Gohil was of Indian descent and the only other attributes to his cell, aside from stacks of legal paperwork, was a little shrine with a photo of a Hindu deity.

Summertime in Coldingley felt a bit like winter in Lowdham. There was perpetual shade and darkness, save for the brief periods of outside exercise. Why such prisons could not just leave the exercise yard unlocked, as at Lowdham, defied common sense. With 12-metre fences topped by rolls of razor wire, along with cameras and patrolling guards, the strict curtailment of outside exercise was unnecessary. If not on weekdays, why not weekends? It formed the subject of yet another complaint.

I had been putting quite a lot of them in. So much so that, one day, I was taken aside to meet with the 'Residential Governor', Miss Jassell, together with a Senior Officer ('SO') called Miss Close.

Jassell was a short middle-aged lady, with a brown complexion, whilst SO Close was tall, of a large frame, with close-cropped silver hair. She had been described as a 'butch lesbian' by some inmates.

"You're generating a lot of paperwork," Jassell said, from behind a large desk.

I began to explain my underlying concerns: firstly, the issue with the Court of Appeal, followed by the prohibition in using computers for self-representation and also the fact that I wasn't in an open prison. Technically, being under two years from release, I fit the eligibility.

"We've got no say on what the courts do," Jassell replied – ignoring all the other issues. "As from today, I am allocating SO Close to be your caseworker. In future, instead of making a complaint, you can just go to her."

She had no interest in further discussion, and when I next put in a complaint it was simply redirected to SO Close.

'This matter is best dealt with by putting in an application or speaking with your wing staff.'

She repeated the same statement, for each subsequent complaint lodged.

Despite the annoyance caused, the fact the prison took a 'light' approach to dealing with my 'paperwork' made me surprised. A 'heavy' approach would have involved a downgrade in IEP level on some pretext and, eventually, a transfer to a less accommodating prison. Whether their comparative amicability was down to my judicial review, or having Asperger's Syndrome, I wasn't sure.

On one occasion I asked to be allowed to start 'a small-scale ant farm', citing the lack of contact with nature. The request somehow generated more paperwork than any other, with Jassell herself stepping back into the fray and writing, in underlined capital letters: *'SO CLOSE HAS ALREADY DEALT WITH THIS MATTER.'*

On 13th June they convened a meeting with the mental health nurse who had recommended my move to 'E' wing a month ago.

The meeting reviewed my use of complaints and application forms, encouraging me to desist. It was legally difficult for them to threaten disciplinary action if I didn't, and probably in most prior cases of dealing with disruptive prisoners they were used to violence or vandalism, rather than someone pestering them with a pen.

The meeting ended with SO Close giving me two of their blue flexi-pens, as all mine had ran out of ink.

Chapter 22: Battling the System

For all the harshness depicted of US prisons, they existed in a country with a written constitution, and a far more defined separation of powers between the judiciary and the executive. In the UK, the official head of the Justice Ministry was a politician, a cabinet Minister, whose personal views and ambitions were changing the very fabric of the penal estate, and indeed the courts. He was overseeing drastic budget cuts to both, causing increasing staff shortages and lock-downs. Prisoners' food was hit: the formerly hot lunches changed to a choice of cold baguettes or sandwiches, about the equivalent of a kid's packed lunch, whilst hot weekend breakfasts ended.

But it was Grayling's removal of Legal Aid that was most significant. This meant no further free representation for things like re-categorisation, adjudications and general treatment. And could we represent ourselves as an alternative? No, because there was effectively a blanket ban on using computers for legal purposes. Similarly, gaining access to up-to-date, relevant legal reference material was dependent on library access. With the staff shortages kicking in, even weekly library visits were being cancelled across the prison estate.

The Prison Service loved it, of course. No more pesky lawyers to challenge their decisions: they could now do what they wanted, with little fear of the consequences. Those who raised concerns over the curtailment of Legal Aid for prisoners were fobbed off with references to a 'robust internal complaints procedure', 'the IMB' and the 'Prisons Ombudsman'. No matter that the first was essentially a joke, the second useless, and the third a mixture of both.

Suddenly, my judicial review took on new proportions. If I could win, gaining a ruling that prisoners had a general right to accessing computers for legal purposes, then it would result in potential injustices being prevented. It was not just about civil matters, but the ability of prisoners to rectify miscarriages of justice, too - where their prior legal representatives had failed to do so.

The right of prisoners to have access to computers and legal reference material to adequately defend themselves was well established in America. Dedicated law libraries were in every US prison. They had won this through taking the fight to court. Now, the responsibility fell upon me to do the same. I would not walk away from it now, even if the prison suddenly made an exception and bestowed computer access; not even if they sent me to open conditions. I had a moral duty to pursue the case right to a final hearing.

***

In early July, with my re-categorisation for open conditions just round the corner, I received a surprise letter from my (latest) probation officer, Shaz Western. Apparently there'd been a recent 'MAPPA board' meeting, and they had *approved* a 'Release on Temporary License' (ROTL). This, she wrote, could represent a 'test of my suitability for open conditions'.

ROTLs were given out sparingly and only to the most trusted prisoners. In essence, they represented a form of absolute freedom, a chance to actually get outside prison! The very concept was hard for me to grasp. Always before, probation officials had – at best – been 'hands off'. In other cases they became an actively hostile force, unseen but working in the background, as implied by Deborah Benson at The Verne.

Now a turning point had been reached. The break I'd been looking for had finally come.

Equipped with the letter, I attended my first 'ROTL board' - headed by governor Ballantyne and a resident 'probation advisor'. With the prospect of walking free being so close, if only temporarily, I was jittery when Ballantyne asked questions.

"I don't find you suitable at this time," he concluded at the end. "However, it seems you would be perfect for D Category."

Rather than being disappointed, his statement buoyed my hopes. With D Category – open prison - the worse aspects of incarceration would be over: the long confinement, lack of access to outdoors, meaningless and excessive security... it would be like Lowdham Grange, except without the walls and fences.

I temporarily suspended all complaints and applications, hoping they would see it as a gesture of cooperation.

Then the decision came on 24th July: *'Your re-categorisation review to 'D' has been denied.'*

At the same time, a letter arrived from Shaz saying she would not support open conditions without a few successful ROTLs from closed conditions. In other words, the absence of one precluded the granting of the other.

In the days that followed, complaints and applications hit them like an avalanche. Another thing, which I learned from Kramer, was the Freedom of Information ('FoI') requests. By law they had a duty to respond to these, and I fired off four in the space of a week to the relevant Ministry of Justice departments.

I soon got called to see another governor, Miss Stobart, along with SO Close.

Stobart was a lady in her 30s with long black hair, who might have been pretty if not for the warped frown on her face.

"Take a seat," she said, then gestured to a pile of paperwork on the desk in front of her. "Look at this."

It looked like an accumulation of the entire wing's various applications over a week. Then I realised it was mine, with a few complaints and FoI requests thrown in.

"Just what am I meant to do with it?"

I shrugged. "Well, it wouldn't be there if I was in open conditions."

Stobart's eyes blazed. "You think you can play games with us?"

"Well, -" I began.

"From now on," Stobart interrupted, "I'm restricting your complaints to two a week. If you go over, you'll be put on Basic."

"You can't do that," I replied. "If taken to court it would be declared unlawful."

"I really don't care. The same goes with unnecessary applications and these – what are these?"

She held up an FoI request.

"It looks like some kind of request asking about the local bird life," SO Close said behind me.

"Unbelievable," Stobart said. "So it all ends here - got it? You'll be reconsidered for D Cat again, in a year's time, like everyone else who has had their review. Putting in complaints won't change anything."

"Will I get this decision restricting my complaints and applications in writing?" I asked.

She rolled her eyes. "Yes, you'll get it in writing. I suppose you think that will help you take it to court?"

I didn't say anything.

She smiled smugly. "The courts are on our side. I've spent long enough as a governor to know that. But go to them, if you want. It makes no difference to me."

SO Close escorted me away.

Shortly after, I received two bits of news that left me buzzing for days: the last Open University module had resulted in a 'Distinction', and the long awaited decision from the High Court about my 'legal access' judicial review had arrived. I unfolded the sheet of paper, expecting some stiff judge to throw back all my efforts, and saw the following statement:-

'Permission is hereby granted. It is at least arguable on the facts of this case that the Defendant acted unlawfully in failing to facilitate access to and use of IT facilities given the passage of time since the request was first made.' – HHJ McKenna

I almost leapt into the air, remembering the smugness of Stobart and others like her. What would they think now?

The courts *did* care. Judges were not under the control of governors, or even ministers. Policies and decisions could be challenged successfully, even by those who represented themselves – *even by prisoners*. It was the greatest victory I could remember for a long time, except it was just the first step in a long journey. Permission had been granted but that did not mean I had won. There would be a substantive hearing next, after the Defendant had filed a defence. Judicial review was unlike other legal proceedings: you needed to get the permission of a judge for a case to be accepted, making the process very difficult for applicants. Yet, in order to challenge a government policy or the decision of a public official, the only way to do so was through judicial review. It was the only clear intersection where members of the judiciary could hold the executive to account, but traditionally there was a 'doctrine of deference' that tilted the scales in favour of public officials. The burden of proof on anyone bringing a judicial review was much higher than any other civil proceedings.

Not only that, but I faced an opponent with qualified legal representation who, in turn, had access to as much resources as they wanted. They could dredge up quotes from previous cases, or refer to oblique court procedures. The best I could do was present arguments rationally and scramble around for references to similar cases in the little time I got in the library. All the while, my tools were a paper and pen.

This inequality of arms and the higher bar set by judicial review made my battle akin to David versus Goliath. But the poor odds of winning, coupled with the wider principle I was fighting for, just spurned me on. Moreover, I knew that not all judges fully subscribed to the 'doctrine of deference'; some were willing to stand up for the rights of individuals, especially where a higher principle of justice was at stake. Past cases proved that, even though in each instance there had been barristers on both sides. For me, a self-representing prisoner, I wondered just how far the impartiality of a good judge could stretch.

Few self-litigants managed to leap the first hurdle of getting permission for judicial review. Even fewer had won their case at the final hearing. And yet... it was possible. No, it *had* to be so. If things continued as they were, then prisoners across the entire country would be barred from using IT facilities and legal reference material to represent themselves and to utilise the courts as a means of last resort. Nor could they turn to a solicitor after Legal Aid had been taken away. It would be fine for the rich, who could afford legal representation, but everyone else would be denied the mere possibility of meaningfully defending themselves against abuses of power and miscarriages of justice.

At the beginning of this journey, I saw prisoners as stupid and dangerous – none more so, ironically, than when I was in the midst of robbing banks. Now I realised that such a conception was childish in its simplicity: the people around me were far apart from the caricatures portrayed by newspapers. Many of them had taken turnings that any law abiding citizen could easily relate to, and follow in the same direction if not for chance. A portion had fallen foul of the justice system, and should not have even been in prison.

The system around me broke them down. It engineered and manipulated, lied and impeded, until the only thing left was hatred and disillusionment. It made first time offenders into serial criminals. One only had to look at the criminology studies to realise this in a detached scientific way. Yes, prison was needed, for some more than others. And there were systems that could sensibly incarcerate, punish and rehabilitate those who offended

– instead of casting them all into a pit of criminalisation.

I thought back to the former university student who had got into a fight and ended up at HMP Hewell and the young 19-year-old Jay at HMP Dorchester who just wanted it 'to end'.

For all the sadist prison officials, as the few checks and balances were removed or made ineffective, it was certain more lives would be destroyed.

**

As weeks passed, I returned to the usual volume of paperwork. The prison acted swiftly.

After two 'IEP warnings', they ejected me from E-wing and sent me to 'B'. They even seemed to pick the worse possible cell: on the middle of a noisy spur, with no writing table, walls streaked with suspicious brown stains. The move was akin to moving from a relatively clean hostel to a drug-infested squat. Even before I had dragged my two heavy prison-issue bags of paperwork into the cell, someone asked "got any burn?"

I looked around into the face of someone who might have starred in *Lord of the Rings* - as an Orc.

"Yer cil, mit wanna klen it."

He walked away after saying this, before returning a minute later with a lit cigarette in his mouth. "So got no burn?"

"No, sorry, I don't smoke."

This drew a long stare. He muttered something under his breath, hawked, and spat a thick brown splodge in the corridor.

Maybe it meant '*Welcome to B Wing*'.

I walked away in search of cleaning utensils. Each landing had a store cuphoard, but it required a screw to unlock it. In theory, that should not have been hard, but the first screw just said "I'm busy", before returning to sipping from his mug. It took two more requests, to two other screws, before one finally came upstairs to unlock the cupboard. I filled a mop bucket with disinfectant, grabbed a mop and brush, then plodded back to the cell.

Three inmates gathered outside, all talking amongst each other. They went silent when I approached, staring at me intensely, but I just ignored them and started cleaning.

"Yo, mate!" a voice shouted.

He looked like he somehow managed to access the gym regularly. A long scar ran from his chin to his ear.

"What you in for then?" he quipped.

The other inmate beside him – shortest and youngest – started to say something.

"Armed robbery. What are *you* in for?"

All three of them paused. B wing was renown for being the worse, not only due to its poor conditions, but because of the inmates. The alarms that went off usually only saw screws run in only one direction. Fights, bullying, self-harming, suicide... B wing had the whole she-bang. If I was to survive here, I had to nip the bullying right in the bud.

"I'm in for ABH," scar-face said in a different tone. "How long you doing?"

"13 years."

It was an automatic response – the question had been asked countless times before the appeal.

At this point the shortest inmate vanished back into his cell. I went back to cleaning, leaving 'scar face' and his spitting companion to watch outside.

"Last guy in yer cill committed suicide."

I paused sweeping. "Good to know," I responded casually.

"What prisons you been in, mate?" scar-face blurted.

I told him – at least the recent ones - and apparently he knew Dorchester.

"Fucking shit hole," he frowned.

"Wers than 'ere?" his companion asked.

"You got to be kidding me," scar-face started, then they began conversing together and wandered off.

It took around forty minutes of cleaning, and two changes of the mop bucket, but eventually my new cell was semi-habitable. I had no way of cleaning the metal grate though, which jutted a few inches from the window. Some prisoners chucked out the contents of their buckets from the windows rather than waiting to use the sluice, and one above me clearly did it on a regular basis.

Lock-up came swiftly after dinner, and I just had enough time to use the communal recess. Of the three toilets, one was cordoned off and the other was overflowing. The 3-metre urinal had a swamp of floating fag-ends, whilst the four sinks were stained and speckled with various spittle.

It is about survival, I thought, once the screws locked off the spur and activated the sanitation system. Immediately a steady stream of prisoners came out, one by one, some taking a few minutes to use the communal recess and others spending much longer. Shouting was endless. The inmate in the cell to my left had a high-powered stereo, going by the continuous booming vibrations that went on until past 1am. Gradually, however, the noise died down – although silent periods could often be suddenly interrupted by a loud prisoner getting unlocked.

I drifted into sleep. A few hours later I awoke again, as often happened, for no discernible reason. Fleetingly I thought someone else stood in the cell – a darker patch of shadow – but there was nobody.

***

Seven nights passed in cell B-111. They should have replaced the middle 1 with a 0. The constant noise, the defective sanitation system, the intimidation... it made the prospect of even a month longer – let alone two *years* – seem intolerable.

And yet, I'd faced worse. The system was punishing me for having the audacity to challenge it, thinking the move would break me down, but it did the very opposite. Kramer's class action against Coldingley's sanitation system was on-going, and the move to 'B' wing galvanised me into getting more people involved. So I stuck up a few hand-written notices with toothpaste, declaring that the conditions of the sanitation system were in breach of Article 3 of the European Convention on Human Rights and adding my cell number. Some faces started to appear, including an obese man in his forties who claimed to be a member of the Hell's Angels motorcycle gang and sported their emblems in tattoos on both arms. With him, I collected a list of names to forward to Kramer's solicitor, adding them to the previous ones he had gathered months earlier.

Aside from 'B' wing itself, there was also my cell. It didn't feel right. Yes, there was the oozing detritus on the window grate that could never be removed without the touch of a high-pressure water hose, and added to most nights from the cell above. Then there was the shouting of unlocked inmates and noise from adjacent cells. But what kept waking me up, in the middle of the night, caused most distress. I didn't feel alone.

As a seven-year old, in what used to be the dungeon of Berry Pomeroy castle in Devon, I had felt the same. But this time there was no option of running to my parents' car.

I took to leaving the cell light on, using a t-shirt to cover my eyes. But on one occasion the light flickered off and I awoke, sweating. Heart rushing, I leaped up and kept pressing the light switch, begging it to work, and to my relief it did. All around the floor, my paperwork lay scattered.

The next day, when striding down a corridor en-route to PICTA, thinking of how much I hated the system and governors in particular, a suit appeared around the corner. It was a tall man, in his fifties. He had a high forehead with receding ginger hair that edged towards silver.

"Where are you heading so fast?" he asked.

"Who are you?" I responded curtly.

"I'm the Governing Governor. *Who are you?*"

"Someone being kept against their will," I threw back angrily, then kept on walking.

Governors were always coming and going, and Coldingley had just received a new one. In the meantime, I had filed an Interim Injunction at the High Court, citing the enactment of punishment as a result of the court case and occasions where my legal mail had been opened. This had principally occurred when I had been moved over to 'B' wing, with a few envelopes marked 'opened in error' - but how they could have overlooked the huge 'Rule 39 Correspondence' wording at the top of the envelopes was a mystery. The opening of legal correspondence was unlawful in and of itself, so the interim injunction called upon the court to order the prison to cease doing it. I also asked the court to expedite the final hearing, given that I wanted the best possible chance with the CCRC representations.

It wasn't long before I encountered the Governing Governor again, who introduced himself as Eoin Mclennan-Murray. I braced for a tirade of threats, but instead he spoke amicably.

"So you're the legal headache," he began, almost smiling.

I wasted no time in explaining how that had come to pass.

"But we have no control over the Court of Appeal," he objected, echoing Jassell.

I sighed. "It's not just that – you could have given me open conditions; you ignored the advice of probation about ROTL; you won't let me make proper legal representations with the CCRC; you keep opening my legal mail. Look, why not just transfer me to another prison?"

I thought he'd grimly nod his head, but instead there was a long pause.

"I've looked at your file. You've been to enough prisons."

"Fine," I replied in frustration. "Then you will just have more legal proceedings to deal with."

His whole demeanour changed and he dismissed me with a few words about "sensibly weighing up your options."

***

The light in B-111 had gone off again!

This time, however, I couldn't move.

It was something that had never happened before, like a great weight pressing down on my chest. My thoughts scrambled wildly, heart rushing, eyes wide. Something stirred in the dark – a form without edges, yet *there*.

I sprung up and managed to hit the cell light in one jump.

There was nobody. Nothing.

The cell was the same, whilst the wing was totally silent. It was one of the only occasions when I would have welcomed noise.

When unlock came, the initial relief soon changed to disgust. Blobs of spit and discarded fag ends peppered the corridor. There was meant to be a wing cleaner somewhere, but I never saw them. A few times the more hostile inmates scrutinised me, a couple of whom threw snide comments my way. As for the guy in the cell above, he expelled his excrement at greater frequency as the days passed. Because the glass in my window was partially broken, I made a make-shift paper barrier, stuck together with toothpaste, to prevent his waste splashing into the cell. It only half worked.

One time someone left a huge turd in the recess sluice, as if they had crouched there and done their business when being unlocked at night. It was *partly u*nderstandable – all the toilets were in a horrific state – but the resulting uproar lasted for hours. The same prisoners who had no problem in spitting everywhere were appalled by someone leaving a shit in the sluice. One went to each cell door, screaming: "you done a shit in the sluice?"

He came to mine, but I didn't bother engaging with him.

"Yo! Jackass, you done a shit in the sluice, you cunt!"

Angered, I swiftly hurled my foot against the door, causing a huge bang. "No. Fuck off, idiot!"

Any other response would have only been an invitation for all the bullies within earshot.

After a short pause he started hurling abuse and threats.

"All mouth!" I shouted back. "I'll see you in the morning!"

Violence in prison was no joke, and the last time it happened on B wing an ambulance had to be brought in. The victim, sliced up by a 'shiv', never returned.

In America, I remembered how another prisoner had shown me how to melt a plastic toothbrush and insert a blade from one of the prison-issue razors at the end. It didn't take long.

When the door opened in the morning I wore prison issue vest and shorts, pumped up by doing sets of push-ups, ready for anything. Sure enough, within minutes, someone came.

He was the scar-faced guy I had met when first coming onto 'B' wing.

"Be careful what you fucking say," he blurted.

I stood strong, keeping within easy distance of the shiv, but he didn't seem to have one himself. "What do you expect if you accuse me of shitting in the sluice?" I angrily retorted.

His fists were balled, and I stood ready to dodge. But instead, he took something from his waistband, flashing briefly under the fluorescent light.

I whipped down my own shiv from the shelf, holding the blade edge down.

"Shaun, don't get us locked up again," another prisoner drawled behind the half-closed door.

This was followed, to my surprise, by the spitter. "Yer nart wantin dis mans".

Shaun backed away, glaring. "Fucking bastard. I'll see you later." Then he stormed off.

Word got round that another altercation was brewing, and the obese biker came to my cell.

"That Shaun is a right cunt," he said. "What are you going to do?"

"Nothing," I replied. "It's his move."

The biker stepped a bit closer and spoke low. "You should

just report him."

"No way," I replied. "Prisoners should be supporting each other, working for the same thing. Everyone has a story," I said vaguely. Even as I said it, Shaun's face appeared.

He looked at the biker. "I want to talk to this guy in private."

I'd never seen the biker move so fast as he scuttled out.

"I was proper annoyed last night," Shaun started. "I won't tell you why – it wasn't the shit in the sluice. And the way you spoke to me, that fucking made me angrier. You think you're better than me?"

"No," I replied.

He looked into my eyes. "Good. You want to settle this then?"

"Sure."

He held out his hand, and I shook it.

I was still cautious, keeping a wary eye on his other hand and watching for the smallest flicker of movement.

Instead, he just opened the door and left.

The biker knocked a few minutes later. "You alright?" he asked.

"Yeah."

"What happened?"

"Nothing," I told him plainly.

He wiped a hand across his mouth. "Oh, right. Now, about this Sandra solicitor, has she done a class action before?"

Thus passed another day on B wing.

***

The PICTA job, at least, was still active. It offered a much needed escape from the wing, as well as a chance to converse with Gohil.

He thought my move to 'B' wing was a good thing.

"They've shot themselves in the foot," he observed. "And probably don't even realise it."

From the corner of my eye I noticed someone else walking over in our direction.

Gohil followed my gaze, muttering "oh, God."

Robby.

"What are you two conspiring about?" he began.

Gohil said something about urgently needing to complete preparation for a Cisco exam, leaving me alone with Robby.

After I mentioned the move to 'B' wing, he ended up going into a long diatribe to do with his probation officer. He told me she was refusing his release on 'spurious grounds' and, since he was doing an IPP sentence, no end lay in sight.

I sympathised, but, after ten minutes of hearing him talk non-stop, the sympathy was running out.

Finally he paused, taking off his glasses and frantically rubbing them against his blue prison t-shirt. "So what do you think of this prison?"

"Well, I've been in worse places. What annoys me most about prisons is how the public never see how they really are. I mean, I just read some article in a newspaper last week and it could have been written by someone who lived on another planet. How they can just -"

"I've come across some right barmy stuff," Robby interrupted. "In one prison, I remember that exercise was cancelled due to – a cloud. And you know, back in 1999, you remember there was an eclipse?"

I did indeed; I had seen it as a child.

"Guess what happened at HMP Elmley."

"They cancelled exercise?"

"No," he grinned. "They locked the whole prison down, all day, because they said the reduction in light increased the risk of escape. But that wasn't the crazy thing."

"Oh?"

"No. I remember asking an officer what was going on. He said 'an eclipse is forecast'. So I asked why they couldn't just do lock-down for an hour or so. The response to that was 'it could be late'. These are the kind of people who control our lives!"

I watched him return to doing computer work, remembering other incidents of crazed decisions I'd come across in custody. The 'exercise being cancelled because of a cloud' had happened to me several times, and in one place there was a sudden ban on bananas because security thought that inmates could get high by smoking the skins.

Later, Governor Mclennan-Murray arrived and beckoned me into Andy's office.

"I don't know what your experience of other governors has been like," he said, "but you will find I am reasonable and pragmatic. I've spent 30 years in the Prison Service, and I didn't join it to screw up people's lives."

The man was an enigma to me, considering my hatred of his rank.

"I want to work with you," he continued, "but at the moment you are working against me. All these legal cases – in the long run, they are going to get you nowhere."

I reminded him about the ROTL application that Governor Ballantyne had refused, giving me the impression I would get D Category instead, only for that to be refused too, and probation requiring ROTLs before they could support me going to open conditions. I also expanded on the way I was fighting a miscarriage of justice, adding that time in America had not been properly taken into account in accordance with the law. As for the conditions on 'B' wing, I described them as 'more fitting for a Third World country.'

"That's a lot of issues," he sighed. "I can't wave a magic wand and get all of them sorted. But if you drop this judicial review about computer access we can come to some arrangement."

Did he mean expediting my 'D' Category review or just granting me access to a computer? I didn't ask, because that judicial review was not for negotiation. I was committed to taking it right to a final hearing; to cave in would be to become a conspirator to injustice.

"I can see you care strongly about this issue," he remarked.

"But this is what I propose to you: you will get IT access for making representations to the CCRC, but not the ones where you are suing the Prison Service; I will get you moved back to E wing, and finally I will support a programme of ROTLs that will then allow you to move to open conditions."

It was an impressive list of promises, but there had to be a catch. "What do you want in return?"

"Good behaviour, no more pointless complaints, no more legal proceedings or encouraging other inmates to make proceedings, and a commitment to focusing on preparation for your release rather than making problems for the Prison Service."

"I can't drop the proceedings that have already started."

"Well, maybe some of them could be settled. Think about it."

Chapter 23: Lords and Labels

*'Justice must not only be done but should manifestly and
undoubtedly be seen to be done.'*

Lord Hewart

On 29th August, after a long Bank Holiday weekend, I was
loaded onto a GEOAmey van and taken, once again, to the High
Court of Justice in London. The Court was huge, with multiple
divisions, and judicial reviews were heard under the Queen's
Bench Division. It was the oldest judicial branch in existence,
going right back to the time when a person could take their case
to the ruling monarch. However, the last time a real monarch
actually sat there and decided on a case had been in 1318.

How beautiful was that Court, yet how dark was its workings.
Here, cases had been thrown out by unsympathetic judges, rulings
cast down upon those who simply sought justice but instead were
sent away empty handed. The majority of cases were spear-headed
by money. Claims in which millions of pounds were at stake were
decided every day. Rows of elite barristers and QCs strolled the
corridors, even as the High Court judges prepared to drive back to
their plush London apartments and country mansions.

My hearing was before Mr Justice Collins. I knew nothing
about him, but he was actually a Lead Judge and would later
decide on several prominent cases involving the Secretary of State
for Justice, striking some of Grayling's policies down as unlawful.

Three GEOAmey guards led me into the court handcuffed, only to be confronted by a frantic clerk.

"No, no, he can't come in here like that," the short man said.

"But we have been told not to remove the handcuffs," one of the guards said.

"He's an escape risk," the other added.

"No I'm not," I frowned. Escape was the last thing on my mind.

"No, no," the clerk echoed. "This judge will not allow it. You need to take the handcuffs off."

The guards glanced at each other, then back at the blazing eyes of the clerk.

The handcuffs were removed, but they stayed close beside me.

It looked like I had entered a lecture hall. It was packed – each row of benches occupied by a mixture of people in wigs and others in plain clothes. They all scrutinised me with mixed expressions, but my attention was directed at the suited man facing the court room. *Was that the judge?*

"You may be seated," he said casually. "Or, if you prefer, you can stand."

"Oh, thank you....Your Honour."

I knew the address had been wrong, but couldn't think of the right term. Nervously, I began a subdued summary of the application: how I was still being denied access to IT facilities and legal reference material; how the prison had enacted punishment out of revenge for my proceedings; how my legal correspondence was being interfered with.

The judge started addressing questions to someone behind me – presumably, the barrister for the Defendant. She stood up and spoke in an American accent.

"Oh, I'm not sure about that, M'Lurd," she responded when the judge asked why it costed me 10p for each side of photocopied paper.

"It does seem to me," the judge continued, "that the apparent blanket ban on access to IT facilities and printing is unlawful. But this hearing is for the Claimant's Interim Application, not the substantive one, and I note the Defendant has yet to file a Defence."

"No, M'Lurd," the barrister said, "and in fact we have not been served many of the documents referenced by the Claimant in his application."

I rose my hand.

"Mr Jackley?"

"Actually... My Lord, I have here a signed statement from a representative of the Defendant, proving the documents in question were served."

Over a week ago I had given some documents to the prison's litigation officer, Simon Farrow, but took the precaution of having him sign a note for proof of receipt. The court clerk scrambled forward, threw a piercing glance at one of the guards beside me, then handed over my note to the judge.

"It would appear the Claimant has affected service, going by this," the judge remarked.

"Yes," the barrister behind me said demurely.

"Nonetheless, it is difficult for me at the moment to order any kind of relief. What I will do, however, is expedite the full hearing for October this year, and to waive the judicial review fee for that hearing, to save the Claimant applying for fee remission. Mr Jackley, have you anything else to say?"

"Well, actually, your Lordship will be aware that there is some interference of my legal mail that has become of great concern."

"I saw that. Have you got any evidence to substantiate your claim?"

I pulled out some legal mail envelopes that had been marked 'Opened in Error', together with applications and complaints regarding the same matter. These were quickly scooped up by the clerk, who threw an even angrier glance at the same guard.

"It says opened in error," the judge said. "So does this one."

He paused, glaring at the barrister.

I glanced behind, seeing that she stood next to a short man with yellow hair - none other than Simon Farrow, Coldingley's 'litigation officer'.

"The opening of a prisoner's legal mail without them being present is something I regard seriously," the judge intoned. "I do fear, however, that it is somewhat separate from this case. Nonetheless, I hope the authorities at HMP Coldingley will take note that if legal mail of the Claimant's is being opened as submitted to me then it is unlawful. Has the Defendant anything to say about the matter?"

There was some whispered conversation behind me. "No, M'Lurd, the Defendant is not aware of the Claimant's legal correspondence being interfered with and denies the same. It may be the case, sometimes, that an envelope is opened in error by a member of staff, but I am assured that this would be accidental and rare."

"Very well. Let us hope such... accidents... will be prevented from occurring again, then."

It was his concluding point, and I was led from the courtroom and swiftly handcuffed again when exiting.

On the journey back, I realised all the spectators had probably been legal students and junior barristers, though why they chose to pick my hearing to take notes was unknown.

The GEOAmey van wound its way through London's streets. Never before had that city appeared as beautiful. The colour, the life, the grandeur... I was struck by it all; the amount of greenery; the people so young and free.

By the time I arrived back at Coldingley, it was evening association. Missing dinner was not an issue, though, since I plunged into writing an 'Extended Grounds' for the judicial review. The 'substantive hearing' had been expedited to just over a month away – much sooner than it would have otherwise been – and the judge's comments had drawn my attention to a few things that needed highlighting. My interim application may not have yielded any formal relief, and yet it had been far from a failure. I'd embarrassed the prison system, and the next time a legal letter arrived, I found myself being called to the staff office. As well as signing for it, I had to also confirm that the envelope was unopened.

***

Most prison wings sported a plaque that declared the Prison Service's so-called 'Statement of Purpose'. I glanced at the one facing the entrance of 'B' wing.

'...*to treat people with respect and decency...*'

It reminded me of the words engraved on the steps outside of HMP Dorchester.

All these plaques and notices were nothing but false images misleading the public, whilst conditions worsened across the prison estate. Nearly all mainstream news coverage was still about how good prisons were and, even when they were depicted badly, that got blamed on the conduct of prisoners themselves, rather than the structural shortcomings of the system.

Only those who have been in custody understand how it really is. To those inside, prisons are built upon the bricks and mortar of inefficiency, unfairness and irrationality – with the occasional half-hearted dollop of rehabilitation thrown into the mix, just in case others were watching. It was even doubtful if prisons complied with Article 10 of the International Convention on Civil and Political Rights, that: '*all persons deprived of their liberty shall be treated with humanity and with respect for the inherent dignity of the human person.*'

Was squashing two people into a 6 by 9 foot space designed for just one person, as at HMP Dorchester and so many other UK establishments, 'decent'? How about having someone defecate in the same space, whilst another person's excrement splashes in? If this was decency, then one might as well dig a hole and call it a house. As for rationality and fairness, it was about as twisted as a fairground ghosthouse. Every day, across the prison estate, arbitrary decisions were made on categorisation, IEP level and ROTL that were for all intents and purposes immune from challenge. Basic things, like accessing the library and spending time outdoors (albeit for 30mins walking around a concrete yard), could be cancelled without notice. The list went on and on. This is not to say there were exceptions – like the way prisoners were supported and funded to undertake distance learning courses – but these were akin to remnants from another age, which could be removed at any time with the stroke of a Minister's pen.

The courts had a responsibility to rectify this state of affairs, but I was about to see just how far their willingness would go.

∗∗

Less than a week after coming before Mr Justice Collins, they moved me back to 'E' wing. No longer did I have to tolerate banging music and shouting till beyond 1am, or the insidious pouring of excrement from the cell above. No longer did I awake at 3 or 4 am, sweating and afraid of something I could not see.

Now I still awoke around the same time, but solely because of an infection that had started just before I left. A fever swung from cold to hot in a matter of minutes. Somehow, I dragged myself onto exercise and went to PICTA, only to be sent back by Andy after I could barely stand up.

"You look terrible," he remarked – as did Gohil, holding a tissue in front of his face.

For days I stayed locked up, drinking as much ginger and lemon tea as possible. All healthcare could provide was paracetamol. Chomping on raw garlic cloves and ginger helped. Both were anti-bacterial and anti-inflammatory – once you got past the fiery taste. Then, when the fever returned, I resorted to 'The Bomb'. It was my last defence line: an evil concoction of chilli powder and salt, with chopped lemon, garlic and ginger, plus a liberal spoon of honey. Ginger and garlic were the only 'fresh vegetables' that could be purchased on the canteen. The recipe had been passed to me by Ady in Dovegate, who boasted that it was the cure for every type of prison lurgy. "The only other ingredient you need," he said at the time, "is whisky." Needless to say, the final addition lay beyond my reach.

I filled my plastic mug with the six ingredients and poured in hot water, letting it brew for a few minutes. Then I gulped the lumpy mixture down – wincing. It took several gulps, but eventually the mug was drained.

One week and twenty mugs later, I was well enough to attend PICTA.

The legal proceedings crept along, with Simon Farrow occasionally coming to provide documents from the Treasury Solicitor. He could often be short-tempered and rude, storming off at the slightest comment. One time he was insulted by another inmate on the wing, apparently due to his campish demeanour, which resulted in him meeting me at the PICTA workshop instead.

As for Governor Eoin Mclennan-Murray, he had a habit of going on random 'walkabouts'. He wasn't afraid to approach prisoners and to actually respond to their issues. Thanks to him, Coldingley introduced a 'New Ways of Working' regime, resulting in unlock being between the hours of 08:00-19:15, every day. He also expanded the number of work places, bringing in more outside companies where prisoners could earn bonuses through increased productivity. There even talk that 'B' wing was undergoing a 'refit', and the number of alarms started to decrease. I thought of what conditions were like elsewhere. Kramer, now at HMP Elmley, wrote of 'daily lockdowns', with ambulances arriving at the prison more frequently than G4S transit vans. Letters in *Inside Time* echoed the same.

The Treasury Solicitors threw their full weight against my judicial review, which required the drafting of further documents to counter their submissions. Whether the judge deciding on the case could plough through so much paperwork was doubtful.

"They will just look at your initial application and the T-Sols response," Gohil remarked one weekend. "You should focus on one or two key points – at the moment you are going everywhere," he added.

It was hard not to 'go everywhere', though. I cited precedents in America and quoted Articles in the International Covenant on Civil and Political Rights (an extension of the Universal Declaration on Human Rights).

Gohil sometimes looked deeply depressed, not bothering to shave, with dark patches sliding down from his eyes. "It's the CPS," he complained, "they are determined to prevent my appeal from getting heard."

There was a particular police office 'out to get him', apparently, after Gohil had made allegations of corruption.[12]

"And all these idiots are getting me down," he continued.

"Who?"

"All of them. That one across the landing, he was in here, and you know what he said? 'There's no smoke without fire'. Pah! I'm sick of it."

I sympathised. There was a general perception, both among the public and even prisoners themselves, that appeals against conviction and sentence were either doomed to failure or groundless. Either the system was seen as rigidly impassable, or infallible.

"Prisons are part of the justice system," I noted one day in PICTA, "yet at the moment they might as well be segmented from it. Fair and lawful treatment, access to the courts – if only as a matter of last resort, adherence to published policies and procedures... all these things are being cast aside."

I paraphrased Lord Justice Sedley, who had concluded:-

---

12   Years later his case was reported in the media, vindicating much of what he said.

'If the Rule of Law is to mean anything, it has to mean that the prison system is no less answerable to the courts than any other limb of state, both for how it serves and protects the public and for how it treats those in its custody.'

"You know," Gohil said, "you should really think about what I said about joining the legal profession. Did you write to the Law Society to ask them about whether they accept people with your type of conviction, like I said?"

I shook my head.

At this point Robby walked over.

"What is it with you and this Governor? Twice he's been in here talking to you."

"Yes," Gohil chided, "how come you get to see him more than me?"

"It must be all my legal proceedings. You know, he's actually a decent man. I've come across plenty of governors, and he outshines them all by far. Surely you've both noticed this prison has improved since he arrived?"

"Is this the same person who was moaning to me a few days ago?" Gohil laughed. "It's a pity I can't record that and play it back to you." He punched my shoulder lightly, then returned to his seat.

"So you are suing the prison," Robby smiled.

I had told him this before, but whether he had listened is another matter. Once he started up a conversation it could go on for some time, so I just smiled back, said "yes", and turned to look at my computer screen – pretending to be intensively dedicated to Cisco's programming.

"What is the case about?"

It was no use – I couldn't ignore him, so proceeded to provide a brief summary.

He nodded frantically, interjecting the odd 'ah', and for a moment it seemed I might escape his usual tirades.

I was wrong.

"You think they really care?" he blurted. "You really believe the courts would ever favour a self-representing prisoner's case?"

"Well, there are plenty of examples of prisoners winning legal cases against the system. Governor's decisions, even entire policies, have been struck down before. Some judges are good, and uphold justice, regardless of the power imbalance."

"Sure! Every now and then they throw a scrap of bone to give the appearance that the system isn't completely fucked. Usually it's to some guy with a big wallet and decent legal team behind them though, remember that!"

"Hmm. But there is a recognition, surely, that justice cannot just be cast aside. It is a principle too high and important."

"Justice," he scoffed. "It's nothing but an illusion. What do you think is justice?"

I paused, unsure how to answer. Talking to him was like playing a game of chess. But the answer became obvious once I looked away from his burning gaze.

"Justice is... fairness... balance... accountability."

"Yes," he replied softly. "And tell me, exactly, where would those things exist in the current British 'Justice' system?"

"They do exist," I argued, "to varying degrees."

"You see what I do not. Maybe you haven't fought long enough, like I have. Maybe you're just too young and naïve."

I frowned. What did he know of fighting against the system – someone who had only been to three UK prisons in the space of four years?

"I hope you win your case," he said. "But I'd be surprised."

"Well, I hope to surprise you, then."

"We'll see."

He started to walk away, then suddenly turned back to me, eyes wild.

"Look around you!" he blurted.

A few others turned in our direction.

"Okay, half of this lot are morons. But then, is that their fault? Maybe, maybe not. But for them and others, we all are here to sustain something! What do you think that is?! It's the same as your precious court system, the same as that governor you say is nice, the same as..."

At this point, Andy himself started to waddle over. Already I could hear him asking us to 'get back to work'. But he didn't need to – before he got too close, Robby loped back to his computer, and I went back to mine.

I stared at the screen. Robby's words were chaotic, but he conveyed exactly what Ady had told me at Dovegate. The prison system needed people to re-offend - for without prisoners, it would not exist. All those who depended on it for a livelihood – solicitors, barristers, judges, police officers, prison officers, probation – would be out of employment. But, perhaps more importantly, the system as a whole would be at a loss. For without a group to constantly stigmatise, how could it justify punitive laws and oppressive policies? Where would it be if people lost their fear for each other? In times of crisis and civil turmoil, who could be looked to as reprehensible scapegoats?

It needed prisons and those it incarcerated just as it needed crime. The society we lived in was not some enlightened, egalitarian utopia that sought to increase every citizen's happiness and wellbeing. Its sole priority was to preserve and uphold the status quo. Look deep enough and there were examples of that everywhere. The rich grew richer, and the poor were marginalised. Power and money always won, because they determined the rules. And thus the status quo endured.

For people like Robby, though, the costs of its endurance were high indeed. He was looking at an indefinite duration in prison, for a term that had already long elapsed, because he refused to 'play probation's games'. He adamantly spoke his mind, regardless of the consequences, arguing against anything he disagreed with.

They would never let him out; not whilst his IPP sentence was maintained. He would spend the majority of his productive years – if not his entire life – behind bars. Not for his offence – of breaking a restraining order – but because he spoke his mind. And for that he would be deprived freedom, a family, employment and outlets to contribute positively to others lives.

In essence, his sentence comprised a social and civic death.

***

Another summer receded, forever lost. I thought of a past no longer possible – not just my own, but that of lands far away, untouched by the same system, but now choked by it. Closed off as I was from the world, I also knew it was on the same trajectory I had left it five years ago. Through the unending greed of capitalism, it was being eaten up and destroyed. As beautiful as the world remained, how much longer would it last?

Sometimes I just wished to be a fleck of dew on a grass blade, reflecting the infinite sky. As a breeze caressed my brow on the prison's concrete yard, I longed to just float away with it, never to be captured or chained.

17 months remained. I knew, in the space of just a few, conditions could swing from relative tolerance to the deeper levels of hell. Sometimes – despite all that had happened and being within sight of release – I also thought of ending it prematurely. Without my mother, it would have already happened.

All these moves, cancelled visits and disappointments were taking a toll on her, too. I had not dared arrange a visit at Coldingley, for fear that yet another transfer would take place. '*We can meet when I get to an Open Prison*,' I last wrote, all too aware that the chances of getting to one were slim.

The only difference now was Eoin Mclennan-Murray. He still baffled me, and I didn't bring myself to trust him. Despite the Colemans, Swinburnes, Lloyds and McAllistors, most prison officials I encountered had proven themselves dishonourable and uncaring. 5 years of mostly being treated like a number – like a 'con' – cemented my perspective.

Even when Mclennan-Murray entered E wing with a young lady from the Howard League for Penal Reform, I thought it was some trick.

"This is Stephen," he said, introducing me.

She was interested in hearing about the judicial review and told me more about the Howard League, who campaigned for fair treatment in custody and a reduction in the number of young people going to prison. Sometimes they went so far as to defend individuals in cases through mounting proceedings of their own, although the capacity for 'interest groups' to launch judicial reviews was next on Grayling's target list.

Perhaps it was the huge escalation of cases: in 2001 there had been 5000, when now that number had more than tripled[13]. Or perhaps he just hated the idea of citizens having the capacity to hold officials such as himself to account, likening judicial review to *'a promotional tool for countless left-wing campaigners'* in one of his vitriolic *Daily Mail* pieces.

Akin to their response to the Legal Aid cuts, the legal profession was almost unanimous in its condemnation of Grayling's latest 'reforms'. Even some judges spoke out. There were street marches, critical articles in the more informed newspapers, a warning report issued by the Bingham Centre for the Rule of Law, and serious concerns raised by Parliamentary Select Committees. Did this change what Grayling wanted? No, he just watered things down a little. And the goal posts were made even narrower for those finding themselves in the unenviable position of completing a Form N461 (judicial review claim form).

Grayling also restructured the IEP system. He introduced a new 'Entry Level' tier for people who first came to prison – kind of in-between 'Basic' and 'Standard'. Moreover, prisoners could

---

13   In this respect the observation of Lord Justice Sedley may have some bearing: how 'the better government becomes, the less scope there will be for judicial review of it.'

be demoted by prison officers to 'Basic' with reduced checks and balances to prevent abuse. Effectively the IEP system could now be used as a means of explicit punishment (as well as rewards), but with none of the procedural safeguards of adjudications. The effect of being on 'Basic' was often worse than many of the punishments handed out through formal disciplinary proceedings. The IEP changes also resulted in prisoners being prevented from receiving stamps from family and friends, which effectively put a limit on how much mail could be sent out for those on 'Basic' (since they were only allowed £7.50 a week to spend in which to buy stamps from the canteen). A few heavy legal envelopes could easily exceed that amount.

The Prison Reform Trust issued a report titled 'Punishment Without Purpose', that concluded Grayling's IEP changes *'were in large part motivated by political considerations'*, noting how reduced standards of decency were fuelling increased incidents of suicide and self-harm[14].

But it was a particular aspect of Grayling's latest policy that proved his undoing: a ban on prisoners being able to receive books from family and friends. Suddenly, a swathe of journalists, campaign groups and even celebrities started to take notice. It would become known as the 'Prisoner Book Ban', despite Grayling's protests that books had not been specifically targeted. Actually, he was partly right: there was no ban on books, simply a blanket prohibition on prisoners receiving items from outside. Yet Grayling was no stranger to lies and misrepresentation, spouting blatant falsehoods like prisoners previously being allowed items of food and clothing from outside, which had never been the case. He wrote an open letter to the poet laureate, Carol Ann Duffy, stating he *'could not possibly allow prisoners to receive regular parcels from home and in doing so put in jeopardy the efforts of prison staff to keep drugs and other illicit materials out*

---

14   'Punishment Without Purpose' (2014), Prison Reform Trust, London.

of prisons'. No matter that such parcels were never allowed in the first place, and that the few items allowed in by staff were meticulously searched and X-rayed beforehand.

Did such politicians have a compulsive need to lie, or did they just think they were so powerful that it could never possibly affect them when found out?

That someone like Grayling could gain such power was scary. He not only presided over the Ministry of Justice but, as 'Lord Chancellor', over the courts as well. His very position was a paradox – a dangerous overlapping between the judiciary and the executive, with him being able to influence the selection and promotion of judges. Through his unique position, he was able to allow his personal views to change the very administration of the courts – something in prima facie breach of the Constitutional Reform Act. Despite all this, nobody was holding him to account.

Part IV: FORGING AHEAD

"I never saw sad men who looked
With such a wistful eye
Upon that little tent of blue
We prisoners called the sky."

'The Ballad of Reading Gaol', Oscar Wilde

Chapter 24: The World, Without Glass

2013 was a year that could have been sprouted from Venus' sulphuric mists and aged in a Martian sandstorm. Ejection from The Verne... the dungeons of HMP Dorchester.... an appeal that effectively failed... followed by more mishaps at HMP Coldingley. Thus, when the night of the 31st December became the 1st January 2014, I joined the few that banged on their cell doors, beating away the memories of the darkness that lay behind.

The only question was: what lay ahead?

Perhaps the most significant court hearing of my life was around the corner. On a personal level, it was nothing compared to the sentencing and appeal hearings, but on a wider basis it could mean the difference between establishing a structure of access to justice, or letting the same dark system take its course.

The governor, Eoin Mclennan-Murray, seemed to be on a mission to surprise me. Not only did he pay a visit to my cell one day, spending a good hour talking and even having some biscuits and tea that I had made, but his words might have come from a dream.

"I am willing to grant you a ROTL for your court hearing."

I glanced at the cell door, just in case he was telling a joke for the benefit of Simon Farrow.

"And I will be recommending that you be given 'D' category."

How was it possible for such a convivial, rational man to hold power in the system? I pondered. Not only was he the governing governor, but he also held presidency of the association that represented all governors across the UK. I heard he'd additionally tried to assist Gohil with his transfer to open prison, whilst getting a lifer who had been in prison since the age of 17 a job in Reception to help demonstrate his trustworthiness. He seemed to *want* people to progress and be given the best chance of re-entering and resettling in society.

What made the governor's stance all the more exceptional was the political climate, which strongly favoured increased punitivity, as overseen by Grayling.

Two weeks after receiving this news came an unannounced lock-down. I stayed in bed a little later, thinking it would be one long day otherwise, but just on the threshold of sleep a guard opened the door.

"Mr Jackley!" he boomed. "You are required to attend an MDT."

MDTs were Mandatory Drug Tests, and I'd only been called for four before, across the entirety of my sentence. Maybe it had something to do with my forthcoming ROTL, yet such tests were meant to be random.

"Give me a few minutes," I told the guard as I got out of bed.

"I'm giving you enough time to get dressed, no more!" the guard shouted.

Tired and annoyed, I put on some clothes and shoes.

Behind me, the cell door closed and locked.

I assumed the guard had been called away for some emergency incident, but just to make sure I pressed my 'cell bell' and spoke to another guard over the intercom. "You've been put on report," he said.

"What! Why?"

"You refused to attend your MDT."

"What are you talking about? I'm ready now – the officer just left."

As indicated before, certain screws took exception to my complaints and legal proceedings. They didn't like the idea of a prisoner who acted 'above his station' and who did not 'accept his sentence'. Undoubtedly, they had heard about my forthcoming ROTL and chance at finally getting to an Open Prison. The presence of the new Governor had held them back from outright victimisation, but now they could claim I'd 'refused to attend a MDT'. The consequences of that were far more serious than any incident that led to me receiving an IEP warning. It didn't matter that no refusal had actually taken place – an officer's word would always be trusted above that of any prisoner.

So much for 2014 being better than 2013! Again, just when a break presented itself, the chance got swiftly snatched away again. My forthcoming ROTL would be cancelled, and with it the progression to 'D' Category. I would remain in closed conditions till my last day in custody.

Fuck them, I thought. They could throw me into segregation, transfer me to another prison, and take away all my puny prison privileges, because none of it really mattered.

Only freedom, the life that had been taken away, and my mother, had any sense of meaning.

They held the adjudication just two days later in a room on the Segregation Unit. As soon as I entered, I saw Officer Spong – an especially hostile screw - who swiftly put me in a Segregation cell.

"I hope your new room is to your satisfaction," he gloated.

The adjudication was heard by Governor Stobart, who I immediately asked to recuse herself.

"What?" she said.

"I request you recuse yourself, and let another governor take this adjudication, because I think you are biased."

She laughed. "I'm not going to 'recuse' myself. I make fair decisions, and I will make one in your case."

Then the officer who said I'd refused an MDT gave a brief statement, which I questioned. He didn't look at me when answering, instead staring ahead at the wall.

"Right, I've had enough of your questioning," Stobart said after a few minutes.

"As for the Prison Service regulations," Officer Spong started, then started citing the relevant protocol about prisoners being required to attend MDTs, as if I disputed it.

Stobart coughed. "Thank you, Officer Spong. Mr Jackley can be removed for a few minutes whilst I make my decision."

"Can I just ask why there is no tape recorder of this hearing?"

"We never have tape recorders for adjudications," Stobart said.

This was different from America, where equivalent disciplinary proceedings were always recorded.

Spong put me back into the cell, slamming the door with extra force. So this would be my new home for the next couple of weeks.... or months.

If they thought I'd be daunted by the prospect of segregation time, they were in for a surprise. Five months in the SSCF Hole of America was worth triple that here.

The door unlocked and a new officer appeared. "The Governor's ready," he said.

I wondered where Spong had gone – he wasn't even with Stobart. I'd expected him to be there, grinning over her decision and relishing the chance to strip-search me when formally moved to Seg.

Stobart's face was impassive. "My decision," she began, "is that you are guilty."

I blinked expressionlessly.

"Your punishment is seven days spent in segregation – suspended for 3 months. You will get a formal statement of this decision soon."

I hardly believed it until being led back to E-wing. Perhaps Stobart had spoken with the Governing Governor beforehand, or at least knew of his intervention in my case. Of all governors, she was renown as one of the harder ones when it came to adjudications.

As for my 'Basic' status, it did not result in me having to leave 'E' wing again and indeed I was placed back on 'Standard' only three days after the adjudication hearing.

More importantly, the planned ROTL on 5th February had not been cancelled. Even after being told this by three different officers, a part of me was still unsure if they were lying.

***

The gates slid open, inch by inch, and I was greeted by....

The World!

It had been over 68 months. 2064 days. In all that time, I'd been fettered, closely guarded, or trapped behind walls and fences. The light dazzled, with every colour sparkling, and the air carried a thousand different scents.

I walked tentatively out onto the street - a caged animal hesitating in the face of freedom after years of captivity. Officer Byrne was there as an escort, but he wore civilian clothes. Rather than detesting his presence, I felt reassured by it.

"So when was the last time you were out on the streets?" he asked.

I told him.

"Long time. You'll get used to it, soon enough."

We went to a bus stop and waited around 15 minutes. All around there was something to see – even the crisp packet drifting alongside the curbing entranced me. I had some money given in Reception – around £35 – but when it came to paying the driver the coins felt strange. They clunked out of my hand awkwardly, and the driver pushed most of them back.

"Don't forget your ticket!" he called, after I got half-way down the aisle.

Some of the other passengers glanced up, most of them being elderly. A young man boarded a bus with an older one close to a prison: did they realise I was a prisoner?

The thought was embarrassing. When we arrived at the train station, I asked Mr Byrne to buy my ticket.

"Alright then, but next time you have to do it," he said, taking the £20 note from my hand.

We boarded the next train bound for London, finding a seat behind two female students. I noticed a lot of things: people constantly using mobile phones, which were different from what I remembered; the scents of aftershave and perfume; the random announcements about reporting any suspicious behaviour. Then there was the speed – everything was faster. It wasn't just the train, but the cars, and people themselves. Several times I needed to stand back and let them rush past, sticking close to Mr Byrne.

After a little small talk, he grabbed a newspaper, which reminded me of the legal paperwork I had in a bag. We read through our respective interests until the train arrived at Victoria.

Once again, the sheer haste of people led to me walking in Mr Byrne's shadow, right to the surging throng before the Underground. It was just past 10:30, but to me it seemed like rush hour. And yet, slowly, I remembered. I had been here before, alone and confident. Then the city had been like so many others – from Bangkok to Perth to Barcelona. Now it was a place of wonder, trepidation and curiosity. A few times Mr Byrne glanced at me, and once he took a phone call. "Yes, everything is okay. He's still with me, behaving well."

We alighted from Temple underground station and walked up to The Strand. Cars zoomed past and beeped; huge double decker buses loomed down upon me. And there, up ahead, was the imposing architecture of the High Court of Justice, except this time I entered like everyone else. After passing through some metal detectors, my eyes widened at a huge hall, with spiralling columns that rose up like trees into a stone sky.

It was like entering the grand hall of Moria.

"The court room is this way," Mr Byrne said, after speaking with someone at the Reception desk.

I paused, still marvelling at the cold beauty of this place, as two barristers floated past with robes trailing along the patterned marble.

We ascended a flight of stairs, passing through sets of doors into a long hallway evenly spaced with desks. At the far end I saw a familiar face: Simon Farrow. He was conversing with the barrister I'd seen at the hearing six months ago.

"Glad to see you made it, Stephen," he smiled. "This is Jessica Radke, from the Treasury Solicitor Department, who I believe you have exchanged many letters with."

Jessica came forward and shook my hand. "It is nice to meet you after so long."

Then it was the barrister's turn. "Thank you for providing your Skeleton Argument well in advance," she said, smiling.

Such was their friendliness that I almost forgot that these were the same people who had kept me up many nights trying to find ways to counter their arguments.

We filed into a court room and I took a position within a few metres of the barrister on the same row of benches.

The judge entered, a Mrs Justice Andrews. She was slightly overweight, with a bouffant of red hair.

I rose after she had made a short introduction, smoothing down my suit. The case was mine to present, and I gradually went through the grounds for judicial review. At times it was difficult, like navigating rocky rapids, but at other points the current was smooth. The judge occasionally interjected a few questions, which I did my best to answer. As she made notes from the bench, she sometimes nodded her head and said 'yes' – which, if anything, threw me off track a little. To present one's case in court was no small matter, least of all before a High Court judge about a matter that would have an impact on tens of thousands of people across the country for many years ahead.

Mrs Justice Andrews called for an adjournment before the barrister presented the Defence. I got a sandwich with Mr Byrne in a nearby café - with each bite, it was like an explosion of tastes.

On return to the court room, I felt confident.

But the barrister knew what she was doing. I wasn't sure how many other cases she had defended, but followed a carefully subscribed trajectory: presenting a background, then a complex interweaving of case law and prison regulations. The submissions were inevitably contentious, and I struggled to keep pace with noting down my objections. She relied on many things, but essentially claimed that I had not followed the 'right procedures' in applying for an 'Access to Justice' laptop and that there were 'technological workarounds' that meant no effective blanket ban to printing legal material actually existed. On top of that, she placed great emphasis on the fact that I had actually been allowed to use a computer for my CCRC proceedings (thanks to the Governor).

Mrs Justice Andrews appeared to accept all the points made by the barrister, although she occasionally asked questions. Then it was my turn, but there were so many things to cover that it was hard to keep on top of it all, especially when the judge interrupted with questions that then led the barrister to respond. I spoke too fast and without the benefit of extensive legal case law to refer to.

The judge retired for a short while, then came back into the court. "This is a case brought by Stephen Jackley, a serving prisoner at HMP Coldingley," she began.

I listened as she rambled through her long judgment. She attached great weight in the way HMP Coldingley had eventually granted me access to IT facilities for my criminal proceedings – this input, it seemed, tilted the case substantially in their favour.

However, she did make some observations around the photocopying costs being too high and the lack of adequate access to the library to do legal research. These were just general points; they did not have any direct bearing on her judgment.

I saw it coming at least 15 minutes before she concluded. "As such, I cannot find in favour of the Claimant and must dismiss this judicial review."

"No costs are sought, M'Lady," the barrister said a few minutes later.

"No. Well I am sure you will be somewhat disappointed by this outcome, Mr Jackley, but I would like to commend you highly in the manner of your representations, which have altogether been very impressive."

Without hesitation I thanked her and asked for permission to appeal.

"In order to grant permission, I need you to provide some grounds," she said.

I outlined the wider public interest elements of the case in the wake of Legal Aid cuts, and the fact that some elements around Article 6 of the European Convention on Human Rights needed to be taken into account.

"The Claimant has asked for permission to appeal," the judge said. "It is my decision to refuse permission, but of course you are welcome to take the case to the law lords at the Court of Appeal. The normal time to lodge an appeal is 30 days, but bearing in mind your situation I will grant a 90 day extension, taking the deadline to April. Would that be enough, or do you need longer?"

"Yes, that should be enough, My Lady. Thank you."

The judge rose and bowed, with the barrister and myself reciprocating, then left.

They were all friendly afterwards – too friendly. The barrister and solicitor even offered to buy me a drink 'in the Court restaurant', to which Mr Bryne coughed and reminded them I was due back at the prison by 5pm.

Simon Farrow ended up coming back with Mr Byrne and me. He was in jovial spirits, cracking jokes on the train about random things. "You did well," he told me at one point.

I just frowned.

"No, really. I couldn't represent myself in court. You fought a good battle – and at one point I really thought we had lost."

"It's a pity you didn't. This case was not about me, like you know. Now I am obliged to appeal it."

"This one is a real anomaly," he said to Mr Byrne.

"Don't I know it," the prison officer replied.

"I think the Governor is right about you, though. You are willing to fight for others. But do you really think prisoners should have computers and... 'law libraries'? Not everyone is like you, Stephen. Most would just abuse such facilities, and others wouldn't know how to use them."

"It works in America," I pointed out. "If people cannot access free legal representation through solicitors, they should at least be given the *opportunity* of representing themselves properly. Without access to justice then there might as well be no justice to begin with."

"Well, whatever. We won; you lost – you need to accept it."

The two prison staff then commenced talking openly about others at the prison and their next holidays, leaving me to make some notes for the appeal.

***

As I worked on the appeal, wider changes were happening outside. Not from Grayling, this time, but from the climate.

Flooding not seen in over 100 years spread havoc across the country, with whole towns and villages being evacuated. Images of people paddling along former roads flashed across the TV.

I looked up from the paperwork and sighed. What did they expect? Pump unprecedented levels of CO_2 into the atmosphere, raze rainforests, pollute seas and lands... there's going to be consequences. And the worst was yet to come. Severe weather is one thing, but what about more general changes like rising sea levels, weakening of the Gulf Stream, melting permafrost? Kiss goodbye to London; the UK would slide into the conditions of a 2nd world nation, with justice and democracy being submerged well before.

12 years ago I knew this. And 7 years ago I began the path that seemed the best way to try and change it.

I thought back to the voluminous waves heaving across the red sea that crashed across Jacob's Ladder Beach in Sidmouth. To feel the wind sweeping across the miles of raging water; to taste the salt of its spray. Did I ever imagine, in the storms of that childhood, what was happening now? Not just the world shuddering to man's excess, but being in prison, at 27 years old, with 6 years of hell preceding my footsteps.

No – not once. I thought of spaceships and wondrous journeys; of finding love and companionship. Life was like sailing a rainbow back then, although the bright colours were all too often mixed with rain. Now... what? I could not say it was like sailing through a storm, but more like drifting through a pitch-black tunnel of turpid waters. A light shone ahead, even so, and it was drawing closer.

I had not seen the Governor for over a week after the hearing, but I still trusted he would keep his word. I'd left the prison and come back of my own free will – nobody could deny that I could have just run. What would the person who had thought so longingly of escape three years ago make of this? Had I become diminished in some way? Either that, or I'd become more sensible. Running would've achieved nothing but swift recapture and longer years in hell. No, the idea of escape was simply that – an idea, long since forgotten. There was no logical reason to prevent me from going to Open Conditions.

And yet, on 21st February, I was told that my recategorisation review decision resulted in remaining 'C' Category.

Had the Governor been playing a game, keeping me sweet with promises and pleasantries to put a cap on the legal proceedings? Now that the main case was lost, could he just walk away smiling?

Maybe a battle was lost, but the war wasn't against them over. And outside, a much larger one was brewing, with Russia rolling tanks into Crimea. The Ides of March, indeed.

Then, one day, a letter arrived under my door from the Governor:-

'I have previously indicated to you that my view is that you do not present the risk that others feel you do and since this is a matter of judgement I am minded to re-categorise you to D and retain you at HMP Coldingley. Whether I am able to move you on to an open prison will very much depend on what progress you make here and what plans you make for resettlement.'

He went on to note, in regards to my ROTL applications I had lodged to use a public library for legal research, that such a thing would be counter-productive in 'the current political climate'. Further litigation, he observed, would only result in the sharing of information with 'Policy Leads' (at the Ministry of Justice), whose decisions would never really be to my advantage.

The Governor was asking me to work with him again – ceasing further litigation and developing a resettlement plan. It was a fair request. I only reminded him that the 'legal access' case was not yet over, and nor could I drop it.

There was a bit of a setback to this appeal when, a month after being posted, the court returned the entire bundle of documents on the basis that a single box on one of the twenty-two pages had not been ticked. This meant having to resend it, by which time it would probably exceed Mrs Justice Andrews' deadline. Consequently I had to apply for permission to serve outside of time, which demanded a whole new set of grounds by itself. Such is the way the British courts function.

***

The Governor remained true to his word. On 14th April he informed me that I'd been downgraded to 'D' Category and due to start work with the outside gardens team the following week.

"I am taking a big risk on you," he said. "This decision is entirely under my discretion as Governor, and nobody else's. If you don't come back here next week I will have to answer some very serious questions."

"You don't need to worry about that," I assured him. "Thank you for all you have done."

He nodded. "I'll check on how you're doing next week."

Thus it was, four days after Good Friday, I left the prison again.

It was strange. They gave me a special hi-vis jacket, but aside from that I could have been a regular member of the public. The trees had sprouted into renewed green since my High Court visit; the sun felt warmer. There were three others working with me, who spent most of their time in a small portacabin. On the first day, they showed me the area we could all walk around – outside the prison wall and parking lot. Our job was to keep this area free of rubbish, clean the visitors' waiting area, and attend to any other duties required by the gardens department.

A small pond lay just outside the perimeter, which the prison had created a few years ago with local school children, along with 'bug hotels' consisting of wood piles. I smelled the trees and grass, heard the birds singing; all the things I had missed for 6 years. On the edge of the treeline I dug small holes without being told to, planting acorn seeds that had fallen like a dense carpet between the branches. Maybe some of them would grow into oaks.

At the end of the day, we walked back through the gatehouse, to get a 'pat down' search by staff in Reception. Officer Spong was working there, and immediately picked me out for a 'routine strip search'. I wondered if he was a closeted gay, or merely delighted in being a sadist. He was around my age, with close-cut black hair and a slight limp. Would he attempt to 'plant' something on me in the search? Such things could be easily done. But on this occasion he appeared content just to sneer and exaggerate how far I had to extend my tongue.

I figured his provocations would only worsen, so remembered some advice Geoff at Parkhurst had once told me.

"If you come across a sadist screw, and can't challenge it, the best

thing you can do is be nice. Smile, even compliment them. You'd be surprised at the results."

So the next time I encountered Spong I just did that, smiling and asking how his day had been.

Amazingly, from that day onwards, the provocations stopped entirely.

Whereas such mendacities might have been a source of temporary concern, one day I returned to my cell and found something of much greater importance. After waiting since June last year, the CCRC had written back with their decision.

They had refused my application.

Freedom of Information requests I later submitted revealed just how few cases they referred back to the Court of Appeal: of 1,450 applications received by them in 2013, only 31 were referred. Was the fact they only referred 2% of cases indicative of the remainder being without any merit? I doubted it. They applied a number of stringent tests before referring a case, one of which was labelled the 'real possibility test'. Effectively this was where the CCRC tried to predict what the Court of Appeal would do: where they predicted a lower than 60% chance of a referred case being successful, they did not refer it. In the words of Michael O'Brian (who spent 11 years in prison for a crime he didn't commit), the 'real possibility' test was nothing more than *'second guessing what the Court of Appeal might do, acting as judge and jury'*. O'Brian had actually been exonerated by the CCRC, yet he later reflected that it 'had changed beyond all recognition' and 'become a spent force'.[15]

In my own case, they had refused to refer it back to the Court of Appeal because the material I had brought up 'was not new' – despite it not being considered by the court. They applied their clairvoyant ability to predict an 'unrealistic prospect of success'

---

15   Michael O'Brian (2012) 'Prisons Exposed', Y Lolfa Cyf (Cardiff).

– something which was for the Court to determine. Their report used weighted language and at other times contradicted itself. Some grounds I had raised, such as the manner in which the prosecutor submitted his Skeleton Argument, were just ignored. As for my time spent in America awaiting deportation, those two months had been flicked away by the CCRC's speculation that the sentencing judge had already somehow taken it into account, despite never mentioning it. In doing so, there was a prima facie breach of the Criminal Justice Act.

My first course of action was to draft a lengthy appeal letter. It was the beginning of a bitter two-year battle that culminated in a judicial review, and yet I discovered that the CCRC is a law unto themselves, with each and every judicial review against them – including those backed by QCs – failing. The courts gave them absolute deference, deeming their decisions flawless.

First the Supreme Court, then the CCRC – and between it a judicial review that should have succeeded. I was getting a sense of why some people just left society altogether and why others jumped off bridges and took overdoses. Were all mankind's systems really nothing more than houses of cards, professing to uphold standards and values that, in reality, were nothing more than facades? And, if justice could not be found in the courts, then where could one hope to find it?

This game I had unwittingly been forced to play a part of spanned every structure, every institution, and every role. Those who moved the pieces were never seen – the richest and most powerful – just as the money they funnelled indirectly to their figureheads (who people thought made the decisions) could never be traced. Meanwhile, the 'law abiding citizen' moved through their lives believing lies, rewarded with the illusion of money. They accepted the scraps thrown down to them from their wealthy masters like mangy dogs, not realising that if they only Stood Up and United, then their very dreams would be possible.

JUST TIME

Few could see it. Few even really cared. They were drugged by TV and sugar; by fake entertainment and promises as empty as the words '*I promise to pay the bearer on demand...*'

Those who took a different path were either outcasts or criminals.

And yet: why couldn't things be just a little different? Why couldn't the CCRC just refer all cases of merit? What would be the harm?

I thought back to all the people I'd come across who received longer than necessary sentences and whose very convictions seemed suspect.

No, of course the CCRC was not in the position to do that. They'd soon be shut down by the body that funded them – the Ministry of Justice, overseen by Grayling. And this man wasn't finished with his wrecking trip, either.

***

I had worked on the outside gardens for a solid two weeks when a new order filtered down from the Ministry of Justice.

Henceforth, it declared, all High Risk prisoners not in Open Conditions will no longer be eligible for ROTLs.

Apparently several had absconded, and Grayling wanted to show he was 'protecting the public', despite the system functioning for decades before his arrival.

Generally all those sentenced for 'violent' offences – of which robbery was classed under – were put on 'high risk to the public'. In the eyes of probation, this risk level could never change until I was released, regardless of what I did. My latest probation officer, Paul Hadaway, made that very clear.

Previously, I could have challenged my risk level with a solicitor, but now Grayling's Legal Aid changes meant that the only way to do that was through self-representation – without access to IT facilities or legal reference material. I was not alone; one of the other outside workers also had been put as 'high risk', and he couldn't leave the prison on ROTL either. Likewise, there were prisoners across the estate who could no longer challenge their recategorisation levels, preventing them from progressing, which in IPP and lifer cases stopped them from being released.

That bald-headed psychopath who headed the Ministry of Justice knew what he was doing: by cutting off Legal Aid first, he had made it nigh impossible for those subject to his later policies to challenge them. He probably didn't count on the fact that there would be some, like me, who would represent themselves – but then again, what did it matter? A self-representing prisoner, with a pen and paper... when even people outside of prison, who had access to computers and the law reports, could barely run the gauntlet of representing themselves? The picture must have made him laugh. Most prisoners could barely write properly, let alone fill in overly complex court forms and manage even more convoluted legal processes. And if some did – well, the judges would look down upon these upstarts and smash them back down. Yes, Grayling was no idiot.

I was not giving up, though. The Governor's hands were tied, but mine weren't. Despite all the knockbacks, I drafted another judicial review – this time against the new ROTL policy. Meanwhile, I was sent to work on the *inside gardens,* which was nothing compared to my previous role. It largely involved strimming and picking up the detritus thrown from prisoners' windows. The grass grew tall and green there for a reason: it got plenty of nitrogen. It was, again, a no-win scenario. The new probation officer, similar to the last, would not approve open conditions without me being further 'tested' on ROTLs. Yet, thanks to Grayling, I could not access ROTLs without being in an open prison.

I resigned myself to spending the remainder of my sentence at HMP Coldingley.

Then, on the 26th June, the Governor visited me at the inside gardens shed. "I've managed to get you a transfer to Standford Hill," he announced.

"Really?" I almost shouted. "That's great!"

"I had to pull a few strings. Luckily I know the governor there, and she owes me a favour."

I was so happy I could have hugged the man.

"Thank you, I will remember what you've done. I don't know how to repay it."

"Just focus on your resettlement and don't come back to prison," he said. "I don't want to see you again – but I mean that in a good way."

As he walked away to speak to someone else, a weight lifted from my shoulders. Yes, there was uncertainty ahead, but almost for the entirety of my sentence, reaching Open Prison had been the goal. It was the doorstep of freedom – a place where I could actually pursue plans for release.

Gohil had written to me two weeks before from Standford Hill (he had got transferred there, thanks to the Governor's intervention in his case). The prison, he said, was very good – there were no locked doors, no walls, no fences…

Kramer, too, had written similar observations, having managed to get there a month ago. Now it was my turn to enter the open estate, with only ten months to go until release.

Chapter 25: Standford Hill

'Where lies the final harbour,
whence we unmoor no more?'

Moby Dick

On the 28th June, I arrived on the Isle of Sheppey in Kent. The first thing I noticed when leaving the van was the lack of walls and fences. Reception staff went through my property, giving me everything I had been allowed at Lowdham Grange, and then I was greeted by a prison officer and his orderly.

"Welcome to Standford Hill," the officer said.

I followed them up a road lined with flower beds to 'A' wing, induction. It resembled a contemporary prison wing inside, except there were no bars on the windows and all the doors were without locks.

Kramer enthusiastically greeted me outside. He looked much healthier.

"You're in for a treat here, Stevie," he beamed.

Standford Hill had a regime where prisoners were always unlocked, albeit each wing was closed between 9pm-8am. There were expansive grounds, a gym that could be accessed every day, and even a swimming pool. Originally a Royal Air Force station in World War Two, it now housed around 400 prisoners.

"On weekends you can hire mountain bikes and cycle around," Kramer said. "There's a few dodgy screws, and you have to wait 3 months before going out on ROTL, but apart from that it's the bee's knees."

"Just keep your litigation and complaints in check," the orderly said quietly. "That prison officer who greeted you has been told to keep an eye on what you do. Apparently you've been taking cases to High Court judges?"

Kramer burst out laughing. "I was in Elmley three weeks ago," Kramer said, "and they practically waved me goodbye with all the claims they had to deal with."

Both Standford Hill and Elmley prisons were integrated into the 'Sheppey Cluster', along with nearby 'B' Category HMP Swaleside. The conditions at Elmley had deteriorated rapidly under Grayling, according to Kramer. "Lock up every day due to assaults or staff shortages, hardly any work, people being dragged out to Seg – it's the opposite of this place."

I was just relieved to finally get to an open prison. After being sentenced, I envisioned coming to one roughly two years before my release - the normal eligibility for well-behaved prisoners - but now it was less than half of that.

In England, there were just a handful of open prisons, with the first being built in 1933. They were modelled on the premise of penal reformer Sir Alex Paterson, that 'you cannot train a man for freedom under conditions of captivity'. However, times had changed. Now the population consisted of people on short sentences, many of whom had been to prison before, because this group generally had a lower 'risk' than long-termers. Measurement of 'risk' was not about likelihood of reoffending, but rather on how risky a prisoner was *perceived* by probation to the general public based on their offence. An open prison will not get the blame if someone reoffends on release, but if a prisoner absconds it is a totally different matter. That is why reoffending is not a factor in considering suitability for open conditions.

The media had played its part in changing the system, with a chain of stories about 'rapists and murderers' who had 'escaped' from 'holiday camp' open prisons. Grayling, ever courting the right-wing tabloids, quickly put pressure on governors to avoid taking on 'risky' prisoners, i.e. those convicted of 'serious' and 'violent' offences – the very ones who would have been given long sentences. It did not matter that I had never been in prison before, that my chances of reoffending were assessed as very low, that my custodial behaviour was generally good, and that I had a medical condition which could reasonably be assessed to increase the need for gradual reintegration.

Without Eoin McLennan-Murray's intervention, I would have spent the rest of my sentence in closed conditions. No ROTLs would have been given either. Re-entering society would have been a short, sharp shock, likely causing me difficulties with adjusting. Backed up by the reports that overflowed with descriptions of someone who was an 'extremist', an 'escape risk' and 'violent' – with nothing to prove otherwise – my new probation officer would have easily pressed the recall button, for me to spend another 6 years in custody.

But someone with power intervened, and a new course was unravelling.

Despite the relative freedom I had experienced at The Verne, together with the brief period of ROTLs at Coldingley, getting used to Standford Hill took time. The extensive grounds included a small grove of trees, where rabbits hopped beneath the branches. Most unusual was the 1 ½ mile walk around the prison perimeter, which required getting special yellow bibs from the gym. Walking through those fields was like returning to the countryside of my Devonshire home, not seen for almost 7 years.

Kramer managed to get me a job at the 'Resettlement Office' – effectively working as an orderly, helping others with their resettlement plans. A 'Business Ventures' course in Education took up the other half of my week and allowed me to create a detailed plan for a social enterprise idea. The tutor was very relaxed, bringing in online material she had printed for the class because internet access was prohibited.

It turned out that Gohil had been transferred a few days before I arrived at Standford Hill – something to do with the police. Such authorities had immense power, alongside probation.

***

It didn't take a lot to be moved from Standford Hill. The slightest misbehaviour and they just showed up at a prisoner's cell, handcuffed him, then literally marched over to HMP Elmley. It was down the road, with its high walls serving as a warning for all of us.

In the first weeks, not a day passed when I worried that I'd be subject to the same treatment. My behaviour was impeccable – including refraining from 'generating paperwork' – but who knew what policy Grayling would next introduce? Maybe he'd say that, as well as ROTLs, all 'high risk' prisoners should now spend the entirety of their sentences in closed establishments? Or perhaps Paul Hadaway would influence the prison to transfer me. This feeling of insecurity stopped me, once again, from arranging a visit with my mother. And, on 8th September, it seemed I had made the right choice.

A GEOAmey van came to Reception, and they ordered me to board it. They told me it was related to a hearing at Guildford County Court, about the Coldingley sanitation claim - but that had been settled in the wake of Governor Mclennan-Murray's actions. I told them this, to no avail. On top of that, I was ordered to pack all of my belongings and take them to Reception, which could only mean a one-way trip.

The four hour drive to Guildford was painful. Nobody else came with me. What other prison waited to squeeze away the small steps I had taken to prepare for release?

At the court, I waited another hour in the holding cell before a female guard appeared.

"Van's here for you," she said.

"So I was brought here for some fake hearing just to be transferred to another prison?"

She frowned. "What are you talking about? Oh... no, there was a mistake. You're going back to Standford Hill."

Even as the van headed back in the same direction, I wasn't sure whether to believe her.

"This kind of thing happens a lot," she told me, passing yet another packet of crisps under the door. "One prisoner got taken to court twice in the same week. He didn't even go in front of a judge."

No hearings, no actual reason to travel hundreds of miles for thousands of pounds – just another quirk of the system's inefficiencies.

Despite the 8-hour round journey, relief and gratitude overcame me when being let off the van at Standford Hill.

A few days later, my new probation officer paid a visit. I was taken to see him by the resettlement governor, John Coccia. Apparently they had both spent a good amount of time talking beforehand. Coccia was actually the husband of the Governing Governor, whilst many other members of staff were related to each other – something quite common in prisons.

Beside the resettlement governor stood a short man in his forties, who squinted at me despite wearing glasses. "Good to see you, Mr Jackley," Hadaway said.

I was initially polite, until he started spouting absurdities about my 'risk of escape'. He ostensibly had serious concerns I would do a runner, adding that my move to open conditions had also been opposed by the police.

"I've been here for three months, Mr Hadaway. And before that I was getting ROTLs from Coldingley. If I wanted to escape, it would have happened by now."

"There's also your distorted thinking," he went on. "In my view, all your legal proceedings just parallel your offending behaviour, and are indicative of higher risk."

"Let me get this straight. You're saying drafting civil claims that get heard by judges as serious matters is like robbing a bank?"

I had heard about how some probation officers liked to 'push buttons'. Indeed, the encounter with Deborah Benson at HMP The Verne was still fresh in my mind. But I could not let such ignorant comments just slip past.

Hadaway made clear he wanted me returned to closed prison. His plans had been thwarted by Governor McLennan-Murray, who seemingly held more power, but his friendliness with Coccia caused concern. I left the meeting unsure what to do. Putting aside the immediate concern of being returned to closed conditions, this was the man who would have total control for my 6 year 'license period' in the community.

Fortunately, I was still in contact with Mr McLennan-Murray and he responded to a letter I wrote outlining my concerns, noting that he would be contacting my probation officer and that nobody at Standford Hill had requested my return to closed conditions. Indeed, Hadaway at least completed his new 'OASYs' document, which meant I could finally access the prison's 'job club' in a building on the edge of the grounds, together with 'supervised outside work'.

The 'job club' was the only place we could use the internet, aside from on approved ROTLs, and two weeks later I discovered to what extent that had changed as well. Every internet browser brought up 'Google' as the default search engine, whilst a plethora of 'social media' had emerged – including networks useful for finding work.

**

One of Standford's Hills many resettlement links was with a charity in London, which provided suits – donated by city professionals - to prisoners who were going to job interviews[16]. I applied to visit them, as well as arrange an appointment with

---

16   Suited and Booted.

another charity called 'Crisis' that sought to help prison leavers get employment. A date was confirmed by Rose Gordon, a nice officer at the Resettlement Unit. After almost four months at Standford Hill, and with just six months to go before my release, I was finally getting a ROTL to prepare for release.

But it was not to be. On the 24th October – just five days before the scheduled ROTL – it got cancelled. No reasons were given, and it contradicted the assurances that had been given by Resettlement and my Offender Supervisor.

So there I was, being refused a structured ROTL directly linked to my resettlement, whilst others serving far shorter sentences were let out for 'town visits' over a year from their release. Indeed, the man doing six years in the cell next to me had just come back from a 3-day 'home leave'.

"You've got everything there for a judicial review," Kramer noted.

He was right. As it stood, I was on course for leaving Standford Hill without any ROTLs whatsoever.

Additionally, out of frustration with the CCRC and not being able to correct my sentence length, I lodged an appeal against my conviction. Some case law existed to back up a substitution to lesser offences for some of my convictions, as well as issues arising around 'mens rea' (criminal intent). Even so, I realised the grounds were flimsy at best.

One weekend, Kramer and I took a walk around the prison grounds collecting berries for his co-defendant, who boasted of making 'a mean crumble'. There were so many blackberries along the hedges of one particular field, that, within an hour, we had collected enough for several crumbles.

A few others joined us, who I would not have normally spoken to, but Kramer was friendly to everyone.

"I'm getting out next week," one of them said. "Just done a 5 stretch, conspiracy. The misses can't wait."

"You get any home leaves?" Kramer asked.

"Just two," the other said.

This was something, like myself, that Kramer had so far been denied – on the basis of having to do more Resettlement Day Releases. He had a five-year old son, so had a strong need for 'establishing family ties' (the professed purpose of home leaves). Despite this, he only had another three months before being released – which he'd hoped to spend on Home Detention Curfew ('HDC').

The other guy sympathised. "When my mother died, just a year ago, they only let me go to the funeral in handcuffs. Then three months later I am out on a town visit."

"You're the one who did some High Court case, ain't ya?" his companion asked me.

"This guy," Kramer interjected, "has drafted legal claims himself and stood making representations before High Court judges."

"You get anything out of it?"

"Sometimes," I replied, not sure how best to summarise the results.

Later, after giving the berries to his co-defendant, Kramer challenged me on just letting the ROTL rejection pass.

"You're happy just to sit there whilst prisoners doing half your time and who've been in and out of jail all their lives go out every week? Let me tell you, if it weren't for resettlement day releases, even I'd be proper fucked."

I told him about Eoin Mclennan-Murray and the effort he had made to get me to Standford Hill, involving 'calling in a favour' to the governor. I worried that starting any kind of proceedings would undermine this.

"There's plenty of guy's involved in some court matter," he replied. "And what about that HDC thing – that's a total joke!"

He referenced how we had both been told, all through our sentences, that we would be eligible for 'Home Release Curfew' in the last 4 months before release. Indeed, we had even been given official dates for when it could be accessed.

Only now, when we had applied, we received responses telling us that we were not only ineligible for HDC, but that our respective cases wouldn't even be considered.

I had spent 2 months awaiting deportation to the UK, which by law should have been accounted for in the sentence. Now, another 4 months was being added on. So, in effect, I stood to do 6 months extra.

Speaking further with Kramer, I realised that more was at stake than just getting out sooner or accessing ROTLs. It related to a wider principle of fairness and justice, which many others would be facing. To have even the faintest hope in changing that, yet to turn blindly away from it in self-interest, went against everything I stood for. Nor could I so lightly sweep aside the vow I had taken at Dorchester and Guys Marsh: to challenge the system's wrongs, right to the bitter end.

That Hadaway was stubbornly retaining me on 'high risk' status and actively trying to get me moved to a closed prison only encouraged me to challenge the ROTL and HDC issues. Indeed, the whole 'high risk' policy in itself was an injustice – another issue that Grayling had warped to capitalise for political gain, thereby impeding the reintegration prospects of thousands.

So, a few days later, two separate judicial reviews were filed.

Chapter 26: Before the Gates

London - this time with Officer Rose Gordon from Resettlement. Barely three weeks after filing the judicial reviews, the prison suddenly relented and decided to grant me a day visit for renewed appointments with Suited and Booted, as well as Crisis[17]. The caveat was that, unlike others on ROTL, I had to be escorted.

Kramer came with us, for he had appointments at the same charities.

Boarding the train, then the Underground, still felt unusual. Everyone was in one almighty rush. Nobody stopped before the homeless people begging on the streets – whose numbers had increased so much since my last days of freedom. How had things become like this? Society was meant to be advancing, not regressing. It reminded me of something Governor McLennan-Murray mentioned: how the prison system went through cycles of increased punitivity, followed by periods of progressive reform. Did society do the same?

Rose, Kramer and I went to see a man at Crisis in the East End of London. He was keen to support my business idea, which aimed to provide opportunities to the most disadvantaged people in society and challenge negative stereotypes through the power of writing. All too often, those who got published belonged to a middle-upper class elite, resulting in a skewed perspective on the 'lower' classes and people suffering multiple disadvantages. The depiction of prisoners was one example. If excluded groups could publish their accounts properly and

---

17   A charity to help people with experience of, or being at risk of, homelessness. Also helps people leaving prison.

have their voices heard, I thought, then society would change for the better. People would start being more accepting and less judgmental towards those who were different and who ended up taking alternative paths. In turn, it would be harder for men like Grayling to do what they liked.

From Crisis, I went to Suited and Booted, based in a converted church in London's commercial heart. After taking measurements, they ended up giving me a three-piece suit from multiple shelves of clothing. It made the tatty, frayed suit from my sentencing hearing days look ready for a bin.

"Very smart!" Officer Rose exclaimed.

"Have you picked a tie yet?"

"No, I was thinking of a blue one."

"Red would suit you better I think," she said.

"Almost didn't recognise you there," Kramer joked, in his own new outfit.

Indeed, walking out onto the street, we would have been mistaken for lawyers or businessmen. Nobody could have guessed we were on a day release from prison.

We returned to the Isle of Sheppey two hours later, after getting a bite to eat.

"I am booked to go out on another RDR [Resettlement Day Release] with you in just over a week," Rose told me.

I had applied for other RDRs, to visit the prison's nearby town of Sheerness, but I didn't realise any of them had been granted until then.

***

19th December came, and the Resettlement office organised an early Christmas party, replete with chocolate, cake, cheese, crisps, sausage rolls... and mince pies.

I loved mince pies.

If they were warmed up with a little sherry it would have been a real treat, but I still managed to consume an entire box.

Little did I know, they only had one box.

"Hey," another orderly said, "who ate all the pies?"

Kramer made an apt guess, swinging round and grinning at me. "That thin bastard, that thin bastard – he ate all the pies."

A few days later I went with Rose to Sheerness, drifting around the small town for a while, then returned with her to the prison.

After that, my subsequent ROTLs were unescorted, with the first one involving a bus to Sittingborne. For the first time in 79 months, I walked the streets completely free. The weirdness of it passed with me sampling various different food, but even a sandwich from Subway was sufficient for the entire day. Standford Hill had a locker area conjoined to Reception, so prisoners could store their mobile phones, money and other items before they entered the prison. A few took the risk of smuggling stuff back, but there were 'pat down' searches for everyone who came in, as well as random strip searches.

Despite this, over Christmas, more than a few got quietly drunk with alcohol they had managed to get onto the wings. I shared vodka with Kramer and some others that Christmas and even a thimble left me feeling tipsy.

Unfortunately, the prison didn't value Christmas lunch too highly. I ended up with a few strips of something that might have been turkey or chicken breast, some sludgy sprouts, and a thumb-sized ball of stuffing. Then a wedge of sordid stuff termed 'Christmas cake'. Whereas before I might not have previously realised how bad the prison food was, after a few ROTLs I truly got a sense of its poor quality.

At 3pm I tuned into the Queen's Christmas Broadcast that ended with a somewhat ironic message: *'Even in the unlikeliest of places, hope can still be found.'* Did she know her words would be heard by serving prisoners?

The RDRs ended up being granted practically every week, allowing me to spend time in the public libraries of Sheerness and Sittingbourne and complete research for my business plan (as well as discretely typing up and printing legal papers – which, needless to say, would have been blocked if found out by the prison). I also continued studying for my final OU module.

Seeing the end of 2014 made me slightly sad, for it had brought far more progress and positivity than any other year – certainly a polar opposite from the preceding one. A week in Standford's conditions equated to about a month at Lowdham Grange, or 3 months in places like Dorchester.

Then, as 2015 began, a judge granted permission for the ROTL judicial review, identifying a 'point of general public importance' around the ROTL policy itself. After the experience with the legal access judicial review, I thought it best for Flo Kraus to represent me. She agreed, provided it was heard at Leeds High Court, which I had no problem with. So, in reality, I now had to manage one judicial review – the HDC one, with Kramer.

The hearing came sooner than either of us expected: 31st January. We travelled there together on a ROTL, going over the merits and risks of the case.

"The principal problem," I observed, "is this relates to primary legislation. Yes – it could be reasonably argued to be retrospective, but statute takes priority over public law principles."

"So you think we will lose?"

I looked at him as the train rushed on to London. "To be honest, I think that is the probable outcome. Judicial review is so hard, even for those represented by barristers, to win against the actions of public authorities. If we win – and yes it could happen – I will be surprised."

The hearing was before Mrs Justice Lang. She was thinner and less amiable than Mrs Justice Andrews, but noted there were several points of merit in the case. One of her conclusions was that the prison authorities, by informing me and Kramer that we were still eligible for ROTL after 'LAPSO[18]' (the relevant Act) had taken place, were culpable of maladministration. This did not win us the case though, and the crucial point I depended on – that a declaration of incompatibility would be made due to LAPSO's retrospectivity – was rejected by the judge.

The T-sol barrister stepped forward and then attempted to claim costs, making reference to other proceedings I had brought.

"It is clear we are looking at a vexatious litigant," she argued.

I pointed out that my proceedings had been granted permission in the first instance and none were declared vexatious.

Still, the barrister persisted.

The judge asked me and Kramer to outline why we should not be subject to a cost order. The answer was simple: we didn't have the means. "Full fee remission was granted in this case, Your Lady," I added. "Both of our assets have been confiscated. Moreover, I remind Your Ladyship that the preceding judge found merit in this case – granting permission for judicial review. I respect your decision in this hearing, notwithstanding his observations."

"Very well," Lady Justice Lang stated. "It is my decision that the Claimants not have an order of costs made against them."

Earlier, we had been intercepted by a journalist outside the court room, who asked for comments on the case. I cautiously told him it was about challenging an injustice, with both of us being led to believe we would be eligible for HDC only for that eligibility to be automatically removed upon the enactment of LAPSO. He asked us some questions about our sentences and which prison we had come from, eventually convincing us to pose for a photo outside of the court's entrance.

Afterwards, I wondered if this would cause problems with Standford Hill. Officially, we were not meant to talk with any media without formal approval. Yet what were we supposed to

---

18   Legal Aid, Sentencing and Punishment of Offenders Act 2012

do – ignore him? Moreover, nothing contentious had been said. I just hoped they would overlook it with the pleasure in winning the case – although, strictly speaking, it was not Standford Hill that had won but the Secretary of State for Justice: Grayling.

There was actually a visit from the venerable man shortly after. The closed prisons of 'Sheppey Cluster' were locked down to coincide with his arrival, and even Standford Hill had restricted movement. One officer part of the 'Grayling welcoming committee' recounted how the upstanding Minister had requested 'not to come into contact with any prisoner'. This was in contrast to the visit of Sadiq Khan, then Shadow Secretary of State for Justice, a few days later. Why they both timed their visits like that I never found out, but Khan's arrival did not result in any lock-downs or restricted movement. Indeed, I met him myself when he came to the Resettlement Office.

He asked a few questions to the orderlies and I took the opportunity to mention a proposal I had written for the Howard League in regards to setting up a supervised system for prisoners to represent themselves in legal cases. "It has become necessary from the cuts to Legal Aid," I told him by way of background, which he had been reported in opposing.

"It sounds interesting," Khan smiled, watched over by an anxious entourage of prison officials.

"Have you got some further information, or a proposal I can look though?"

It so happened that a copy of the typed up proposal from Sittingbourne library lay on my desk.

"Thank you," Khan said. "I'll take a look at this on my train back to London."

After this, a prison official immediately accosted me. "What did you give to him, Jackley?" he demanded.

"Just a proposal about justice in prisons. I can give you a copy, if you'd like?"

"The last thing I need is *you* interfering with visits like this.

And yes, I'll be getting a copy of that document from you later."

He never did bother to pick up my proposal, however.

I wondered, later, if Khan had taken the time to read what I'd given him. Did he really believe in equal access to justice, as well as rehabilitation? And by those terms, it meant being treated fairly, decently and humanely, whilst given the opportunity for self-betterment. Otherwise, prison became just time: a simple passing of one day to another, having no real impact save the flimsy rhetoric of 'removing dangerous people (temporarily) from society' – no matter that they' be re-entering it even worse.

Of course, the system could never hope to be perfect. I'd entered seeing how bad it could get, even when everything was in relative order. But, across the years, I'd also witnessed a deeper structural shift. First, random changes in the regime; 'minimal standards' like 30 minutes of daily exercise and library visits being cancelled. Then, the few 'privileges' like gym, family visits and evening education classes cut back or removed altogether. Throw into this the tendency of some prison officers to abuse the power given to them, when the safeguards to do so are removed, and you have a toxic cocktail ready to explode. Some erupted more easily than others, but ultimately all would leave the gates worse than when they entered.

The mechanisms meant to hold the system accountable - a robust internal complaints system, dedicated Ombudsman and Independent Monitoring Boards – had been stripped to a state of ineffectiveness or total powerlessness. The very last defence, of being able to freely access professional legal representation and going to the courts as an option of last resort, had now been removed too.

In the background of all this, politicians could play with policies to their heart's desire – changing the requirements for things around ROTL, entering open prison, the procedures for disciplinary actions, the 'IEP' scheme; essentially, everything that underlined the daily life of those in custody.

And, after enduring it all, a prisoner re-enters the world with a life-time of guaranteed discrimination. For those receiving less than 4 years, they might not be forced to declare their convictions, but the information could still be easily obtained. Most employers wouldn't want to have an ex-offender on their books. Even obtaining such a basic thing as car insurance would be difficult. Still, with a bit of persistence and luck, someone leaving prison could start again afresh – as a law abiding citizen.

But what of those who have been inside some form of prison all their lives – from care homes to YO institutes to adult jails? Or those entrapped by mental illness, drug addiction and severe trauma? Whose opportunities seem as limited as the space granted by a 4-sided concrete enclosure? Whose values, which form the basis of their interaction with the world, are only reinforced by one unending conveyor belt of punishment?

**

Probation was the other side to imprisonment, and I began to realise it suffered from similar flaws. Hadaway had been dragging his feet about allowing me home leaves to visit my mother – it should have been something planned six months ago, yet I was now within three months of release. My mother's disability meant it was difficult for her to visit prisons, but such considerations had no relevance in the eyes of my probation officer. I missed the old one – Shaz – who'd recommended I be given a ROTL when in closed conditions, well over a year ago.

I ended up writing to Hadaway's manager, risking some act of vengeance from him, and in early March he finally responded to the prison. My first home leave, for 11th March, was granted! I was going back to Sidmouth, my childhood home, to spend three days with my mother.

The week before, Kramer had left Standford Hill. After 6 ½ years in prison, he was departing the gates for good. It was a bittersweet moment, for although I would miss him, it also meant that he could finally get much needed time with his partner and young son. We promised to keep in touch.

With Kramer gone, I essentially had nobody else to talk with. The prison authorities also undertook a full search of my cell, which included going through my paperwork. I couldn't recall such a meticulous search before, not even in closed conditions. Nonetheless, despite a concern they would 'plant' something, nothing resulted from it.

A further 'hiccup' occurred on the 9th March, when Flo lost the ROTL judicial review. Apparently the judges (two of them this time) were very unhappy at how I'd primarily written the Skeleton Argument, initially thinking it was Flo's. They went on to declare the case as 'without merit', despite the single judge granting permission with an observation that it raised an important point about the new ROTL policy. Flo told me they'd spent most of their time going over the ROTLs I'd been granted since the case was lodged, despite the fact that it related to the policy itself.

Despite these things, 11th March eventually arrived. Hadaway, alongside two police officers, had visited my mother beforehand, and demanded that I see him in Exeter at the probation offices as soon as I arrived.

What to say about those resulting three days from 11th-13th March? They flew by, like a dream in another world. On return to the prison, I just felt immensely depressed. It was deeper than the other depressions I had encountered – an agonising feeling of loss. Not only had I received a real taste of life outside, sleeping outside a prison for the first time in almost seven years, but I'd properly seen my mother, whose only real contact had been through letters. To have that, and then voluntarily come back to prison, was akin to walking away from Eden and into Purgatory.

Now I understood why some who went out on home leaves never returned.

***

The next big step was attending a Prince's Trust course in Chatham, which required a series of ROTLs. I wasn't sure if these would be facilitated – not least because of the delays Hadaway created before I was granted a home visit – but it turned out this form of ROTL did not require his approval. Unlike him, my Offender Supervisor was a pleasant man who saw no issue with me leaving the prison – after doing so countless times before – to attend a course directly linked to my rehabilitation and reintegration.

So, for four days in a row, I travelled to Chatham and joined a group of eight young people to learn about setting up a business. Only the course coordinator knew that I came from prison, although she later shared this with my assigned mentor (Peter). He was a very amiable man in his 50s who volunteered for the Prince's Trust to help disadvantaged young people. Later I would be granted a few RDRs to meet him, where we discussed various things both within and outside of business.

The Prince's Trust, Crisis, Suited and Booted, and the Prisoner's Education Trust were the four charities who made a genuine difference to my eventual reintegration back into society. Without their support I would not have been able to complete my degree and start a business. In turn, I would have faced unemployment due to the prejudice that employers have against people with criminal convictions. This is why so many take the self-employment route, although for some industries having a conviction did not matter so much.

On the last day of my Princes Trust course, I found a £10 note crumpled up at the end of the train station platform – covering my day's expenses in food and travel costs. Smiling, I wondered if Fate was swinging towards a kinder form of irony.

Having spent 4 consecutive days outside prison, coming back to the old routine was difficult. Unlike most, who could access real jobs and build up savings for release, I had to take up a

'CVSE' role unique to 'restricted ROTL' (i.e. high risk) prisoners. It entailed working unpaid with a small group supervised by a prison officer in civilian clothing, doing work like those subject to 'community service' sentences. After digging a hole for a while in some community centre allotment or picking up plastic refuse from alleys, most days were spent in the back of a van listening to the meaningless chatter of my peers.

At least I managed to access 'Resettlement Day Release' on the occasional Saturday, upon submitting written plans that had to be approved by my Offender Supervisor. It usually involved going to Sittingbourne Library and finding something new to eat, but on one occasion I was confronted by a huge yellow lion.

"I am the Library Lion!" the costumed man exclaimed.

I said "hello" but then looked behind to see the 'lion' doing an exaggerated creeping motion, as if stalking me.

Ignoring the act, I found a computer and commenced typing up an OU module assignment. An hour later, a paw landed on my shoulder.

"The Library Lion offers treats!" the costumed stranger said, holding a tray of biscuits in his other hand.

I took one and thanked him, watching him 'creep' towards somebody else and do the same. A few kids then started to file in, and the 'Lion' entered a state of frenzy.

Fortunately my entire RDR did not have to be spent in Sittingbourne Library in the presence of a crazed man dressed as a yellow lion. I had arranged to meet with Kramer at a nearby pub. Needless to say, this was not on my resettlement plan for the day.

He was in jovial spirits, talking about all that had happened since being released. We enjoyed a good lunch with beer (also not on the resettlement plan), which he insisted to pay. Then he abruptly swung in the opposite direction.

"Are you alright?" I asked.

"Keep looking ahead. There's a screw just walked in here."

The prison often sent its staff to visit the nearby towns, keeping an eye out for prisoners on RDRs. If we were spotted it would be reported back, and that would probably result in problems with future ROTLs. But the screw just headed for the toilets, giving us an opportunity to slip out.

Kramer needed to get back to Essex – he had a job driving trucks – so we parted ways.

When I returned to the library, the 'Library Lion' had gone. I began to finalise my assignment, when suddenly something landed on my shoulder – something yellow.

"The Library Lion welcomes you back!"

I glanced back and smiled thinly, watching as the costumed figure pranced away to annoy someone else.

That night, back in my cell, amid the cacophonous noise, I dreamt of a huge yellow lion that chased Hadaway down a street with a tray of biscuits in one hand and a law book in the other. He was not exactly a source of good will, so perhaps my subconscious had been too generous with the biscuits.

When this probation officer wasn't making demands, he simply chose not to communicate. On my second planned home leave, I was left in total uncertainty as to whether it would go ahead, simply because he had not responded to the prison about approving it. By not responding to emails, letters or phone calls, the leave was inevitably cancelled.

March moved to April, and three weeks remained. I counted the days down, just as I had done at the very beginning. 21… 20… 19… 18… 17…

Concerns that formerly occupied my mind, like attending work on time and filling in the canteen sheet, became irrelevant.

Hadaway's insistence that I go to a 'probation hostel' on release took prominent concern. Such places were rumoured to be full of drugs and nonces, with a sizable majority sent to hostels getting recalled due to the problems they encountered. I remembered how Ricky at Lowdham Grange had instead chosen to spend the entirety of his sentence in prison, rather than go to a hostel. There was a kind of increased punitivity with such demands, for others serving the same sentence length could go straight to their families. Again, it was all about 'risk'. Those assessed as 'low risk' weren't required to go to hostel, nor did most of those on 'medium'. Despite this, and everything that had happened, I was also lucky. For every 'high risk' long-term prisoner in open conditions and receiving ROTL at the end of their sentences, there were hundreds - if not thousands - who were not. Had it not been for Coldingley's governor, I would have joined them.

How different things would be if judges, instead of walking away from those they condemned to prison, instead 'kept an eye' on their progress through custody. They could intervene, when needed, and perhaps have the option of even reducing a person's sentence through exceptional circumstances. If change and rehabilitation was actively demonstrated, then they could order that more of a sentence be spent in the community rather than in prison. Such a model had in fact been trialled in some jurisdictions, with a focus on young offenders, and the results were promising. Sadly, I doubted if a country like the UK, ruled over by Ministers like Grayling, could ever embrace such a model. To find progressive proposals thriving in this system would be akin to discovering some unicorns dancing in a forgotten wilderness.

***

Ten days from release, another sudden change was announced. Initially Hadaway wanted me to go to a hostel in Exeter called 'Fleming House', but now he changed it to one in Bristol due to a shortage of spaces in Exeter. It didn't matter to him that Bristol was four hours by public transport from my mother, or that I had zero links to it. There was no consideration that many of my preparations for release were based on going to Devon. All that mattered was his need for me to be in a hostel.

However, it had one plus: at least, by being based in Bristol and presumably classed as resettling in that area, I would need a new probation officer.

Now it was May; the last one I would spend in prison. I could feel the richness and vibrancy of Spring, after so many years of darkness. It had cycled around all those years without me; even as wider society went through its own cycles of destruction and unrest. But how many times could Nature rebound from mankind's growing pressure? Was any discernible ending not defined by doom?

Epics, fables and legends always allow the end to be flooded with truth and light. But how can that be so in today's world, when the pace of environmental destruction, inequality and injustice is so unremitting? Man does not have the moral responsibility to manage his technological innovation. It is destroying him, together with the world.

Should we blame the good-hearted innovators, or that part of human nature which appears to be incontrovertibly dark? A darkness that destroyed the Native American tribes, which enslaved the African Nations, and which ruthlessly annihilated countless indigenous peoples.

Evil is self-perpetuating; it spreads through its effects. Consider the case of prisoners – people who have (in theory) committed harm against others. Whilst it is hard to generalise this group, some common trends do arise. Most come from poor, marginalised, under-privileged backgrounds. Is it then fair to say that their crimes arose from some intrinsic seed and could not have been prevented? Or was the route to crime paved with abuse, lack of opportunities and pressures that leave no other alternative?

It only takes the right circumstances to thrust someone on a path of crime, or to commit a totally uncharacteristic act that was triggered by extreme, unrelenting pressure. Blame cannot be solely laid upon the head of an offender. This is why society must recognise the importance of forgiveness, and realise a person can change for the better. For, if it routinely condemns individuals, it must also condemn itself.

If criminals can be reformed, so can society. If enough time and effort is invested to develop someone's potential as a contributing citizen, even if past wounds cannot be completely healed, then there is hope for society as a whole to become more just, equitable and sustainable.

But the routes and processes that have caused social instability and environmental destruction must be addressed. These are about structural frameworks that underpin the foundation of present day society. They have become so imbedded, on a historical and cognitive basis, that they cannot be demolished in one movement. What are these routes and processes?

The pursuit of money – and the belief that 'the economy', exclusively defined by 'GDP', comes before all else.

That the people and the government must be separate.

That people, groups and communities can make little difference to their own and others' lives.

The reliance on top-down technology and throw-away consumables.

The failure to consider or take responsibility for the wider impacts of unsustainable production and consumption.

These are the abusive care homes, crime ravaged estates and acquisitive criminal sub-culture of today's society. As each year passes, they grow stronger and more imbedded. The harm they create expands with each new generation, as power structures use them to prevent change.

Meanwhile, the very same minority with unparalleled wealth and power were the same who gained it, and held it, through exploitation of people and destruction of the environment. Entire swathes of legislation had been shaped around their interests – almost to the point of completely eclipsing the founding purpose of law: to prevent harm and damage. Once you truly grasp this and see the system for what it is, formerly invisible chains that bounded you slip away. That doesn't mean an invitation to wreck what good exists in the system, or cause harm. On the contrary, it's a calling for justice – real justice. The kind that encompasses fairness, equity, and safeguarding the future for all.

And, on a planet speeding towards disaster, the time for action is fast running out.

***

Daffodils and tulips upraised their buds in flower beds, as bluebells spread beneath the shade of trees. Sometimes I wandered into the quieter areas, away from others, and thought of all that had happened, along with what was yet to come. I took a book and a notebook with me on these occasions, listening to the currents of thought that flowed from my heart and tracing them on paper:-

> *As the eve lengthen*
> *I think of mountains far*
> *Blackbirds singing on shed roofs*
> *Sparrows grouped in three*
> *On the grass, a rabbit grazing*
> *As peace permeates the sky*
>
> *Spring-time solitude, freshly begun,*
> *One last week to ponder*
> *How seven summers were lost...*
> *I think of open oceans and forest dells,*
> *To walk amidst their sighing splendour*
> *Counting one's tears until no more can fall.*

Seven years were lost, and nothing would change that. Part of me wanted to re-enter society and spend the last two years of my twenties experiencing as much as possible, whilst the fringes of youth were still within reach. But it was pointless, for these years too would soon pass. What mattered were the things I left behind and the impact I created around me.

We were all sent into this world as souls with a hidden purpose, a reason more than just surviving and passing on our genes. That was on a basic level, but the wider one meant making the world better for those who would succeed us. Or at least, that is what I thought, as I sat under a Sycamore tree in Standford Hill's grounds.

Next week, my journey through Britain's prisons finally came to an end. I walked to Reception and was handed the £46 discharge grant with which to restart my life, then headed to Bristol.

Afterward

My journey through Britain's prisons would have been very different without the interventions of some people: prisoners and staff alike, who offered a hand of friendship and support. I am grateful to all of them.

Many years have passed since I left those Spring grounds of Standford Hill. But the British prison system still lies at the mercy of politicians, some of whom have no restraint in playing political games that do nothing to improve reintegration and indeed do the very opposite. Suicides, self-harm, violence and a stubbornly unchanging reoffending rate are the only result of their input. I witnessed this most dramatically in the last two years of my sentence, but nothing has changed to prevent others from doing the same. There are tens of thousands of people in British prison, most of them young and with multiple disadvantages, with very little in the way of genuine support to reduce reoffending. Locking people up and finding more ways to make their sentences harder does nothing to stop them from going back into crime. Treating them unfairly and without regard to the Prison Service's own policies and the public laws that oversee their administration only creates bitterness and resentment, which will be reflected upon society when they are released. There are other ways.

Prisons are part of the justice system, and this means that people in custody should expect to be treated fairly, humanely, and with opportunities to improve themselves. It also means that they should be able to access the courts, as a route of last recourse, in a place where abuses of power are most likely to occur.

For anyone reading this book who is already in prison I have one message: Don't Give Up.

And for those outside: value your freedom - and what you can do with it.

The Nine Hell Levels		Examples
1A	All things on 'necessities list' – each subsequent level has all the positives below it	Open prison
1B	Outdoor exercise, work, regular gym, friendly acquaintances	HMP Lowdham Grange
1C	Leisure activities, visits, good cell, good canteen	
2A	Work, exercise, contact, gym, leisure activities, canteen	HMP The Verne
2B	Clean living area, good food	Metropolitan Detention Centre / HMP Parkhurst / HMP Coldingley ('E' wing)
3A	Time outside cell, limited contact, limited canteen	HMP Dovegate
3B	Reasonable food	HMP Hewell/ HMP Guys Marsh
4A	Very limited exercise, letters, clean cell/ communal area	North West Correctional Facility / HMP Gloucester & Dorchester
4B	Poor food	HMP Garth ('Bullies Den')
5A	No outdoor exercise, activities or leisure	

5B	Limited books and writing	Southern State Correctional Facility (The Hole)
6A	No fresh air, no exercise, no contact, no food	
6B	Constant surveillance (24/7), no books or writing	Punishment in The Hole
7A	No hygiene or privacy, minor torture (beatings)	
7B	Major beatings and mental torture	
8A	Constant torture, no sleep, no natural light or fresh air, constant surveillance	
8B	Lasting injuries, deep pain	
9A	Prolonged torture followed by death	
9B	Rancid decay – experimented on and changed, slow death	

Note: Mental state can overrule any environment, generally affecting the Hell Level by around one whole level, but it can be more.

'The Rules'

'The Golden Three'

1. Trust NO-ONE.
   No foe is greater than he who fools you he is a friend; no opponent deadlier than he who keeps his knife hidden.

2. Don't Let the Bastards Bring You Down.
   There will be many among the bad and broken who will seek to cast you down – don't let them succeed! There will be many whose aims are dark, devious and sadistic who will cross your path, but keep on walking!

3. Believe in Yourself.
   Weather the storm, draw strength from every battle, seek the truth amongst lies. Keep on fighting, finding the fire within to hold back deepest darkness. Remember the heroes and Righteous who stood like pillars in seas of adversity; trust the voice that guides in peace and shines with love. Rise like a star that never dims, roll like valleys beneath an azure sky, with foresight to see and never falter.

4. Never Give Up.
   Never stop seeking, never stop trying. If every door is locked and barred – seek a window, whether within or without. Look for silver linings on the more foreboding of thunder clouds; with courage and an unassailable will, forge onwards.

5. Don't Seek Improvement When All is Well (or as well as it can be).

   Often those who sought paradise end up stumbling in hell. Do not pursue tales of betterment when you are already satisfied – be thankful for what you have. If stranded at an oasis, think hard before going off to seek a river.

6. Expect the Worse, Hope for the Best – but Also Expect the Unexpected.

   Be prepared for the worst case scenario, as if it's a given that it will occur – but at the same time, Hope. For Hope alone is the greatest weapon against despair – a tool in which to carve a passage through the caverns of hell. Also remember Fate's fondness for unpredictability and irony, so look outside the borders of past experience and expectations.

7. Think Before You Act.

   In times of stress, anger, anxiety or simple fixation there will be intense desires for a certain immediate action. The temptation to launch into a supposedly irresistible endeavour can be strong – as strong as the lunar pull on tides. Such urges are more often Siren calls in rocky waters. Look before you leap, think before you speak, contemplate before you implement.

The Fighting Song
As written and sang in 'The Hole'
(Foxtrot Unit, Southern State Correctional Facility,
Vermont, USA. July 2008)

If there's one thing I've learnt, if there's one thing I know
It's *don't let the bastards bring you down*
Keep on fightin', keep on fightin'
Fight till ya breath rasps out in pain!
They can lock you up, they can break you down,
They can beat your body, try to ravage your soul
But they can never conquer
The righteous spirit within.

Keep on fightin', keep on fightin'
Fight till ya heart breaks outta ya chest!
Just remember those fighters, endless and nameless
From King and Gandhi to Joan D'Arc
Fight and make a Nation within your heart.

Printed in Great Britain
by Amazon